When Your Kids Go to College

Lucantonio N. Salvi
and
Michael J. Hunt CSP

Paulist Press
New York/Mahwah, NJ

Library of Congress Cataloging–in–Publication Data

Salvi, Lucantonio N.
When your kids go to college/Lucantonio N. Salvi and Michael J. Hunt.
p. cm.
ISBN 0-8091-3502-7
1. College students—United States—Psychology. 2. Parenting—United States. 3. Parent and child—United States. I. Hunt, Michael J., 1941- . II. Title.
LA229.S24 1994 94-19323
378.1′98—dc20 CIP

Published by Paulist Press
997 Macarthur Boulevard
Mahwah, New Jersey 07430

Printed and bound in the
United States of America

Contents

In memory of my parents,
Jane and Michael Hunt

M. J. H

With deepest gratitude to my mother,
Gina Salvi,
and in memory of my father,
Nunzio Salvi

L. N. S

INTRODUCTION

From the moment your son or daughter sent off that first college application, you have been inundated with information. The colleges have been sending you reams of data about courses and programs, as well as about all the services and opportunities they can provide. This flood of information will not only continue throughout his or her college career but will go on for years after that. As you get ready to see your son or daughter off to college, you have probably also been very attentive to newspaper and magazine articles about college life and have eagerly watched any television reports that describe what life on campus is all about.

Most of the parents we have talked with feel overwhelmed by all the information, and frustrated because it does not seem to address their real questions. At the same time, most parents are fearful about asking these questions too directly, especially of their sons and daughters, because they do not want to seem to be prying. Often we hear parents sounding insecure about their role as parents once their son or daughter is off to college because they are not quite sure what that role is now. All parents have some fears and worries. And nearly all parents are very cautious because they also know how easy it is now to make the mistakes that only serve to make a college student less open and communicative.

In the pages that follow we want to tell you about life on campus, what to expect, and how students think and feel about their parents. We provide some examples from our own experiences of how students interact with their parents and of what students and their parents go through during the college years.

But most of all, we want to offer two things that we know can be decisively helpful to every parent of a college student. The first is an assurance. For almost every  college student we know, their relationship with parents is the most enduring and important element in their life. Because we also know how college students can talk and act, we are pretty certain that you may not always feel or hear this importance when you are communicating with your son or daughter. College students everywhere have to sound independent, autonomous and often rebellious. But as people who often talk with col-  lege students (when parents obviously are not present), we can assure you that you are *the* important relationship in their lives, their constant point of reference and the greatest influence on their lives and values.

The second thing we would like to offer you is an invitation. We have often seen how parents and children enter into a whole new, adult relationship during  the college years. Frankly, the change required for this to happen must come largely from parents who shift from an authority based model of communication to one  that is more open, more adult and more reciprocal. We have also seen many examples of parents who do not make this transition and continue to deal with college students as if they were still children at home. These examples only serve to emphasize the importance of making the change and transition as wisely as possible.

These pages, then, are an invitation to form a new, adult relationship with your sons and daughters and become the beneficiary of a valuable new experience in your own life.

You will quickly discover that this book is written from two quite different perspectives which, we think, complement and complete each other. The first perspective is that of a graduate student who is only a few years removed from his own undergraduate days. Luca Salvi, a native of Washington, D.C., graduated from Georgetown University. Presently he is a joint–degree candidate at the Georgetown Law Center and at the Fletcher School of Law and Diplomacy at Tufts University. He has been very active with the Catholic  campus ministry program at Tufts where he has worked extensively with undergraduates and established a very successful retreat program.

The second perspective is that of a college chaplain, Fr. Michael Hunt, a Paulist priest, who has served as a chaplain at Boston University, Wayne State University, the University of California at Berkeley and, since 1984, at Tufts University. He is also the author of *College Catholics: A New Counter–Culture* (Paulist Press).

In chapters 3, 4, and 6 of this book, Luca Salvi addresses the question of how caring parents can avoid becoming intrusive parents, the issues of drinking, drugs and sex on campus and the very practical issues of grades, careers and the economic investment that today's college education represents. In chapters 1, 2, and 5 of this book, Fr. Michael Hunt discusses the fears that parents have, the fact that parents are the experts when it comes to their children, and how religious faith is passed on and plays an important role in the lives of college students.

As we planned and discussed this book, we quickly

realized that our different ages and experiences gave us very distinctive perspectives about college life and college students. In working together with students at Tufts University, we had already discovered that combining those perspectives greatly enhanced the service and ministry offered to students and could see how students drew great benefit from our different perspectives. Now, in these pages, we hope that our two perspectives can add something of value and insight to your own, knowing as we do from our experiences that you, the parents of college students, are the most important people in the lives of your sons and daughters.

1
Why Parents Have Fears

For most parents, it is an exciting but intense trip. Whether you actually bring your sons or daughters to their new college campus, or see them off at an airport or train station, you are brimming over with strong emotions. You are filled with pride as you look at this suddenly grown–up adult child, who is now old enough to vote and almost ready to live without constant care and supervision. But there is also fear and anxiety, usually carefully hidden, because parents know how difficult this first adjustment to college can be, and you know too well the dangers that linger on even the nicest looking campus. It does not help, of course, that your son or daughter is cutting short the farewells, acting cool about the whole thing, and anxious to see you leave the airport or the campus. You don't take that too personally because you recognize that it is really an act as your son or daughter is already bracing for the onslaught of homesickness that strikes every new college student but would rather die than admit it. You want to say you understand, that the homesickness will pass, but you constrain yourself and remember that homesickness is a word that must not be mentioned now.

Every year after the welcoming ceremonies and at a chaplains' reception for the new students and their families, I see the parents, excited but anxious, saying their farewells. And I see the new students, desperately trying to look so perfectly nonchalant but already feeling the dreaded but unmentionable malady of homesickness. Finally, it happens. "Let's get this over with and say goodbye."

In the next few weeks, the homesickness does recede, just as you knew it would, and your son or daughter is filled with news of new friends and the excitement of a new life. You become accustomed to the separation and look ahead to the first visit. But soon a new concern manifests itself – the unknown. Usually you are kept up on all the news from school, but you also realize that the news is carefully edited and you are not there anymore to see for yourself.

Will My Questions Sound Like Prying?

Is she eating properly? What kind of people are these new friends she's all excited about? What really goes on at these parties he's always talking about? What are they up to when your phone calls go unanswered for a couple of days? You hear a lot of news but you also strain to catch the parts that are carefully left out. You trust your son or daughter but still you worry and wonder.

It does not make much difference whether your son or daughter is now at a college a thousand miles away, or living at home and commuting to school. You still feel a new awkwardness about asking questions. Not long ago, you felt quite comfortable in asking those probing questions that would account for a teenager's every waking moment. Now that's all changed but you still want to know all the details. Like most parents, you want to ask a million questions, but you want the questions to sound less authoritarian and less demanding. Are you studying enough? What are these new friends like? What really goes on in those coed dormitories? Are you keeping up your religious observances? Catholic parents wonder if they should ask if they are going to mass now that they are on their own and away from home.

Parents hesitate before asking questions. Do I really want to know? Will my questions sound as if I'm prying? Will I just provoke a defensive or evasive response? How long should I wait patiently for the subject to come up naturally, or, better, until the student brings it up? Some parents will convince themselves that they no longer have the right to know everything from a son or daughter who is now technically an adult. Other parents like to remind themselves about who is paying for this college education and that they have every right to know how their "investment" is turning out. Most parents vacillate back and forth between these two attitudes, frustrated by not possessing all the information they would like to have. In some families, one parent is very inquisitive, while the other can seem indifferent. Of course, the student has long ago developed the skills to play off those parental differences. Some parents scheme to find other ways of extracting information from friends of their son or daughter, or from other parents who did the spade work and got the information payoff.

Fears Are Normal But Disguised

Susan showed up in my office one afternoon about halfway through the second semester of her freshman year. I recognized her from Sunday mass where she always greeted me cheerfully and seemed to be enjoying her first year at school. But now this afternoon, she was almost in tears, brimming over with anxiety. As she took off her coat and sat down, she explained that she was facing a horrendous problem with her parents. Time was running out on her and she had only a few days left to make her official transfer from the College of Engineering to Art History. As she detailed her decision to forsake civil engineering and become an Art History major, she brightened up, obviously thrilled at the prospect of her new course of study. But then the dark clouds quickly returned as she told me how upset her parents would be. Actually her parents had encouraged her interest in art but always reminded her that it was not a practical way to make a living later on. Their urging and advice had led her to enroll in Engineering but by the Christmas break she knew she wanted to change to Art. Now she had to tell them that she was making the change, and she knew they would be very upset and, as she kept saying, they would be really angry at her.

Susan was probably correct to envision a forthcoming emotional encounter but she had identified the wrong emotion. Her decision was not about to set off her parents' anger but rather their fears. There could well be some angry words when Susan told her parents about her decision but it was their fear about her future, her economic prospects, her career and, perhaps, their own economic insecurities that would alarm her parents.

As we talked that afternoon, I could see that Susan had never imagined her parents as having fears. College students think of their parents as having strong opinions, or values, even sometimes prejudices, but fear is something college students do not envision in their parents. According to students! Now Susan is assembling a series of examples of people she has already met and who have established themselves in fine careers in the field of Art History, especially in Museum work. I realize that she is not doing this for my benefit, but our conversation has now become a rehearsal of how she will explain her decision, while trying to allay her parents' fears about her future career prospects.

Sometimes students think their parents mean well but are just hopelessly out of date, or misinformed, or set in their ways, or prejudiced, or maybe even stupid. It almost never occurs to students that the parents are operating out of fear. Yet when most parents see their children off to college, fear becomes a constant anxiety. Even when the relationship is a good one and all the objective indications like grades are fine, parents have fears of all the things they do not know or control. Like college students, parents can mistake the emotion they are feeling for something else and it can degenerate into anger and irritation. Fear, however, is the most normal and predictable response to the departure for college. You love someone more than life itself, you have taken care of this person for nearly two decades, and you have protected your child from a thousand dangers. All of a sudden, in an instant, that child is somewhere else and you are not there anymore. What else but fear would a parent feel as they drop a child off at college?

On a brilliant August day, while driving back to Boston from New York, I pull off the interstate in northern Connecticut and head for a Dunkin' Donuts in search of a large coffee to fortify myself for the last 100 miles of my drive. As I am standing on line, a woman comes over and introduces herself. She quickly explains that she is the mother of a freshman at Tufts and recognizes me from the mass she and her husband attended on Parents' Weekend last fall. When I indicate that I know her son, she invites me to join her and her associate who have stopped in to take a break from their real estate selling. I ask how Larry is spending the summer, and her brow wrinkles with a measure of concern as she explains that Larry is not spending the summer at home. One of Larry's friends at school is from North Carolina and Larry is spending most of the summer living with his friend's family there and doing construction work. It's probably easier to get work down there right now, she assures us and herself. But in her face and in her voice, I can see questions. She doesn't ask them explicitly but she is obviously wondering if a chance meeting with the college chaplain could fill her in on what Larry really thinks. In fact, I know nothing about Larry's decision or his view of his family, but on this August afternoon I sense the questions in his mother's mind and see that she has thought it best not to ask Larry directly. Why would Larry want to spend the summer away from home and family when he's been away  from them all year at school? When she explains that she and her husband have never met this friend or his family, there are fears about the unknown just beneath the surface. There was probably no explosive scene about Larry's decision to spend the summer in North Carolina, but clearly it left his parents with questions and some unspoken fears. Tension and emotional stress color the relationship between Larry and his parents and, even if major confrontations are avoided, his parents, and probably Larry himself, are unhappy with the meager communication that flows among them.

Express Your Emotions Constructively

Students and their parents have different emotions and come at issues from very different experiences and perspectives. Both, however, cover up their real emotions, and the results are false signals and garbled messages. Students, especially in the first year, feel lonely, homesick, frightened. Usually students greatly miss their families, their friends and all the familiar surroundings of home. Because it seems so uncool to have any of these "childish" feelings on campus, students expend enormous energy covering up. They deal with these feelings and emotions, if they do at all, by posturing and faking it. As a result of all this covering–up, parents often get the message that they are no longer needed or even wanted. In reality the student giving off this bravado is feeling lost and even helpless without family and parents around. But the charade of independence must go on. No student, especially a freshman, will want anyone, especially parents, to know how much the college separation hurts.

Parents also do a pretty effective job of covering up their real feelings. When a child goes off to college, whether residential or commuter, most parents feel a lot of fear, but they don't want anyone, especially their children, to see that fear. Parents naturally want to be seen as mature and confident, proud that their son or daughter is making the transition to adulthood. They want everyone to share their positive feelings about the college, its programs and their child's opportunities. Most parents are smart enough to know that any expression of fear is prima facie evidence that they have not let go. They convince themselves and anyone who will listen that they are pretty cool parents, dealing very calmly with the separation and the lack of firsthand knowledge. It only takes an article in the newspaper or a show on television about the turbulent problems of college life to revive all the fears again.

And so some parents prefer to raise objections, express strong opinions, or invoke the status of their authority. Instead of talking about their fears, parents begin sentences: "I don't approve of..." or "We don't think that..." or "Experience has taught me that..." To a student who is desperately attempting to bolster some flagging sense of autonomy, sentences that begin in that spirit trigger all the worst mechanisms. A student easily feels that the small area of autonomy that he or she has carved out is under attack. Naturally a young person becomes defensive, evasive and, in some instances, deceitful. "They treat me as though I were still in high school" is the common complaint you hear from students.

Parents quickly imagine, perhaps with good reason, that their son or daughter is holding back on them, not telling them what is really going on. In their frustration and anxiety, parents assert authority, and the student feels under attack and suspicion. Then communication rapidly degenerates.

Some parents, however, are able to see clearly what is going on. Instead of confronting their son or daughter with their iron will or an assertion of authority, they actually reveal their own fears, both the real and the foolish ones, to the student. These parents offer themselves openly as fellow travelers on a journey beset with fears. Of course, most parents do have more answers and wider experience, but in this emotional crisis of separation, they wisely place themselves on the same wavelength as a student. When they offer this part of themselves, they are often met with understanding, a ready flow of honest information and, not the least important, a deepening of their relationship with a son or daughter. A student is always surprised to see this vulnerability revealed, especially from someone who only recently was so clearly in charge. When parents frankly and openly talk about their fears, the student's autonomy is not threatened at all but may well be enhanced by his or her own efforts to reassure and encourage a parent.

Establish Two–Way Communication

Even in the brief conversations that happen around the campus or after mass on Sunday, Andrew had always struck me as someone with an inner peace. One day during a long talk with him, I noticed how often he talks about his father. Whenever Andrew opens up a fairly serious issue in conversation with me, he describes his father's thoughts and reactions to that issue. Finally it dawns on me that Andrew usually talks out all his serious concerns pretty deeply and, more surprising, first with his father. This is not a common or universal experience for nineteen year old college students. I have never met his father, but through my conversations with Andrew I know that his father is a surgeon in his late fifties who often worries about impending old age and who regrets deeply the unhappy relationship he had with his own father who is now dead. I have also learned that he has been taking small vacations alone with Andrew's mother because he wants the two of them to become even closer as their careers fade in importance and their children leave home. I can see that Andrew has little difficulty talking his issues out with his father because his father has told him about his own inner fears and doubts, about his own insecurities and needs. I cannot imagine anyone having more respect and admiration for someone than Andrew has for his father. Andrew has been allowed to see beyond the parent who is a fifty–eight year old highly successful surgeon and has seen the darker, inner fears in his father's heart. As a result, a parent and child have become very good friends.

Andrew's father obviously has skills that you cannot learn in a medical or any other school. If there is a secret to his success in creating an intimate relationship with his son, it is his willingness to name his emotions, like fear, for what they really are. In opening himself up like this, he has invited his son into his life and his son has clearly reciprocated. No one is more a parent than when knowing how to offer the invitation  to transform the parent–child relationship into the kind of friendship that will deepen the bonds they already share.

2
Parents Are Experts

I was looking forward to meeting Carol's parents when she invited me to have lunch with them during their upcoming visit to campus. From knowing Carol and meeting three of her brothers and sisters who had visited earlier, I had already gathered that her parents had done an outstanding job as the parents of six children. Carol had also told me that, after the children had grown up, her mother had returned to school herself to acquire her Master's Degree in early childhood education and was now a specialist in her field. At our lunch, Carol's mother was very excited because later in the afternoon she would have the opportunity to sit in on a lecture by a professor of child study on our campus who was a renowned authority on early childhood development and whose textbooks were very familiar to her from her own studies. I laughed and told her that, from what I had seen of her children, she was the one who should be giving the lecture. But, she quickly explained, this professor was the real expert.

I did not pursue the topic at lunch but it reminded me of an increasingly important question in our society: Who are the real experts? The proliferation of professional counselors, researchers and people on the talk shows have made many parents feel they need to look to someone else, a professional, for expertise and advice in dealing with their children. When a child goes off to college, the urgency to find the right expert on that topic can become a priority. All the emphasis on these professional experts has tended to make many parents feel inadequate or even incompetent about being parents.

In my own experience, nothing could be further from the truth. Parents usually know more than anyone else about their sons and daughters. College students, even in conversations about a family problem or crisis, nearly always give evidence of how well they think their parents know them. Upon reflection, most parents will realize that they do, in fact, have a reliable understanding of their children's needs and talents, their problems and their personality patterns. When a son or daughter goes off to college, parents have had seventeen or eighteen years of fairly intense experiences with their child. An enormous amount of experience and complex skills are there to be utilized by both the parents and students.

It is also true, of course, that the use of this resource may be impaired by some family problems, by secrets that parents and children have been keeping from each other, and by the more common obstacles to deeper communications. Working through these difficulties can place the considerable resource of parents' understanding and savvy at the disposal of a child's struggle for autonomy.

One obstacle that should immediately be cleared away is the assumption that parents must always give way to an expert professional. Relying on their own common sense and reviewing what they have learned over many years of living with a son or daughter, par-

ents can rely on their own insights with confidence and security. If parents take the additional steps of finding the most effective methods of communication, they will most often find that their sons and daughters will be very open and receptive to them. Avoiding unnecessary assertions of authority or vehemently expressed opinions will allow parents to establish very productive two–way communication. Students are naturally disposed to hear what their parents think as long as they do not feel put off by side issues or threats to their still insecure autonomy.

Parents are frequently intimidated by the sophisticated levels of education and expertise that their children are acquiring. Sometimes even a well educated parent has no idea what students are studying or talking about. "What do I have to say to a budding astro physicist or a chemical engineer?" But parents do know the person who is becoming a rocket scientist or a corporate lawyer, and the issues for communication are not arcane academic concepts but the personal and intimate ones that exist between parents and their children. Even when students are dramatically better educated than their parents, they easily distinguish that kind of learning from the life wisdom which their parents possess and which they would like to access.

Family Influence

Nearly all the students have finished finals. The campus is getting very quiet except for the noise of the carpenters who are building the platforms and stage for commencement which is now only ten days away. Tony who is about to graduate has invited me to a farewell lunch. Even though we are in a restaurant packed with people, Tony's eyes are filled with tears and he is fight-

ing very hard not to break down sobbing in such a public place. Since high school, Tony has told everyone he wanted to be a surgeon, but now he is telling me that he has been turned down by every medical school he applied to. Partially, his sadness is anger at himself for not getting the grades that he knows he could have gotten and which would have meant admission. But what is really hurting him now is the realization that, before graduation next week, he will have to tell his parents that he will probably not become a doctor. He explains that they will not be really disappointed but they will hurt because they know how much he wanted this.

A few days later, I bump into Claudia, another senior, in the corridor of a classroom building. She gives me a big hug and whispers that she just found out that she received a fellowship for graduate school at MIT. She tells me that she will call her parents as soon as they get home from work in Wisconsin and says she wants to make sure I meet them on graduation weekend.

A phone call that afternoon from Terry brings a request that I say a prayer for her father who has just been diagnosed with colon cancer. The doctors are very optimistic about his prospects after surgery but he will not be able to come to graduation. To Terry that is a minor point now and she is just praying that the doctors' optimism is on target.

Three graduating seniors are having very different senior weeks, except for the fact that, for all three students, when important things are happening, parents are their first consideration.

How Important Are Outside Influences?

Most parents today respond with some skepticism when they hear someone talk about the great influence of the family on children. Even parents who attach the highest priority to parenting are realistic enough to recognize that many other influences outside the home are at work on their children. Television, friends at school, music and dozens of other aspects of modern culture are beyond the control of parents. Parents and family begin to lose their unique role in forming children even before the teenage years. Parents may regret some of these influences or may not even fully understand them but, in contemporary American society, there is little they can do. Parents accurately recognize that their values and beliefs will have to compete for their child's allegiance with a vast array of contrary or different values that will often attract that child.

Instead of dwelling on how difficult things have become in this regard, it is also useful to recall that, even in earlier and simpler times, the influence of parents was shortened and curtailed because people married and/or left home much earlier than they do today. In any event, parents need to work with the opportunities they have in our present culture.

Even when diminished, the family remains the most powerful and pervasive influence on young persons as they leave home for college. All their basic skills, their images of love and trust, and their capacity for self–discipline will have been either nurtured or neglected in their family experience. Years later, when they have established their own families, they will continue to look at the world in the ways they learned in their early years. All of us modify, enhance or transform what we received as children but none of us are able to re–create ourselves in a completely new way.

Growth Is Expressed in Many Ways

Some college students follow a process of integration in which they use their family experiences as the touchstone for later developments and experiences. Other students seem to find it necessary, at least for a while, to adopt a rebellious and rejectionist stance toward their family experience while they experiment with novel and often contradictory identities. When students follow a process of integration, most parents will recognize the continuity of development, although at times it may not be so apparent. Parents who have to deal with rebellion and rejection have a much tougher task. They will often feel useless and beleaguered, rejected and cast aside. Commonly there is bitterness and silence between them and a child who follows this course. To illustrate the randomness and unpredictability of these outcomes, it is only necessary to remember that, often in the very same family, one child will follow a course of integration while another will set out on a path of rebellion and rejection. The same basic family experience diverges into two or more outcomes.

Every Family Has Problems–Don't Be Afraid To Talk It Out

In either the integration model or the rebellion model, parents do well to reflect, together if possible, on what their family life has been like, on what may have colored or shaped their children at an early age, and then find ways to talk about that calmly and non–defensively. Since every human family has some problems, it should not be taken as an accusation or indictment of their parenting when a college student focuses on these problems. A college course in personality development, a visit to the college counseling center, participation in a self–help group on campus or just talking with friends at school may heighten a student's awareness of such problems and prompt the desire to talk about them on a visit home.

When parents understand that this is probably the first time a young person has seen these problems for himself or herself, they will not be put off when a student seems to exaggerate or over–dramatize the problems. Instead of quickly and defensively insisting that "things weren't that bad," parents are wise to look beyond the student's overblown rhetoric and instead listen carefully to how a young person is processing these new understandings. When they find their parents open and calm about discussing family problems, students will often become much more communicative about everything that is going on in their lives at college. There are hundreds of ways to short–circuit this communication. Only careful listening is guaranteed to keep it on track.

The most hurtful aspect of family problems for most young people is not simply the problem in itself – they soon discover that most family problems are common enough – but rather the sense of uniqueness that is omnipresent among the young. They tend to bury their thoughts about family issues deep inside themselves because, in their youthful naivete, they think no one else has ever had to deal with such a problem. Healing and growth comes, not from the impossible fantasy of rewriting the past, but rather from those conversations that can eliminate the awful uniqueness they carry around as a burdensome secret. When parents are alert to this special syndrome of youth, they will be encouraged rather than threatened to find out that their children are seeking someone outside the family, a counselor, a chaplain, or another adult, so that they can talk out their perceptions of themselves and their family. By calmly listening, parents also make an enormous contribution to the dissipation of this painful sense of uniqueness.

For many families today there has been a problem which, though common enough, was big enough to hold the whole family in its grip and make it unavoidable for everyone involved. A divorce, however amicable or necessary, will inevitably be a central issue for everyone in the family, especially the children. Nearly everyone is now familiar with the oft–repeated insight of some psychologists that very young children internalize the divorce of their parents, thinking that they did something bad to cause their parents to break up. Without questioning the validity of this insight, at least in some cases, it is important to reflect on at least two resulting feelings about parents' divorce that are much more pronounced among college–age young people.

The first is that young people are rarely neutral, at least on the feeling level, about the actions of their divorced parents. Rightly or wrongly, rationally or emotionally, most young people feel that one of the parents is more directly responsible for what happened. Clearly this judgment will be very much shaped by whose version they have heard the most and by factors like custody, remarriage and visitation. Frequently, however, their judgment is not the one which the more involved parent has tried to inculcate. Both parents will have to deal with that judgment if they are going to have a valuable relationship with a son or daughter. It is particularly important and very difficult for the parent who has received the more negative judgment to hear that expressed, but unless it is fully talked out, the relationship with that parent usually atrophies and becomes one of mere familial obligation or worse.

However much parents attempt to put a good face on their divorce, they need to understand that their children will eventually come to a judgment on what they have experienced as a real loss. That judgment will assign greater or less responsibility to the parents, and it becomes the prism through which a young person will see his or her now divorced parents.

The second result of divorce is a painful question that becomes embedded deeply in the consciousness of a young person. Is real and lasting commitment possible? Can two people really love each other for life? Am I fated to repeat my parents' discovery that lasting commitment could not be sustained? This troublesome question will be at work as they enter relationships, look toward marriage and sort out their own future. It is not easily put away.

Most parents who have gone through a divorce will recognize the blaming mechanism and the skepticism about the possibility of lasting commitment because they have the same questions themselves. Neglecting to talk about these issues openly with children will only serve to remove a most important experience from the realm of communication and attaches only more superficiality to the relationship between parents and children.

Many families today have had to face the problem of a parent's addiction to alcohol or some other drug or a similar problem with one of the children. The most prominent symptom of the problem of addiction is denial that there is a problem. The addicted parent or child will, of course, deny a problem for a long time but spouses, children and siblings who are not addicted also enter into this denial rather than face the harsh reality that someone close is addicted. In those families where recovery from addiction has happened in a holistic way, all the members of the family have learned how to talk openly with each other about the problem. Silence about the problem is the manner of dealing with the problem in families where denial prevents recovery. In this situation, an intervention is probably called for and one of the members may decide to initiate it. Whether this is a spouse or a child, it is important to seek experienced and knowledgeable counsel about how to arrange an intervention that can succeed.

When a carefully planned intervention is able to bring about the recovery of the addicted member, the cycle of denial and addiction can be broken and treated. Even here, where some outside counsel is almost always necessary, it will be calm, non–judgmental communication that brings the family to a new and healthy life together.

Even this very brief and cursory glance at some serious family problems and how they might be healed by better communication serves to reinforce the basic premise of this chapter, for families confronting such problems as well as for families who have less significant issues. The role of the family is paramount for college students as for all of us. True, it should be added that this influence is for both good and ill. Nonetheless, in my experience, families who have faced serious problems and dealt with them well become only more influential, closer and more helpful to all members. The second part of this chapter's premise is that parents who learn the skills of non–judgmental, non–defensive communication will come to experience a growing and rewarding friendship with their college age sons and daughters. Those families with deeper problems obviously have some urgency about moving in these directions. Families with less serious problems also have everything to learn from the same process of understanding their essential role and learning how to talk with each other.

Parents Are Not the Last To Know

When a tragedy happens to a college student, the parents often express their sense of helplessness by telling me that they had no idea that their child was so depressed or had been using drugs or was involved in some major illegal activity. "Of course," they tell me, "parents are usually the last to know." Even when the problem is of a much lower magnitude, like an academic wipeout or a disciplinary problem at school, parents frequently express the same sentiment. In my experience, however, this is really something parents have been taught to feel by a culture that is constantly pointing to real experts somewhere out there. In fact, parents do know and are often the first to know when there is a serious problem. They may not know all the details which have been carefully kept from them but they do know their children and can intuit precisely and quickly that something is wrong. Parents may need to find out more, often they may need to seek good counsel before taking any action, and they will need to avoid anything that will be counter–productive. But, except in some very rare cases, they will be very much on target.

Then the hard work begins, as parents seek the most effective way to be of help to a son or daughter. All the finest strategies for help in this world will be of no consequence unless parents are secure and confident in their role, their intuitions and their experience. The strategies are there to be found through calm thinking and wise counsel. First, however, one should rely on the experts. When it comes to college students, their parents are almost always the real experts.

3
Caring Parents Are Not Intrusive Parents

Communication, Not Over-Protection

As an only child, Paul had been always close to his mother, and she, until the day he was accepted into college, was always physically present through the ups and downs, the dances, the soccer tournaments, and the broken arms of her son's life. Never having had the opportunity to go to college herself, Paul's mother took pride in her son's achievements, and in a very real sense she voluntarily accepted the task, as she saw it, of a parent to protect and encourage him to make the best choices of the opportunities he had. Because their relationship had been so close, Paul's mother naturally came to expect that their relationship would not change. It didn't need to.

When it was time to go off to college, it was no surprise that Paul decided to attend a good, local university, a little over an hour from home. Moving on campus for Paul, like many other first year students, was an exciting but emotional experience. He realized that he was leaving the security of home for a new and unfamiliar place.

Paul and I were immediately compatible as roommates from the moment we were assigned to live in the same dorm room. But even more importantly, we got along as friends and I would often go with him during the first semester of college to see his family over the weekends. Paul's mother made me feel very welcome, and I felt comfortable in his home away from the hectic bustle of student life.

It didn't take long for my new roommate, however, to become accustomed to the excitement and newness of college. Paul had a knack for taking every advantage of his environment to meet other people—by joining student groups and participating in club sports. Predictably, Paul soon met a freshman woman, Valerie, who, like himself, decided to major in physics. Only a few weeks into the school year, they began to date.

During one of my tag–along trips to Paul's home, shortly after he started to date Valerie, I sat down for a comfortable home–cooked meal with Paul and his mother. Paul excitedly began to tell his mom about his new girlfriend. With little experience dating before college, this new relationship had obviously become very important to him in the two or three months since school began. However, before Paul finished his story, his mother, in a concerned tone, began to interject, "Well, I hope that she doesn't get in the way of classes.... You really shouldn't be thinking so seriously about a girlfriend so early in school."

Although Paul tried to tell his mother about his new relationship with Valerie, it did little good. The maternal fears had been unleashed, and rather than talk with her son, Paul's mother became overwhelmed by her own fears of the hypothetical possibilities of her son's ruined career bought at the expense of a serious relationship he wasn't ready for. Finding no reciprocity in the dinner conversation, Paul decided to leave for school soon after the meal was over.

In part due to Paul's new relationship, and in part as a result of living on campus, Paul gradually began to shorten and space out his trips home. His mother, however, interpreted his behavior as a sign that she was losing the wonderful relationship she had with her only son. She could not understand why he would no longer take every opportunity to visit his family. During phone conversations, Paul became reluctant to share his feelings, especially about his relationship with Valerie; instead, he would later complain to me about having to listen to lectures from his mother about the seriousness of college work. Even worse, the non–verbal messages, like the tone of his mother's voice, infuriated him because he felt that she was trying to make him feel guilty for spending too much time with his girlfriend. He felt trapped between his new college life and the old quasi–dependent life he left back home.

The perceptions of Paul's mother—feelings of loss, the jealousy of someone else apparently fulfilling a role previously occupied by her, concerns about Paul not being able to balance academic work with a relationship—are all real concerns for parents today. Her method of communication, however, failed to recognize the very real change that had taken place in her son's life. In order to communicate effectively, parents need to shift (perhaps consciously) from authority–based communication to shared communication of experiences, hopes and fears.

Resorting to one–sided parental lectures carried very little appeal for Paul, even when he needed the benefit of his mother's advice. Few people would dispute the truism that parents can add a wealth of experience and knowledge to the trials faced every day by their children as burgeoning adults. However, in order to communicate effectively, parents need to be sensitive to the fact that their children have become young adults and that the "because–I-told–you–so" approach can (and should) no longer work. If Paul's mother had conveyed her concerns on a level of parity and reciprocity, Paul might have been much more willing to engage and share his life with his mother, as he wanted to the night I had dinner with him.

Reaching the Right Balance

Recognizing that effective communication requires a new understanding of the parental relationship, the logical question becomes, "How do I reach the right balance?" An over–protective parent, for example, might have a propensity for being too intrusive in the life of a college student. On the other hand, parents who try too hard to stay out of the affairs of the student risk creating an image of not caring or of not being concerned about their child's well–being. The quandary, then, manifests itself as, "too much will alienate, too little will distance."

Because families are so different in the way they communicate with each other, reaching the right balance of communication requires wise personal assessment and common sense. However, the important point is that mother, father, son or daughter understands the perspective and needs of the other side. There is a tradeoff. Such an approach will often not yield the quick results that parents might wish by getting their child to accept things blindly and act on their advice. Instead, sheer parental "authority" can become more helpful when achieved through reasoned communication on a level of parity. More importantly, though, mutuality and reciprocity—prerequisites to a mature relationship—will in the long run provide a foundation for a solid and trusting bond of communication.

When Sally came to college, she had no idea what to expect, especially because she grew up in a small town far from the big city where she now found herself. Her parents, both college and law school graduates, saw her off with the mind set that their daughter had now entered a new, independent stage of her life, not to be influenced by nosy parents. I later found out that they both had made a pact not to intrude in their daughter's life, apparently in response to their own memories and fears of overzealous parents. Soon into the school year, however, Sally began to struggle with trying to balance her school work, extracurricular commitments and pressure from her boyfriend to invest more time in their relationship.

One evening, as I was walking across campus, I ran into Sally, who happened to live in the same dorm building I did. As we walked, she told me about her problems. To my amazement, Sally seemed not only concerned with resolving her issues, but also with finding someone whom she could trust and converse with about her problems. When I asked whether she had tried talking with her parents, she admitted that she had brought up the subject, but that she became frustrated when her parents seemed to avoid giving her any advice. In fact, she said, they seemed to belittle the significance of her concerns, especially because they never said anything at all—positive or negative—about her boyfriend.

Even before college, many parents realize that their own vocal opinions about a boyfriend or girlfriend will have little positive effect on their child's decision and behavior with that person. Often, however, because relationships touch the fundamental core of vulnerability, a parent will provoke an emotional judgment rather than a reasoned opinion whenever the subject is raised. Such protective instincts, however, need not mean that relationships, though a sensitive area, are a taboo zone to be avoided. A parent's input can often be of tremendous value to their children—neophytes in the realm of relationships.

Whereas Paul's mother always sought to retain authority–based communication with her son, Sally's parents embraced the opposite extreme when they decided not to influence any of their daughter's personal decisions. Whereas Paul felt alienated and uncomfortable sharing the most intimate parts of his life with his mother, Sally really wanted to share her experiences with her parents but felt distanced by their lack of any meaningful response. In both cases, the new college students tried to share their life on an adult level with their families. While their parents could provide important opportunities in which to discuss their fears and concerns, Paul and Sally also needed the freedom to make their own decisions and to accept responsibility for their mistakes.

Growing up doesn't have to mean growing apart. It does mean accepting the change from an authoritative role to one of reciprocity—as adults capable of making decisions and handling mistakes. Accepting this transformation also means welcoming a new kind of relationship, one that is deeper, more substantive, and more mature. A new level of closeness will emerge as both the parent and child realize that they can share more of their lives knowing that the conversation is based on respect and an attempt at understanding the other side's perspective.

THE HARD TIMES AND THE DIFFICULT SUBJECTS

All relationships have to endure periods of disappointment, disillusionment and emotion. Blow–ups and fights followed by anger and rebellion are common enough in all families. The way they are dealt with, however, can make a vital difference in the final outcome and long–term effects of the parent–student rapport.

One night during her freshman year, Lisa decided to go to a field hockey team party off campus. Although she was not yet of legal drinking age, she went with some older teammates who thought it would be a good idea to see just how much liquor Lisa could handle. A few hours into the party, she became completely drunk. As Lisa was leaving to go out dancing, the local police had arrived outside the house in response to neighbors' complaints about the noise and recklessness of the party. When Lisa's friends saw the police, they began to run in different directions. Lisa also started to run. Two policemen pursued her, and after a quarter mile chase, they caught up with her and brought her into the station. Not wanting to press charges, the police notified the school that an underage, intoxicated student had been apprehended.

Lisa later told me that she dreaded the moment she would have to tell her father about the incident, even more than having to face the school officials. Deeply ashamed of what she had done, Lisa had already reprimanded herself for making the mistake of drinking so heavily and acting so foolishly. Nonetheless, she had to tell her father about the disciplinary action that the school imposed on her. She decided to tell him in person.

As a doctor, Lisa's father knew full well what the consequences of heavy drinking could entail. Growing up, Lisa had always thought of her father as a reasonable but strict disciplinarian. Consequently, she feared the possible reactions which might come from her confession. He might, for example, threaten to take her out of school or to cut her off financially. Or even worse, he might just refuse to talk to her.

As she recounted the story, Lisa watched her father stare at the floor in deep thought. She kept expecting him to look up with an angry gaze before beginning to lecture and shout. Her expectations were wrong. Her father silently listened, and then asked whether she was all right. They talked about what happened and about the school's actions, but her father did not reprimand her. Instead he related some of his experiences, both from his own days at college and from the hospital. Lisa felt that her father, rather than reacting emotionally, conveyed his concern in a way that allowed her to discuss her fears and worries.

Lisa's father treated his daughter as an adult who had the capability of realizing the mistake she made. His method of communication made her feel at ease discussing the matter, even though it was a subject she was extremely ashamed of. Today, she tells me that she is much more inclined to discuss her fears and experiences with her father, whereas she had never thought she could do so before. To their benefit, Lisa's family is probably closer today than before she left for college.

Just as many students want to talk with their parents about goings–on in their personal lives, there are also certain topics which most college students usually won't talk about. For example, sex and sexual orientation for many families is simply a taboo arena. Given the unique nature of the parent–child relationship, many students feel that mom or dad (or both) just wouldn't understand their problem or would reject their perspective. Perhaps the subject concerns something that the student is ashamed of, like peer pressure to experiment with drugs, or perhaps it involves sexual questions which might embarrass the student if discussed in a parental context.

If a student has decided not to tell parents about something, there might be a good reason. Forcing a discussion might be interpreted as too aggressive, and thus force a retreat. Not only do students have to be ready to discuss whatever might be on their mind, it must be remembered that a parent will in some sense always be the harbinger of right and wrong, reward and punishment. In other words, while parity and reciprocity are important elements to communication with college students, parents will always retain some stature of moral certitude and fear of reprisal from their children. Therefore, as in conversations with friends, non–confrontational ways of inviting conversation usually work more effectively than forcing unwanted topics to surface.

Nevertheless, parents usually have some idea of what is going on in their child's life and can usually spot when something is not quite right. It doesn't take too much deduction before the list of topics is narrowed down, and then there are ways of asking the right questions in order to invite a response in a non–aggressive fashion, letting the person know that someone is concerned and there to listen and help. For example, by telling a story about an old classmate who became pregnant, parents who suspect a similar issue with their child can invite him or her to discuss any concerns voluntarily. The direct approach, on the other hand, might trigger defensive mechanisms that lead to unwanted abrasiveness and arguments.

When fights and arguments do occur, time is needed to repair the damage. However, too much time may solidify the resentment formed by the words of disagreement. Feelings might have been hurt and individual pride has usually been hurt. Few want to admit that they are wrong and fewer want to apologize for acting out of bounds or saying things that they didn't mean. When these kinds of hard times occur, grudges will do nothing to ameliorate the situation, but patience and forgiveness need to be ready at hand.

In adjusting to a new relationship with a college son or daughter, parents might reflect on how they relate to their own friends or family members, people on their own level. They will quickly realize that, while they cherish the closeness and emotional intimacy of these bonds, they would be easily put off by a friend or relative who was too inquisitive or too intrusive. Parents will quickly see that they value most the friendships which are based on parity and mutuality. Why? Because these are relationships among adults. Extending this adult style of relationship to a son or daughter (who was once so dependent) is not easy, but it is critical to begin it the day a son or daughter begins college.

4
Getting In with the Wrong Crowd

Decisions and Consequences

College students live in an artificial world, unlike anything in their previous experience, and surely very different from the way they will live after graduation. Never again does a person live in an exclusive community with hundreds or thousands of single people the same age. Never again does a person experience the diversity of cultures and information. Students in college are constantly inundated with new information but, most often, they do not have the time or discipline to process all that data maturely when decisions have to be made..

The image in the media and the popular culture of the college experience portrays a life artificially free from the pressures and responsibilities of family and work concerns. The truth, however, is that college students confront many decisions that will have serious consequences and a direct effect on their present and future well–being and happiness. When a student chooses to drink, to experiment with drugs, or to enter into a sexual relationship, the consequences may be felt immediately or over the long term, though it rarely feels like that at the moment. Many freshmen, in fact, are unexperienced novices in dealing with these questions, especially when they are driven by peer pressure.

Although college students have entered an "adult environment" where a parent's *physical presence* can no longer supervise, guide or determine the choices being made, the loss of physical contact with a college student does not mean the loss of influence and communication. The psychological and moral presence of parents can play a more helpful or valued role in a student's life than the fear of getting caught ever did when the student lived at home. For this reason, the quality of the relationship that parents now build with their college students will establish to a large degree the openness of a student to parents' advice and insights.

As we discussed in the previous chapter, by cultivating a reciprocal, adult relationship that transcends an authority–based model, parents are able to gain and build trust and confidence. My own experience is that most college students seek the experience and advice of their parents, as long as their freedom and independence do not feel threatened or compromised in the process.

Even though most college students are reluctant to share their own insecurities with their parents (or any other adults), part of the college experience involves their search for answers to difficult or perhaps unanswerable questions. This book hopes to stimulate thinking so that parents may know what to expect from their college students. Difficult times become easier to share when parents are prepared to respond, and the embarrassing moments will become easier to discuss when it is apparent that other people, especially parents, have faced similar experiences, and are willing to talk about them.

Drinking and Drugs

Bob and I got to know each other well during our freshman year because we lived in the same dormitory and we played on the same intramural basketball team. He was a very friendly person, sometimes insecure, but a hard worker who excelled in math and science. Four times a week, he and I would go to the gym with a group of other guys from the dorm to practice for upcoming games. On weekends, many of us would go to the campus pub or a student party to escape from all the work we still hadn't finished from the last week.

Bob's strong work ethic always intrigued me. Yet to me Bob also seemed to be given to extremes. Many of us were very impressed when we found out he pulled a straight–A average after his first semester. He was remarkably diligent and efficient with his time, adhering closely to his study schedule, which somehow allotted time for extracurricular activities like basketball. On the courts, he was an exceptional athlete, just as aggressive as he was rigorous academically. Unfortunately, Bob's pattern of extremes also applied to drinking on weekends.

Whenever Bob drank, he almost always did so excessively. He would change from a friendly, usually quiet person into an aggressive talker who would captivate audiences with crazy antics and with his story–telling gifts. Maybe he had found that alcohol helped him to compensate for his normally shy demeanor, especially around women. Or perhaps Bob drank so much because other people, at least the people he often hung out with, made it look so normal to drink on weekends. Or maybe Bob had a serious drinking problem.

Near the end of second semester freshman year, Bob was walking back to the dorm with his roommate and two other friends from an off–campus party. According to his roommate, who now recounts the story as part of an alcohol–awareness program for incoming students, they were all very drunk and quite rowdy. For fun, Bob said something to one of the students that provoked a playful chase. But as he was running across the street to get on campus, Bob didn't look and failed to see an on–coming car. He was struck by a hit–and–run driver and lay in a coma for three days before he died of internal head injuries.

When I first met Hilary, I was immediately impressed with her quickness of mind and agility of wit. She could easily win a logical argument on topics that she knew little about, and her bizarre sense of humor made her attractive to be around. There was no question that, for many students who knew her, Hilary was a campus personality—someone easy to get along with and always ready to have a good time. What few people thought much about, however, was that she would often drink to carry a good buzz through the night.

I used to see Hilary around campus and, on occasion, I would bump into her on the way in or out of the gym. She was one of two women who had made the tennis team without being recruited. At the time, I didn't know her very well, but I, like many others on campus, held her on a sort of pedestal.

One Friday night, Hilary and a couple of her friends went to a campus party put on by seniors. Although this particular party had been filled with people earlier in the evening, now, by the end of the night, most people had left for home. At two o'clock in the morning, Hilary was still at the party and quite drunk. When she decided to leave, a senior male student she knew only slightly from around campus offered to walk her home. By the time they arrived at her apartment, Hilary had become sick and was barely conscious of where she was and whom she was with.

If Hilary's housemate, Cathy, had not stumbled into the apartment when she did, Hilary might have been raped. She might have died. When Cathy walked into the living room, she was startled to see that an unfamiliar person was in the apartment and that Hilary's shirt was thrown on the floor. When Cathy asked if everything was all right, this male senior abruptly got up and said, "She's drunk; you'd better take care of her," and quickly left.

Hilary soon began to vomit, but Cathy could not wake her up. Fearful that something serious might happen, Cathy called for medical help. Hilary was rushed to the university hospital where she was found to be suffering from alcohol poisoning, and the worried doctors had to pump her stomach.

Bob and Hilary are not the only examples of the dangers of heavy drinking that I have seen. All college students witness heavy drinking, and, most often, nothing as tragic as death or rape occurs. These two stories from my own college experience are not uncommon and they do illustrate the heavy drinking phenomenon so prevalent on college campuses today.

In dealing with the alcohol problem on college campuses, parents need to accept the fact that it is very common and to educate their college student about the reality of drinking. It does little good for a parent to overreact to alcohol or to think that all drinking is evil. Yelling and screaming does not help, but communicating as an adult to an adult creates a better opportunity to help college students gain the maturity and knowledge to drink responsibly.

Despite all the peer pressure, there are actually many students who would prefer not to drink or get caught up in the alcohol–oriented social scene. Parents, whether or not they themselves use alcohol, might point to the validity of such a decision and how they respect and admire those who do not drink. Long before the college years arrive, parents are wise to be sure the option of not drinking is presented positively and not as an oddity. Since a student who does not drink may feel some sense of isolation on campus, parents can provide opportunities to discuss this with a student and, in the process, supply support and reassurance.

Some students find themselves in an environment conducive to experimenting with drugs, especially marijuana and hashish. Other students decide to use drugs recreationally or just every once in a while. Like alcohol, these other drugs can become addictive. Experts in the field of addiction make no distinction between addiction to alcohol or drugs. Both are drugs, have similar long range impact and require the same kind of recovery programs.

Drug use may be different because there tends to be some social stigma attached to drug use, especially with heavy drugs. Drinking, on the other hand, is more socially acceptable. The essential thing for parents, however, is knowing what to do when they sense a student is involved with the wrong crowd and knowing when and how to intervene.

The signs of chemical abuse are any changes in personality, loss of interest in studies or sports that once were important, a new and very different crowd of friends, unexplained absences, trips or silences, late night telephone conversations that are very emotional or strange and any discernible physical or health changes. Parents are often the first to notice such changes and need to watch out for their own denial that a problem exists. One very common form of parental denial these days is when parents, upon discovering a student is drinking a lot, say they are relieved that it's only beer and not a hard drug. Alcohol abuse is not only as lethal as drug abuse but is far more common and, tragically, more tolerated and accepted. Likewise, some parents are hesitant to open up the question of excessive drinking because they do not want their own drinking questioned. Denial which allows a drinker to keep drinking can also lead parents and friends to overlook and excuse a real problem.

Because it is obviously better to educate students *before* they get drunk or high, parents need to find the right approach when discussing drinking and drugs. It should not be a taboo subject. Parents can invite discussion as an opportunity to make sure that college students understand the meaning and dangers of abuse. Some students respond to reason and argument. Others respond to experience. Few, however, listen to stern lectures. In fact, emotional over–reactions can make students secretive or deceptive about what really goes on in their life. Drinking has real and serious consequences, and it is important that students know the consequences and effects of drinking and drugs.

Substance abusers come in all forms, shapes, and sizes. An alcoholic does not have to be someone who drinks alone or in a dark alley. The effects of taking drugs do not have to include some catastrophic consequence or tragedy like those described above. A drinking or drug problem can manifest itself in a variety of ways. If parents are concerned about their child's drinking, a problem probably exists. And if so, there are constructive ways of dealing with the problem. For example, many campuses have offices for substance abuse where parents and students can obtain guidance and information in helping someone with a problem.

A family intervention to get an alcohol or drug abuser into treatment may be necessary. Today there is a wealth of information and experience to help plan a successful intervention. Talk to people at a treatment center, or contact the local AA General Services Office, or use the wise experience of friends and other family members who have done well in recovery. A poorly planned and haphazard intervention degenerates into accusation and acrimony, and does not work. If you believe an intervention is necessary, take your time, find out everything you can about how to do a successful intervention, contact the treatment center you want to use, check your health insurance coverage, and be confident that even the perplexing problem of chemical abuse can have a happy ending. Both of the present authors have close friends who have dealt with their alcohol and drug abuse and have discovered a whole new and better life in recovery.

Many college students who are not alcoholics or addicts nevertheless allow excessive college drinking to interfere with their studies and other activities, thus jeopardizing their grades, relationships and opportunities for graduate school. "Partying too much" does not always require professional treatment but it can mean the elimination of a desired professional opportunity.

SEX AND SEXUALITY

Sex is a major and eternally discussed part of college life. As with drinking and drugs, the sexual decisions that students make can have serious and permanent effects on their and others' futures. For some, college is the first time that a sexual relationship presents itself. For others, it is the time when questions regarding sexuality are discovered and explored. For many reasons, parents can and should play an important role in lending support and advice for what can otherwise be a confused and difficult dilemma for students.

The morality of sex, for many, is a cerebral or intellectual debate that has little to do with reality. This is not to say that many people don't feel guilty about having sex, but it does mean that, guilty or not, many college students do have sex. Therefore, it is important that—since students are going to make their own decisions—parents keep open an invitation to talk about sex, knowing full well how uncomfortable such topics can be.

When John and Elizabeth started dating, both were overcome by feelings they had never experienced before. As John would tell me later, the emotions of their new relationship overtook both of them, and they quickly became dependent on one another. Neither had dated seriously before college, and now they each found themselves immersed in a new, exciting, and intense relationship.

Most of John's friends thought that he and Elizabeth made an unlikely couple. John was very humorous and outgoing, the kind of person who enjoyed spending a lot of time with his many friends. Elizabeth, in contrast, was very serious, very committed to her studies and The Environmental Club on campus. Nevertheless, as John would later put it, "The fact that other people had doubts made me that much more determined to make things work. Having seen my own family go through failed marriages, I wanted to make this relationship work."

As in many college relationships, John and Elizabeth thought mostly about the present. They rarely thought about where their relationship was going or what was most important to them individually. As far as they were concerned, the fact that they cared so much about each other now was all that really mattered. The rest was superfluous.

After dating about three months, John and Elizabeth started to have sex. One night, they went to the Christmas Ball together, a formal event that involved cocktails at seven, dinner at eight–thirty, and appearances at the dance between ten and eleven o'clock. Like many couples at the dance, they both became quite tipsy over the course of the evening. After the dance, and now quite drunk, John and Elizabeth had unprotected sex. A short time later they found out that Elizabeth was pregnant.

They were both unprepared to accept the reality of the pregnancy. John, who did not want to abort the baby, assured Elizabeth that he would do whatever he could to raise the child, and that eventually they might get married. He told her that he was even prepared to finish school at night in order to find a job and support the baby, and he was sure that his parents would be willing to help out under the circumstances.

Elizabeth, however, had no intention of keeping the baby. She wanted to get an abortion, and was adamant about not telling anyone, especially her parents. John disagreed and tried to persuade her to talk to her parents. However she was unwilling to have any discussion with them. Her future was at stake, and nothing would change her mind. Eventually, John realized that the decision had been made, and to support Elizabeth, he accompanied her to the clinic to get the abortion. Less than a month later, their relationship ended.

Today, John still regrets deeply the way it all happened. Because it felt right for the moment then, he now lives with the pain of having acted irresponsibly. He never imagined it would be so hard to live with the memory of bringing Elizabeth to the abortion clinic.

Since then John has talked with his parents. Even though it was not easy, John has found real comfort in sharing his experience with his family. He once told me that he wishes he had talked to them before the abortion. Maybe then he would not have accompanied Elizabeth to the clinic. But he also wonders whether or not that might have changed things.

Even the best relationships between parents and their children will not guarantee that a college student will always make mature and balanced decisions. Some decisions will turn out to be big mistakes. The difference, however, is that a healthy relationship can accept the mistakes and can deal with them on a mature and realistic level. Although John's parents were angry and disappointed with their son, in the end John never lost their support or their love. Today, even if John regrets having unprotected sex, he does not regret sharing his problem with his parents.

During my freshman year, I became friends with another student, Pat, who was in many of my first year classes. Since both of us enjoyed a cynical sense of humor, we got along well.

At the end of the school year, I had been able to get a good pick in the campus lottery for university housing the following year. I was already committed to living with three other students, but it was a five–person place and we were looking for a fifth housemate. When I asked Pat if he would be interested, he quickly responded, and so I arranged for him to live with us.

Over the summer, Pat decided to work and live near the campus in order to take one or two summer classes. He lived with another student from his freshman dorm who had planned to do the same thing. This roommate, who had taken some time off between high school and college, was older than Pat. He was also gay, and during that summer Pat came to realize that he too had sexual feelings for another man.

As soon as we returned for the beginning of sophomore year, Pat decided to tell me about his homosexuality. I could tell he was having a difficult time sharing such a personal realization with someone. Pat told me that he had never had homosexual feelings before that summer, and now he believed that his feelings were a sort of aberration, an exception to the rule that applied only to the man he roomed with over the summer.

As the year progressed, however, it became clear to me that Pat had an exceptionally difficult time dealing with his homosexuality. He became very depressed, and he could never muster the courage to tell his parents the truth. On one occasion, he even asked a close friend of his, Loren, to accompany him home for the long weekend. I later found out that this was a ruse to let his parents assume that she was his girlfriend. When I asked him why he didn't tell his parents, he explained that he was afraid that they would never be able to accept him as a homosexual. In his mind, it was better to hide the fact from them than to risk losing them.

Pat's secret distanced him greatly from his family because he had to exclude them from an important part of his life. Finally, one day, Pat decided he had to confront his family. His parents, although uncomfortable about the subject, listened attentively.

The subject was a difficult one to admit and discuss openly, even though his parents had suspected the truth long before. But for Pat, the truth released the burden of deception he had been carrying for a long time. For his parents, the truth destroyed the rationalizations they created to justify the distance in their relationship. The very act of sharing transformed the distance into closeness by forcing everyone to deal with the truth.

Sex is the most intimate part of our lives and, very naturally, most of us have difficulty talking about it. Parents, however, can encourage students to talk more openly about sex when they decide to listen. Often parents confuse listening with approval or mistakenly express disapproval by shutting off the communication. The best sex education, and the best preparation for the sexual carnival that can exist on campus, is a respectful sharing about sex between parents and their children from an early age. There is a lot of talk about sex on campus, just as there is in the office or the factory, but most of it is either bragging war stories or the proverbial dirty jokes. College students are old enough to absorb difference and disagreement from their parents on sex as on any other topic, if the exchange is open and respectful. Parents can also make the common mistake of thinking that college students are very knowledgeable and nonchalant about sex in their lives. In reality, they are as fearful and confused as anyone else, maybe more so because of the campus climate, and will often relish a chance to share their fears and doubts about sex, intimacy and their own self–image. Most college students are urgently looking for someone to confide in. Parents can make themselves good friends and confidants when they put a premium on the openness and quality of the communication.

Parents cannot solve all their children's problems ever or at any age, but can be a great help and support. College students need the freedom to choose, even when that means making mistakes, even when parents can see the mistakes coming so clearly. Parents who pick up the skills of quality communication can, however, encourage the student to make the most informed and educated decision. Parents can cultivate a relationship that remains open to discussion and one that suggests alternatives but does not force them. Above all, parents need to build a relationship that respects the newly emerging adult, even when that new adult disagrees with a parent's judgment or opinion.

There are times, however, when a parent cannot and should not accept the choices made by a student. A college student who continues to engage in destructive behavior such as drinking or drugs, and who continues to deny that any problem exists, should not expect to have family support. Every parent has to establish the threshold of sensible toleration which might require them to intervene in a student's life.

Parents who are paying for part or all of a college education might wonder about the return on such a heavy investment. Rationally discussing the money involved and the performance of a student can lead to a more mature assumption of responsibility. Some of my own college friends who basically wasted a year or two because of their constant partying are now grateful for a few words of parental concern that woke them up to the high stakes that were involved.

A parent who offers some flexible space and refrains from premature judgments regarding a college student's choices will probably be surprised to find how eager and ready the student can be to open up and talk about very personal worries, concerns and fears. Communication works and, when it flows between a parent and a college age child, the only mistake a parent can make is thinking that the child is the only one reaping the benefits.

5
Keeping the Faith on Campus

Kevin's father, a very successful attorney who specializes in corporate law, has been a trustee of the university for over a decade. Since he himself graduated from the university on a scholarship program that made higher education possible for students from his family's modest economic background, his work as a trustee has been a labor of much gratitude. After years as a trustee, serving on many of the most important committees, he knows the university inside out. This year, however, his relationship with the university has become even more intimate because his oldest child, Kevin, began his freshman year.

Toward the end of Kevin's freshman year, I ran into his father at a charity benefit dinner where he took the opportunity to say how happy he was that Kevin was participating in the Catholic community on campus, attending mass regularly, going on our spring retreat and also being a lector at mass. After sharing some of his own feelings of how important his religion has been to him in his life, he explains that he has been very pleased to see Kevin get involved in the Catholic community very much on his own without, he adds, any pushing on his part. He adds that he has been literally astonished at Kevin's reports of a packed, standing room only chapel for Sunday mass and the strong student response to the Catholic ministry. As much as he thought he knew the university from his service as a trustee, he would not have expected very much of a Catholic presence in what he has always regarded as a highly secularized atmosphere. He has been thoroughly delighted by Kevin's reports, he tells me, but also very surprised.

The perception of Kevin's father about religion on a college campus is a common one, and it is, as he would learn from his son, a mistaken one. On most college campuses there is a very large, thriving Catholic community of students, sometimes along with faculty, staff people and nearby residents. In fact, on most campuses in the United States today, the campus Catholic community will also be the largest worshiping community, defying the secular perception about religion and Catholicism in particular. Because the tradition and teachings of the Catholic Church run counter to much of what appears to be the trend on campuses today, some have concluded that Catholicism is barely present any longer in this environment. The secular reading of college students today is deeply flawed and so bound up in its own a priori ideological commitments so that it easily misses the fact that Catholicism's counter–cultural position may well be the source of its vitality among college students.

Parents for whom religious beliefs and practices are important need to view much of the media image of college students with a large grain of salt. Like the larger American society, a college campus is permeated with religious groups and activities. Many observers have noted a resurgence of religion on college campuses. Jewish chaplains speak of the rise in religious observance among Jewish students. Protestant campus ministries draw many to Bible and prayer meetings. Nearly all religious ministries are deeply involved in social action and volunteer efforts. At those universities with a Religious Studies department, there has been a dramatic increase of interest and enrollment in recent years.

If your religious faith finds expression in the Catholic tradition, your son or daughter will have plenty of opportunities and many companions if they decide to practice their faith on campus. They will not be alone or lost but, on most campuses, will find a large faith community for worship and a host of other activities.

Students will also find a secularist mindset among some professors, administrators and other students that is glibly hostile to traditional religion, especially Catholicism. My experience, however, is that expressions of such hostility, while commonplace, serve mainly to provoke young people into a deeper reconsideration of their own religious faith and beliefs. Many students I have known over the years arrived on campus with a youthful indifference to religion but then dug deeper into their religious identity because of the unfair or bigoted attacks they encountered. Students are furthermore well served, in this regard, by the healthy skepticism they bring to all pronouncements from on high. The fact that now some pronouncements from on high by professors and others denigrate their religious background frequently motivates them to search out the Catholic campus ministry and its programs.

Some students, of course, do drift away and appear to have lost their faith. Others will just linger in the indifference they bring to most larger issues at this stage in their life. Later I will suggest some ways to understand these reactions but, at the outset, parents should know, contrary to much that is reported, that Catholic faith communities are thriving on most campuses.

Your Family's Faith and Practice

Jo–Ann's father had evidently died of cancer when she was still in high school, and her mother was then left with the task of raising and supporting three children. I only came to know Jo–Ann well in her junior year, some years after her father's death. On our spring retreat that year, Jo–Ann had been asked to be one of the student leaders, which involved giving one of the six talks that set the tone for the discussions and reflections of the retreat. As I listened to her talk, I was hearing for the first time the story of what had happened to her family and how her mother had impressively overcome the loss of her husband and become, in effect, two parents for her children. Jo–Ann's topic for the talk was: "Why my religion is important to me." In her freshman year, away from home for the first time, she came to realize what an extraordinary person her mother was, especially in light of the tragedy of her father's too early death. Jo–Ann searched in her own mind for the source of her mother's strength and concluded that it was her mother's deep Catholic faith that sustained and empowered her. And, simply put, Jo–Ann wanted some of that strength and power for herself now and in her later life. She explained that she could not predict what trials or crises would face her in her own life, and she was quite certain that these would different from those of her mother, but she was very determined to have those same resources to face whatever life would bring her way.

When college students have already seen first–hand the value of religious faith in their parents' (or grandparents') lives, even in circumstances far more ordinary than in Jo–Ann's story, they will generally want that for themselves. And they will seek it out. If parents have been open enough with their children to allow them to see how faith really does operate in their lives, how it has served them in trying times, then students naturally gravitate to that vitality and strength. If students feel loved and secure in their relationship with their parents and see some connection between that love and what their parents do on Sunday, they will hold fast to that connection with religious faith. Of course, if young people have only experienced a tepid and formalistic religious life at home, or if they have only experienced a blind dictate forcing them into religious practices, they will most likely discard that religious faith their first week away from home. Yet even in these circumstances, it often means, at least after some time and other experiences, a return or re–evaluation of what had only been a formalistic and external religious veneer.

Parents who attach importance to passing on their religious faith are wise to share the very practical side of their faith with their sons and daughters, sharing with them the instances when faith has comforted them or sustained them or empowered them. Faith is, of course, a sublime and transcendent mystery, but it also works in our lives with demonstrable and practical benefits. When young people have actually seen and experienced those practical dimensions of faith in their own family, it is nearly impossible for them ever to become indifferent to a reality that invaluable.

Religious faith is contagious. We pick it up from other people, especially those close to us. The surest way to pass faith on to others, especially our children, is to let them see that faith in action in our lives.

Faith Lost or Abandoned

There are about as many atheists among college students as there are in the proverbial foxholes. In fact, around final exams, atheists probably do better in foxholes and anywhere else than on a college campus. At the Sunday mass just before final exams, when I mention that our congregation seems to have grown, everyone laughs heartily, even those who are making their once a semester appearance.

Yet it is true that some students, soon after arriving on campus, will formally abandon or repudiate their religious faith. Sometimes this will include a formal announcement to parents, especially if it has the power to upset them. When I speak in a class or at some program on campus, there is always at least one student, no matter what the topic under discussion, who will go to great pains to introduce himself or herself as someone who used to be a Catholic, or as someone who left the Catholic Church in a flourish of honesty and maturity. Since this declaration usually bears no relationship to the rest of the question or remark, I suggest that we discuss that part later at some convenient time and I go on to deal with the matter at hand. Often this does lead to a follow–up discussion, later and in private, where I often learn the real reasons for this disaffection. Most common is a student's realization of the hypocrisy of parents and all the rest of us who practice Catholicism. I always plead guilty to hypocrisy because the alternative would be the final perfection of the arrival of the kingdom of heaven which I am not prepared to announce. Very rarely, almost never, is atheism the factor. College students are, at that time of their lives, extremely tentative about all commitments and lasting solutions. Philosophical atheism is a large chunk of personal philosophy for most students to swallow whole.

A new boy friend or girl friend who disdains religion, or one from a religious background that is very different, or a grudge against parents for a whole variety of reasons, or the posturing of a very sophomoric sophistication, or coming under the spell of some campus professor guru—these are all much more common reasons for the abandonment of religious faith and practice by college students. Increasingly, students come from families where religion was treated with neglect or indifference, or from families where a divorce meant, among other things, that religious and sacramental preparation was one of the things abandoned in the scheduling that was dictated by custodial or visitation rights.

When confronted with the repudiation or abandonment of religion, parents are wise to wait and see what the next stage will bring. A student may be merely experimenting with different identities, or provoking an argument that is really about many issues, or simply going through one of the cycles of "I don't care" indifference that is part of the routine. Similar cycles will often mark their attentiveness to their academic work, to their phone calls home, or to friends on campus. Some students veer dramatically from one trend to another and are easily susceptible to influences a parent may not know about. With the exception of some very determined students, most student opinions and convictions are quite temporary. There is always next semester, next year, and a different person may well emerge. Within bounds, that is part of the college experience and is to be expected, however much it afflicts the patience and practical sense of a parent.

Students roam through these cycles with their religion as with other things, and while parents may well have reason to be concerned, the most important thing is the old bromide about patience as well as avoiding anything that will harden attitudes or close off communication.

Should We Ask Them About Religion?

Gerry has kept in close touch with me over the five years since he graduated. During his four years here, he never even once appeared at a Sunday mass. The unlikeliness of our friendship was established on his first day as a freshman when his parents brought him into my office and announced that he had missed confirmation because they had moved a few times and he was never in a parish at the right time and right age for the sacrament. At that inauspicious introduction, they made it clear to him, and to me, that they expected him to be confirmed and attend mass every Sunday. His parents were so authoritarian about this and everything else that even I, who was about their age, felt first intimidated, then annoyed.

Predictably, Gerry did nothing about being confirmed and, as I said, never attended mass. He and I got to know each other at the beginning of his sophomore year when he came by to tell me that his parents were now cutting him off financially because of his refusal to do their bidding in matters of religion as well as in other areas. Over the next few months, however, he found a way to finance the rest of his college education with some scholarships that became available to him precisely because he now had no family support. Eventually Gerry graduated, went to graduate school and has done very well in the creative arts. In all our conversations over these years, I have never found him to be particularly anti–religious or unbelieving. But, of course, his whole experience of religion has been in the context of threats by his parents to cut him off. I have always recognized that as something close to insurmountable in terms of his response to religion, at least for a long time to come.

While Gerry and his parents are an extreme and rare instance in my experience, I have known other parents who did issue threats about religious practice to students, but in a much more subtle and clever way than Gerry's did. The impasse and subsequent estrangement of Gerry and his parents does serve to illustrate the futility and destructiveness of threats. Especially in regard to religion, which must be freely embraced to have any authenticity, threats have no place at all.

Short of threats or ultimatums, some parents constantly quiz their sons or daughters about their religious practice. In these queries, students often feel an underlying, unspoken threat, and the results can come to be as terrible as from a dire threat.

More frequently, when I meet parents around campus at Parents' Weekend or other events, they will ask me if they should ask their sons and daughters about their religious practice. My response is that such a question is fine if it seems natural and welcome, but that it will be counter–productive if it seems like prying or displays a lack of trust. Most parents, upon a moment's reflection, can easily distinguish the two very different contexts for the question. In fact, most students from families where there was regular religious practice will say something about their religious life on campus. If there is a huge silence about it, I would suggest wondering about what else is encompassed in that silence and why a son or daughter feels the need for such a silence.

Your Faith Is Important to You

When parents talk with me about the religious practice of their sons and daughters, I usually sense that they feel they have discharged their duty by tending to the religious and sacramental formation of their children while they were young and lived at home. No longer are they concerned about what might be described as parental obligations or duties. And they are generally ready to accept the inevitable transition, in religion as in other areas, by which a child works out and decides these matters for himself or herself.

Yet, especially in Catholic parents, I also sense a larger hope that what they have found to be so valuable in their own lives will be there for their children when they need it. They worry now, not so much about their own obligations, but about circumstances beyond their influence which may leave their sons and daughters without the strong anchor that faith has been for them. They hope it will be there and are often anxious about what they see and hear on a college campus.

The anxiety, if it can called that, is really a tribute to the deep and experienced faith that many parents have. Even when they school themselves in the patience necessary to weather the fads and experiments that come with college years, they hope that certain fads and stages won't be the lasting ones. Communication is, as always, the key. If parents can open up in a new and adult way about their faith, its value in their lives, and their own doubts and struggles, they will most often find an equally open response from college students. Nothing is more conducive to the religious faith and practice of a student than the witness of parents. Sometimes quiet and undemonstrative, often deep and unspoken, the parents' religious faith is one of the most formative elements of a young person's make–up. It may emerge and blossom on a different schedule, or even lie dormant for a while, but religious faith has a power of example and influence that is immeasurable. Never does it go unnoticed.

Many, perhaps most, college students, after some time

of skepticism and rebellion, do come to stand in awe of the love which their parents have for them. It may take some rough times on campus or difficulties with relationships and friendships at college for a young person to fully realize what was given to them as gift from the beginning by their parents. As they come to that realization, they begin that wondrous encounter with unconditioned love that all of us must have at the core of our being if we are to love and be loved. In life there are really only two sources of unconditioned love – the love of our parents for us and God's love for us. In time, if we are blessed and if we are attentive, we realize that both have the same source whose name is God. It takes time to make these connections and it requires patience to observe others as they try to make the connections. In the end it becomes faith, but parents, chaplains, and older friends have to let God do his part as well.

6
And You Want Them To Do Well for Their Future

Taking the Academic Part Seriously

Some years ago, during orientation weekend for college freshmen, a university president welcomed the incoming students to their new home. The president's purpose was to calm the anxieties and fears that accompany an unfamiliar environment and to motivate the freshmen to pursue all their interests during their college careers. He stressed that it was up to the students to take advantage of every opportunity, both inside and outside the classroom. The president's message was clear: "Don't limit yourself academically; shop around for classes. Don't limit yourself to only academics; get involved in the college community."

His message is valid for every new freshman class. The vast majority of students will later go on to find a job or apply to graduate schools in an area unrelated to much of their undergraduate studies. The years that students spend in college involve much more than academic pursuits in a particular field. They also open up areas of intellectual and personal growth, a learning process of maturity built on exposure to different perspectives in the classroom, extracurricular activities and interpersonal relationships. We hope that the previous chapters have offered some insight into many of these college experiences.

Parents, nevertheless, rightfully want their college students to secure a good future, often one better than their own. To a large extent, this involves a serious commitment on the part of the student to take the academic part of college seriously. Educational institutions exist primarily to offer *academic* degrees at graduation. Future employers and admissions committees will use college transcripts as a basis for determining whether a student is qualified for work or advanced study. The most successful students, then, are those who achieve a healthy balance between academics and the other realms of college life. In a very real sense, their future does depend on it.

Recently I was fortunate enough to serve as a member of the admissions committee for graduate school. While the committee considered many qualities in assessing an applicant's qualification for acceptance, it would be dishonest of me to downplay the impact of good grades or a high class rank on the members of the committee. Although grades were not determinative, they were an important indication of an individual's talents, skills and commitment to work. For example, a student who scored exceptionally high on a standardized exam, but whose college grades were mediocre or low, might be seen as lazy or unmotivated. In the committee's eyes, there were always other applicants who posed less of a risk because they were consistent across the board and could more confidently be expected to do well in graduate school.

During the course of my work on the committee, we

received an application from someone who coincidentally was a college friend of mine. From my own personal experience, I knew Stacey to be one of the best–read people around. Her reading interests extended from the daily newspaper to classical literature. She was easily on a par with the best applicants in terms of intelligence and creativity.

The problem with Stacey's application, however, was that her record on paper did not reflect what I personally knew to be true. Her grades, while not embarrassing, were not particularly remarkable compared to the other applicants we saw every day. Since she was applying to the program right out of college, she also had little work experience that might be relevant to the course of study at the graduate level. Despite her impressive extracurricular activities, the majority of the committee saw her as a borderline case to be reviewed at the end of the selection process. Eventually she was rejected for admission to the graduate program.

Stacey's case is not uncommon. In any interview or application process, there will always be far more applicants than available openings. For this reason, employers and schools need some mechanism to discriminate between the best candidates and everyone else. Some standard, like a minimum grade–point average (GPA), often makes the difference. A good argument can be made that such a standard is arbitrary, but so also is assessing a person's competency for work based on an application file composed of recommendations and other testimonies rather than a person–to–person interview.

While parents will usually be very aware of the importance of grades for future opportunities, they need to appreciate that, in the college experience, academics are not everything. Students, on the other hand, frequently spend a great deal of their time and energy on non–academic pursuits like sports, relationships and just plain fun. The right balance needs to be discussed without resorting to a false either–or dichotomy. This very important discussion is best initiated during the college application process and in the selection of colleges.

The Economic Investment: Getting Your Money's Worth

Parents are frequently concerned that college students do not appreciate the financial consequences of assuming college costs. Many parents pay college tuition bills, at least in part, and they expect the student to study sufficiently so as to take advantage of opportunities in the future. College is an economic investment, and an academic "under–achiever" wastes good money. So, parents often ask, why pay the bills if the student does not take classes seriously?

Parents face a similar dilemma about finances when students have a choice among a number of schools which have significant differences in their tuition bills. Which one should a student attend? Is there a difference between degrees from various colleges? Cost–benefit considerations may induce a parent to present an ultimatum to a student who is not living up to the investment opportunity: "Shape up academically or we're not paying the bill anymore!"

When money is necessarily a central concern for the family, the best time to deal with such considerations is before a student goes off to college. While some schools are better suited for a particular individual than other schools, the rising costs of education are a reality that limit the options for many students. A mature student will usually understand budgetary constraints and will pick the best option within the family budget.

Some parents do use the threat of financial "cut–off" in the hope that their son or daughter will improve academically or otherwise. The problem, though, is one of cause and effect. Typically, the cause of a student's academic apathy has little to do with money. The threat of losing financial support may not address the real cause for the behavior which may range from personal unhappiness to a drinking problem or a relationship or some deeper issue.

A student's college education is too important to be cast only in terms of "getting your money's worth." Talking to college students as adults will usually be much more effective than threatening to take them out of school. Threats always run the risk of alienating both parties. There is, often, a deeper, personal reason for the student's academic problems. Perhaps the student is trying his or her best, but needs help. There are other options that are more constructive and more effective than seeing everything in terms of the "economic investment" rationale.

Grades, Achievements and Careers

A great deal of statistical literature supports a strong correlation between grades and career/graduate school opportunities. The "best" students usually get the interviews with the "best" companies, and subsequently get the "best" jobs. As my own experience on the graduate admissions committee indicates, good academic standing opens the door to opportunity.

Because they realize that so much can depend on grades, most parents naturally become concerned about their children's future well–being when academics take a turn for the worse. However, grades need to be measured alongside other important needs of the individual student. Parental expectations should not be set too high or be unrealistic. There are many qualities that can never be tested in school. Even in an imaginary school of all straight–A students, there will still always be a bottom 50% of the class.

If students are not achieving their potential, however, it is important to talk and find out the reasons for the decline. The happiness and well–being of the student must take first place in this conversation, and parents need to be clear that this is their prime concern. Some students, for example, find the transition from small high school classes to large university courses to be disorienting. Similarly, the move away from home can be traumatic for a student who is not used to a large campus, a big city or an independent social scene. On the other hand, some students need to wake up to the significance of working instead of partying. The important point is to remain alert to the real reasons for academic difficulties. Parental communication can provide the opportunity for a practical response and effective remedy.

Using College Administrators, Professors and Other Resources

Parental anxiety manifests itself in countless ways. Parents will call the dorm or they will send packages of goodies. They attend the orientation meetings and they will come to campus during parents' weekend. When a serious problem arises, parents often resort to more drastic measures. Some decide to call college administrators, professors or chaplains, without telling their son or daughter, in the hope of influencing the student or finding out information that is not forthcoming from their son or daughter.

Such interventions, made without a student's knowledge, often backfire into creating an even worse problem. Obviously, this caution does not apply to a parent discussing some discrepancy about financial aid with a loan officer. These interventions, however, can gravely damage trust when a parent contacts a teacher or other college official about a personal problem that a student regards as private.

Students want to be treated as adults, and expect their parents to treat them on a level of parity. Students who find out about a parental call to a professor or dean will naturally resent such an act as an intrusion in their life. Parents are wise to undertake such interventions only after a full, frank and honest discussion with their son or daughter and with their agreement.

A similar technique used by some concerned parents is calling a roommate or friend in the hope of gaining information about their son or daughter. A parent wants to find out whether their son is out for the night. Or maybe they want to know whether their daughter is really serious with her boyfriend and whether she is spending all her time with him. Inevitably the student will find out about the parent's call and the bonds of trust can be severely damaged.

All parents want their children to do well for their future and want a college student to take the academic part of life seriously. Grades are important because they open many doors and create opportunities later in life. But always the best way to deal with college students is to deal with them directly. The transition of a college student into a life of autonomy and independence necessitates a level of parity in communication with parents. By building a relationship of shared communication of experiences, hopes and fears, caring parents do not become intrusive parents. In the process, they become friends with another adult. Now that friend is their own child who has become a college student and is on the way to becoming an adult.

7
FINALLY, AND AGAIN . . .

For some, *friendship* will seem an unlikely, and perhaps unworkable, metaphor to describe the relationship between parents and their college sons and daughters. This is because we find it hard to envision alternatives to the two extremes of either the authoritarian parental role or the lax and permissive role which some parents adopt to encourage the independence of their children. Friendship also suffers, in our time, from being too narrowly defined as an intimate, highly personal and secret bond between two people who are equal in every respect.

Yet the great philosophers saw friendship as the basis for all relationships. Aristotle spoke of how it must be the basis of even the political community. In our society, where marriage and family feel the brunt of stress and disarray, men and women who have good marriages speak of friendship as the lasting quality they have discovered in each other. "We have become each other's best friend," these couples often say about themselves.

Perceptive observers of the academic scene are now retrieving the ancient model of friendship as a remedy for the often cold and distant relationships between faculty and students. We are rediscovering the effectiveness of friendship in motivating and deepening the learning process. All of us can remember the profound effect that a teacher had on us, sometimes making all the difference in our later lives. In some way, that teacher became a friend and we were changed because of it.

Experience will quickly reveal for most us how little the differences of age, background, gender or race played a part in these friendships. What a loss to limit the experience of friendship to our exact equals or peers! As parents and their college students move closer to real friendship, the differences of age and perspective become unimportant. Even past misunderstandings and hurts have a way of losing their remembered sting as the relationship grows more mature and open.

With every topic and example we discussed in these pages, we pointed to communication as the way to resolution. Communication is far from being a gimmick or a quick fix. It requires patience, hard work and willingness. Often it means acquiring new and unfamiliar skills. And it takes time. We are reminded of the wisdom of Aristotle who said that friendship required "time and familiarity."

Wherever parents and their sons and daughters find themselves in their journey to friendship and maturity, we are confident that the next stage in that growth will come through enhanced communication. If you have felt at a loss with some of our examples or suggestions, and if you have felt the inadequacy of your communication skills, you are like the rest of us. But there are ways to hone those skills. Talk with other parents, bring up the problems and issues you are facing when you are sharing ideas with your friends, ask them how they talk with their sons and daughters, read some of the excellent books and articles about communication skills that are available today. But, above all, do it—talk with each other and with your sons and daughters. Practice does not always make us perfect but it always makes us better at what we are trying to do.

Everything we have described or suggested does happen. We know college students who have their best and most profound conversations with their own parents. We might wish that was the case all the time. Our first priority in these pages has been to assure parents that it does happen. And it can happen more often. But most importantly, friendship and good communication can become the next stage in your family life, especially with your college age children. Reading or even looking through this book shows that already you are an open and willing participant. "Time and familiarity" are your greatest resources. You have them in abundance. And they are on your side.

10-10-81
From the Books of
Nancy Godwin

FREEDOM TO LIVE

A Positive Strategy for Happiness

by Dr. JOSEPH BIRD *with* LOIS BIRD

SIMON AND SCHUSTER / NEW YORK

Published by Simon and Schuster
A Division of Gulf & Western Corporation
Simon & Schuster Building
Rockefeller Center
1230 Avenue of the Americas
New York, New York 10020

Designed by Judith Neuman
Manufactured in the United States of America
Printed and bound by Fairfield Graphics, Inc.
1 2 3 4 5 6 7 8 9 10

Library of Congress Cataloging in Publication Data

Bird, Joseph W
Freedom to live, a positive strategy for happiness.

1. Self-actualization (Psychology) 2. Self-respect.
3. Visualization—Therapeutic use. I. Bird, Lois F., joint author. II. Title.
BF637.S4B53 158'.1 79-15733

ISBN 0-671-24699-2

Contents

Note to the Reader

This book will not influence your life. It will *change* it. Almost totally. All that is required of you is that you test the formula outlined in its pages—a matter of a few minutes a day for a week or less.

In writing it, we have not attempted to persuade you by evidence, logic, or emotion (except to the extent our own bias may have crept in). We present a method which claims to offer a way in which you can achieve anything you hope to achieve. It is up to you to test the method. If you attempt to evaluate the method "philosophically" or "logically," but hold back on subjecting it to a personal acid test, you will gain less from this book than you might hope to gain from any of a dozen or more "self-help" books. Its value lies only in employment of the formula outlined herein.

We therefore strongly urge you to test the validity of the formula it outlines. It is a formula for the achievement of personal power, freedom, and happiness, concepts which may be philosophically unacceptable to some, values which may be paramount to others. Including the authors.

Foreword

Many years ago, when I first began to see people in psychotherapy, and began to see them as interesting, lovable, and very complex human beings, I became aware of how pervasive human problems and heartaches can be. Psychotherapy, in which I had been trained, offered a learning process whereby the individual might find ways to cope with his or her dilemmas, but as I evaluated the results of my own professional efforts and those of my colleagues, I felt a growing frustration. Life is so short, I thought. Why must it take so long to come to grips with fears and frustrations which prevent us from fully enjoying the days we have left? My professional background was heavily influenced by the precepts of psychoanalysis. And here I found myself, week after week, month after month, probing deep into the memory traces of wounded men, women, and children who were trying to find relief through painful recall of what may have been a very traumatic childhood. I told myself there had to be an easier and quicker way to find peace and happiness, that the "surgery without anesthesia" of psychotherapy was frequently mutilating to the human spirit and often ineffective as well.

These individuals who sat across from me in my office shared a common pain: the frustration and often despair of feeling powerless to control one's life—often on every level. They felt powerless to do anything about their work, marriages, children, emotions, and health. These feelings of powerlessness led inevitably to feelings of self-loathing.

Only if these feelings could be changed could the person lose these symptoms of unhappiness.

The importance of a positive self-image to emotional well-being has long been recognized. Freud was not unaware of it. In the free associations and dreams of his patients, he found the wounds of early childhood experiences which left the individual emotionally crippled, incapable of coping with life's everyday experiences. In the 1940's, Dr. Carl Rogers, a University of Chicago psychologist, introduced "client-centered" therapy which placed heavy emphasis on a non-judgmental role by the therapist in which the client was given "unconditional positive regard." Drs. Albert Ellis and Robert Harper, two psychotherapists in private practice advocating a more directive therapeutic approach, helped the individual examine, and hopefully change, his negative self-sentences, the assumptions he makes about the world and his place in it. In recent years, the swing has been to humanism, meditation, group processes, and various mind-body therapies. All have emphasized the importance of the *person* and his or her self-esteem.

Over the past fifteen years, we have examined, sampled, and worked with many of these therapies. All, we feel, have something to offer. In presenting a new method for effecting change in one's life, we are standing on the shoulders of countless research scientists, theoreticians, and clinicians. Psychology itself is the descendant of philosophy, theology, physics, physiology and, some would claim, even the occult. Any attempt to acknowledge these men and women by name would result only in neglecting to acknowledge our debt to at least an equal number. We have learned a great deal from the mistakes of some. And we have learned perhaps even more from our own mistakes. But one group we can acknowledge, and they are perhaps our most significant contributors: the individual men and women with whom we have worked over the years. They have patiently endured, some for over ten years, our explorations into pathways which have ranged from general semantics to psychodrama, from sensory awareness to neurophysiology and conditioning. At times they must have felt they were being led through a maze in which they were never told what might be waiting around the next corner. And if so, their feelings were more than understandable.

All too often, we did not know where we were going. We knew we were searching, and we knew what we were searching for. Somewhere there had to be an answer to both explain how we human beings became unhappy and incapacitated and how we might find a better world. We could not accept the dreary inevitabilities which were pronounced in the name of "reality." Why must life be a "vale of tears"? Why "into each life some rain must fall"? Why must we accept the "facts of life"? Whose "facts"?

These patient fellow-explorers have been as much responsible for what you will read in the pages to follow as either one of us. Not all have persevered. We would not have expected that. Many have had doubts, and that has been more than understandable. We are also indebted to them. They have challenged us, and more often than they may ever know, have forced us to question our assumptions and hypotheses. We hope they will read these pages, discover where our faltering search has led us, and enjoy the fruits of the labor to which they so generously contributed.

For those of you who have hung in there until the development of the formula and have given it full application, how can I thank you?

This book is written in the first person singular, but the information, counseling experiences, and methodology are a joint effort. Lois Bird, lover, co-worker, co-adventurer, playmate, and mother of our nine children, has contributed insights and leadership into the new world which have left me, time after time, standing in awe. This evaluation, biased by an affection and passion of long standing, is one in which I am certain "our people" would concur. And for myself, when I think of love, fulfillment, aliveness, and omnipotence, I think of Lois.

JOSEPH BIRD
February 1979

1 Freedom . . . Freedom . . . Freedom

This is a book about the most important thing in life: *freedom*. How you lose it, how you gain it, how you keep it. And being a blueprint for the attainment of freedom, this book offers a formula for happiness, for wouldn't you be happy being able to do anything you might want to do, not having to conform to the demands of others, and capable of achieving anything, even your wildest dreams? That's what *I* mean by freedom.

All misery stems from a lack of freedom. If I am confined to bed with the flu, I do not have the freedom to attend the theater. My infected body is my jailer. If I sit day after day in an office when I would rather be doing something else, I am a prisoner, to "economic necessity." If a fear of snakes keeps me from enjoying camping, I am locked in by my phobias. There are probably tasks you feel you have to do which you really don't want to do, other things you would like to do but feel you can't, and limiting conditions which you have accepted as "inevitable facts of life."

But despite what others have told you, you *can* be free. Not partially or relatively free. *Totally free*. Human limitations, natural laws, and a host of other supposed factors are the walls others have built to enclose you. In Fiji, men walk over glowing-hot stones without being burned. Fiji Islanders apparently do not know a human being cannot walk unburned over fire, so they do. You and I have been taught so many limitations on our freedom we have come not just to accept them, but to be unaware of that acceptance. Until I learned what the men of Fiji do, it had not occurred to me that I might safely walk on fire. Of course, if anyone had asked me, which is unlikely, I would have told them it was out of the question; human skin burns. Now I'm not so sure.

If you are skeptical, your skepticism is understandable. The very earliest lessons we are taught are those which teach what we *cannot* do and what we *must* do. And their number increases with each year. But stick with me. I am not going to ask you to accept the premise that you can become totally free without proof.

Most counseling and psychotherapy aim at insight (an understanding of how the individual got to be the way he is), direction (telling him how he *should* behave), or a combination of the two. Most psychotherapists champion freedom. At least in their words. But it is freedom from fixations, obsessions, compulsions, and other "symptoms" that concerns them. If the "therapy" is successful, the patient is "freed" from the neurosis, and able to "cope" with "normal limitations." The psychotherapist never suggests the patient may be capable of freedom in all areas of his or her existence. He probably does not believe anyone is capable of becoming free of *all* emotional hang-ups. Psychotherapists also believe freedom is not man's natural state. They live in prisons which differ little from those of their patients.

I'm not going to bore you with the story of how I learned from "patients" the potential we each have for total freedom and how we can achieve it. First, however, came the recognition that our limitations on freedom—our jail cells—are always three-sided. The three walls dictate what you must do, what you cannot do, and the reasons why.

IL: "It's Life." This is a statement of your perceived reality—how you have been taught things "really are." It may or may not coincide with the "reality" of others. It provides the rationale, the "because" for the IC and IM.

IC: "I Can't." This is what you have been taught, and what you presently believe, you *cannot* do.

IM: "I Must." Usually expressed as "I have to," this is what you have been taught, and presently believe, you *must* do.

These three—the IL-IC-IM—work to keep you frustrated and imprisoned. As I write these words, it is past midnight. Suppose I am locked in by the following:

IL: I need at least eight hours of sleep.

IC: I can't stay up past midnight because I get up at 8 A.M.

IM: I must put the writing aside for the night.

With an IL-IC-IM, the jail cell is secure. The three walls lock you in. You can start by stating either the IL, IC, or IM, then move to the remaining two to complete the triangle. When you get to the IL, it will always be stated as "Because." If my editor were to ask why I am not more productive, I might start with my IM: "I have to put the writing aside early each evening." And if he asks why, I offer my IC: "I can't stay up past midnight." If he wants an explanation, I state my IL: "I need at least eight hours of sleep."

Tonight I might enjoy pulling the cover over my typewriter, but what about last night when I sat in that little bar enjoying the sounds of a jazz group? At the witching hour of midnight, the doors of my IL-IC-IM prison clanged shut and I missed a lot of fun.

LEARNING YOUR *FACTS OF LIFE*

You probably cannot remember when you were taught your first IL. Perhaps it was when Mommie shoved a spoon of pureed beets in your mouth while purring, "Mmmmm—

good!" All those IL's were intended to inform you of what life is all about, what is good and bad, true and false. They were presented to you as "basic truths" ("God made you"), "natural laws" ("The stove will burn you"), and "universally accepted" preferences and reactions ("Snails are ugly and slimy"). In time you *incorporated* them. They became your IL's, your perceptions of reality.

All IL's have one thing in common. They are held and professed with certainty. You are certain of the truth of your IL's just as I am of mine. We almost never doubt our own IL's, and if anyone else questions them, we feel sure those people are stupid, crazy, or "just trying to start an argument." IL's enjoy the status of revealed truths. And we generally seek friends who defend the same "truths."

Our most powerful IL's are those which state something about ourselves—our assets, liabilities, and life circumstances. They were taught by parents and other adults who observed us and described *their perceptions* of us. You may have been told you are a slow learner, poorly coordinated, frail, naturally fat, or high-strung. Each IL was a statement about what you *really* are (in the view of the "teacher"). And each IL carries an elaborate definition. Sidney is forty-six years old. His age has become an IL.

"I have to spend the weekend in front of the TV." (IM)

"How come?"

"I can't go bicycle riding." (IC)

"Why not?"

"I'm forty-six years old." (IL)

"So what?"

"Well, I mean I have to watch what I do." (IM)

"What do you mean?"

"I mean I can't act like a twenty-year-old." (IC)

"How does a twenty-year-old act?"

"You know what I mean. I can't go peddling around on a bike. I'm a forty-six-year-old man." (IL)

I cannot attack Sidney's IL. He has a birth certificate to prove his age. It is his belief that forty-six is aged and infirm, with which I quarrel. This IL supports his IC and

IM, and probably many other things. Sidney learned what it means to be forty-six. He is certain of the meaning, and no argument will sway him.

CORNERSTONE IL'S, IC'S, AND IM'S

Most people possess several *cornerstone* beliefs about the world in which they live. These are statements of "how life is and what it is all about" which influence and even direct the course of one's life. Sidney's "I am forty-six" is a cornerstone belief. It doesn't just keep him from bike-riding. It accounts for the baggy suits he wears, his worries over heart disease, and his increasing problems in sexual functioning. Often these cornerstone beliefs are statements about human "nature" ("Everyone is out for everything they can take you for"), ethics and morality ("Lying, no matter what the circumstances, is always wrong"), the other sex ("Men are interested in only one thing"), abilities ("I can't carry a tune"), physical self ("I have a weak stomach"), the future ("Another depression is on the way"), occupation ("I'm just a mechanic"), and relationships ("I'm a husband and father"). These "truths" can be defined in a variety of ways. How we define them will shape our triangular jails. If one's cornerstone IL is "Everyone is out for everything they can take you for," it can generate the following IC's and IM's:

> "I can't have any faith in my husband [wife]." (IC)
> "You have to question everything you are told." (IM)
> "I can't allow myself to get close to people." (IC)
> "I take everything with a grain of salt." (IM)

These cornerstone IL's are seldom supported by evidence. They are often no more than blind opinions, beliefs, dogmas, and myths. And since they are so general and so all-encompassing, they are the hardest to refute. The confirmed optimist who believes "Every cloud has a silver lining" will have accumulated a lifetime of experiences to prove it. But the pessimist who is sure "whenever you plan a picnic it will rain" can come up with just as many facts and figures to support his view.

IL'S AND SELF-IMAGE

IL's such as these make up the self-image. If I am a confirmed optimist, I think of myself as a good guy, deserving of only the best. If I am a pessimist, I no doubt believe I deserve to have everything go wrong in my world. Whatever self-image IL's we have been given, we tend to lock onto them. They are almost unshakeable. Several years ago I was consulted by an orthopedic surgeon who felt he was worthless. I decided to see how far he would go in defending his very negative IL. I asked him how he concluded he was worthless.

"My entire life has been a series of failures. I'm just a born loser."

"But you're a highly successful surgeon."

"A big practice and a lot of money don't spell success as far as I'm concerned," he said.

"You're also highly respected by your colleagues."

"What do they know? They're not in surgery with me."

"They can see the results."

"So what? The first surgeons were barbers," he said.

"What about the fact you graduated at the top of your class in med school?"

"The school wasn't that demanding. Besides, I had to study twice as hard as the others."

"Have it your way. But your wife and kids think you're the greatest even if you don't."

"I thought of that, and I don't know. Maybe it's pity."

Had I asked my surgeon friend to list his failures, he no doubt could have done so. We tend to gather such "evidence." But self-image is neither "true" nor "false." It is a *belief system,* nothing more.

The overwhelming majority of our IL's can be reduced to one cornerstone IL: "*I am inadequate.*" If you feel other people keep you from doing things you would like to do, or make you do things you don't really want to do, then you must feel they are in control of your life. Hence, relative to them, you are inadequate. Not really of course, but then IL's are not *really* anything. They are only IL's. You must remember that.

2 Meet Your Jailers

Your jailers may be anybody (or, if you're President of the United States, everybody). They become jailers by applying for the job and being accepted—by you. They cannot become your jailers unless you let them (unless, of course, they can physically control you) and, although it doesn't make a great deal of sense, *ask* them to be your jailers.

A fashion expert tells you, "Doubleknit suits are out, and white shoes are *never* worn in San Francisco." If you accept this IL, he becomes one of your jailers. The IL leads to an IM ("I have to conform to Brooks Brothers") and an IC ("I can't wear my comfortable white shoes").

Advice columnists provide us with daily syndicated IL's. Pastors, astrologers, psychotherapists, and educators do the same. If you're into astrology and born under the sign of Taurus, this morning's newspaper tells you, "You may encounter an unusual and somewhat knotty business problem. Don't try to solve it yourself. Consult an expert for guidance." If you're a Sagittarius, "The spotlight is now on your material interests. Indications are that you will receive something of value—and in an entirely unexpected manner." These are not, of course, IL's, although you might, with a little imagination, develop them into IL's. The actual IL may be *The stars control my destiny*.

You may not even be able to recall who the jailer was who initially gave you a particular IL, yet you may continually accept it as authoritative. To use a word psychologists are fond of, you have "incorporated" it. Most of our social IL's are of this sort. Frank and Harry are finishing lunch.

Frank: "I sure hate to leave all this good gravy on my plate, but I guess I'm going to have to." (IM)

Harry: "I don't see why. Why don't you soak it up with your bread?"

Frank: "You've got to be kidding. I couldn't do that." (IC)

Harry: "I don't know why not."

Frank: "Oh, come on, you do too."

Harry: "No. Why not?"

Frank: "Because it just isn't done." (IL)

You may not know who handed down these social rules. I don't. Most of them were passed down to us by our parents; others we picked up from a variety of self-appointed Emily Posts.

"Take off your hat in an elevator." (IM)
"Cover your mouth when you yawn." (IM)
"Don't mix your peas with your mashed potatoes." (IC)
"Good people practice good manners." (IL)

Most of the people who gave you and me those IL's, IC's, and IM's (and in doing so became our jailers) can, however, be identified. They may *still* be our jailers; any jailer is your enemy, and it's important to know who your enemies are.

PARENT JAILERS

First, there are parents. You may be saying to yourself, "Here we go! Shrinks blame everything on parents." Well, I don't have a thing against parents; I happen to be one myself. But we did learn our IL's from someone, and most of us were raised by parents.

Much of what parents teach children is either an IL, an IC, or an IM. Your parents gave you a long list of IL's,

IC's, and IM's simply because they had the responsibility of raising you. They were not laying them on you out of malice. They were not trying to lock you up; they were teaching you how to function in society in a way that would be profitable to you, how to tell "right" from "wrong," and how things "really are in the world." So they taught you:

"Streets are dangerous." (IL)
"School is important." (IL)
"A balanced diet is essential." (IM)
"Little girls don't play with snakes." (IC)
"Santa Claus brings toys only to good little boys and girls." (IL)
"Boys don't hit girls." (IC)
"Children should not pester adults with questions." (IC)

I have an IL-IC-IM from childhood. It has to do with zucchini squash. I hated zucchini squash, intensely, passionately, vehemently.

Me: "I can't stand zucchini."

Mother: "Stop complaining and eat what you're served."

Me: "But it makes me sick."

Mother: "Nonsense! That's all in your head."

Me: "Why do I have to eat zucchini when I don't like it?"

Mother: "Because it's good for you. You want to grow up to be big and strong, don't you?"

Me: "Why can't I eat things I like?"

Mother: "Because you can't go through life doing just what you like."

Me: "I hate zucchini. I'll get sick if I eat it."

Mother: "That's enough of that. You have to eat your zucchini; it's good for you."

I still hate zucchini. My wife understands this, bless her, and never serves it to me. But when I'm invited to dinner and the hostess serves the despicable vegetable, I struggle to down it. Why? Well, I just can't leave it on my plate.

That's one of my IC's. I have to eat what I'm served; it's only common courtesy (one of my IM's), and besides, it is nutritious (one of my IL's). But some day I'm going to look a large portion of zucchini in the face and let the whole nauseous mess just sit there. Then I will have broken out of my zucchini IL-IC-IM prison.

REWARDS OF JAIL

These childhood IL-IC-IM's have some payoff value, however, or we wouldn't hang onto them so tenaciously. What is it we get out of them? Security for one thing. The IL's our parents gave us provide the security of "knowing" what the world is all about. The IL, *hot objects can burn me,* provides me with a piece of information which will help me function more securely in a world of hot objects. IL's can provide a measure of comfort. It is more comfortable to "know" than not to know, and those childhood IL's we were handed were "facts." They were knowledge. They provided direction, even something which passed for wisdom.

Many of these IC's were presented with the best of intentions. Our parents wanted to protect us from danger, frustration, and disappointment. Sometimes they were right, and sometimes they were not. I am certainly not suggesting that knowledge boxes one into a prison. Quite the opposite. Knowledge can free us from many prisons. If I am taught "rattlesnakes are dangerous," I may be freer to hike in rattlesnake country than I would be if I did not have this information. I can learn where to go, and where not to go. And even what to do in the event I am bitten by a rattlesnake. But if I am told, "Snakes are ugly and bad; never go near them," I may be locked out of a part of the fascinating world of nature.

When I was a kid, I was short and skinny. I was about as athletic as a rock. My mother said, "You're just not built for sports [IL]. If you can't compete in sports [IC], and it doesn't look like you'll be able to, you'd better get in and prove what you can do in your other subjects [IM]." Well, for a long time, I didn't do much academically, but I did throw in the towel when it came to sports. From the eighth grade on, my athletic pursuits never went further than a game of Monopoly. I accepted the "fact" that I was going to have to make it in a field not requiring muscles. I had acquired a double IM: "I have to succeed/I have to make it without brawn." Mother may have been right. But I'll never know. If you are told you cannot do X, you may not step off any cliffs and try to do X. This may keep you from getting hurt. On the other hand, it may also keep you from achieving what you might achieve if you didn't hold that particular IC.

Most of us were taught some IC's that have to do with physical limitations. We learned them from mom and dad, teachers, and coaches. For example, "If you are about a foot under average height, you can't hope to play professional basketball." That one seems reasonable, but I'm not so sure. Does the fact that I've never seen a 5′1″ professional basketball player mean that no one 5′1″ tall can possibly play professional basketball? Or does it mean, perhaps, that 5′1″ people very early in life abandon any hope of ever playing professional basketball because of the IC they have learned? IC's based upon physical limitations may or may not be valid. I tend to doubt any and all of them. Other IC's are built on IL's of commonly accepted sexual, racial, ethnic or academic myths. And they are almost *never* valid. The IL may be true ("I am 5′1″ tall") but the IC ("I can't play basketball") doesn't necessarily follow logically from the IL. I might pick up the paper tomorrow to read that the Los Angeles Lakers have signed a 5′1″ forward who can shoot with 90 percent accuracy from midcourt!

Why would you or I choose to hang on to an illogical IC based upon an illogical IL? There are several reasons. For one thing, IC's "legitimately" provide a reason to avoid doing things we find unpleasant. If I don't like running track in high school (and I didn't), that IC from home, "You can't run, it will bring on your asthma," was an ideal excuse. It could also protect me against other IL's ("A program of physical exercise is essential'') and IM's (''and I should run track because it is good exercise''). That IC my parents gave me provided a perfect escape: ''But I can't because it will give me asthma.'' Such IC's, of course, have a way of becoming self-fulfilling prophecies:

''I can't swim.''

''Really? Why don't you learn?''

''It's no use, I'd sink like a rock.''

''That's ridiculous. Anyone can learn how to swim. Why don't you give it a try?''

''You want me to drown? I told you I can't swim. I'm just not a swimmer—and I'm not about to drown to prove it.''

The mere fact that parents and teachers and other big people told us, ''No, you can't,'' did not create an IC. There were many things about which I was told, ''No, you can't,'' things I knew I could do, but that I would suffer punishment if I did. In some cases, however, I may have failed to make the distinction. I may have been told, ''You can't safely climb that ladder to the roof,'' and it may have saved me from breaking my neck. The message was really, ''I forbid you to climb that ladder to the roof, and if you do, I'll clobber you.'' But if I had interpreted that as ''You can't climb a ladder to the roof,'' I would now have to hire someone to fix a leaky roof because *I can't climb ladders.*

You may have a head full of IC's resembling my garage: stacked high with a strange assortment of objects which once served some immediate or potential purpose (at least I think they did), but which now only force me to leave my car standing in the driveway. As a result, you may be in the position of the prisoner who has served his sentence but lives on in a cell because no one has told him he is free to leave.

Your parents undoubtedly also handed you a lot of IM's in order to get you to do what they wanted you to do or what they thought would benefit you. Most of these IM's were linked to IC's which had to do with what you or I wanted to do at the moment (''My Mom says I have to clean my room [IM] so I can't go out and play [IC]"). My childhood, like most childhoods, seemed to be scripted with long lists of things they said I had to do (IM's) and things I couldn't do (IC's). I could hardly wait to grow up so I wouldn't have to do what I didn't want to do and could do anything I wanted to do. I think the disillusionment of adulthood came with the discovery that it had even more IC's and IM's than I had as a kid.

If you were fortunate to have concerned parents who had their own values pretty much together, the things they told you you had to do probably served you fairly well; they provided direction in life. Sure, they were IM's, and as IM's they were one-third of the triangle of the prison, but they did provide goals and useful day-to-day activities parents like to call "assuming responsibility." No doubt they taught you to:

"Brush your teeth."
"Study hard in school."
"Wash your hands after you go to the bathroom."
"Obey the law."
"Say 'please' and 'thank you.' "
"Develop some goals in life."

They seem like reasonably sensible IM's even though they didn't always seem to make complete sense, and still don't. They could never be rational, however, unless they were tied to rational IL's. Which they often were not. The IM "I have to practice piano every day" may make some sense if your IL is "I am a professional pianist." But then it is no longer an IM or an IL. Practicing every day becomes something you *want* to do. If becoming a professional pianist is really *your* goal and not that of your boss, supervisor, parent, spouse, or teacher, then practicing the piano everyday is rational and is no longer something you "have to do."

When we were young, we were sure our parents knew absolutely everything. They had the answer to any and every question we asked. "My Daddy says so" was the answer to all disputed statements. Parents have an almost god-like authority, which can be quite an ego trip if you are a parent. When mom or dad said, "This is the way things *really* are" or "You can't do that" or "You have to do this," they spoke with a voice from on high. Most of us didn't start seriously questioning their absolute authority until we got to our rebellious teens.

TEACHER JAILERS

The authority we hand over to others to supply us with IL-IC-IM's is frequently an extension of this parent-child interaction. As children, we have a lot of surrogate parents. Teachers, babysitters, and just about any adults are afforded the status we give to parents. Teachers probably have the biggest impact since they have the most contact with us. It can be like having your backside imbedded with slivers. I'm still digging out some of those crazy IL-IM-IC's my grammar school teachers gave me.

In the fourth grade I did poorly in arithmetic. I showed a remarkable lack of ability to cope with multiplication tables. "Joseph obviously does not have an aptitude for mathematics," my teacher told my mother. This did not come as news to me, nor was it devastating. I had no liking for multiplication tables, and the judgment of my teacher (an IL) took me off the hook. With no aptitude, I could hardly be blamed for bringing home poor grades in arithmetic. I managed to use that IL effectively through twelve years of school. (When I hit college, the ceiling fell on me. My cop-out no longer was acceptable; I was expected to learn advanced math—with or without any "aptitude.")

As you and I moved through our school years, we were given IL's in history, math, literature, geography, and even art. And always, of course, they were the IL's of the teacher. I learned the Spanish-American War was started by nasty Spaniards who sank the U.S. battleship *Maine* in Havana harbor. The fact that this might not have been the most rational action on the part of the Spaniards, and the fact that William Randolph Hearst and his newspaper campaigned us into a war with Spain, was information I was not given. "Remember the *Maine*" made good sense to me. It was the teacher's IL. In the months following the outbreak of World War II, I learned a lot about the Germans and Japanese—all IL's of my high school teachers. Almost all of it was hysterical nonsense.

RELIGIOUS JAILERS

If you came from a religious home, as I did, the church may have run a close second to the school in supplying you with IL's. Little children are taught to sing, "Jesus loves me, this I know, 'cause the Bible tells me so." The words state an IL. For that matter, the Bible itself (or the Torah, or the Koran) is a collection of IL's. It makes a number of statements of reality which are accepted "on faith" by the followers. Our religious IL's usually come first from our parents and, second, from the clergy and religious school teachers. In terms of power, an IL could not have stronger backing. A very few religious IL's can generate a large number of powerful IC's and IM's—enough to control virtually every move you and I make during our lifetimes.

THE PEER GROUP

Another big source of IL-IM-IC's during childhood is the peer group. By the time most of us reach high school, friends have taken over as the most influential source of values. For a period of four or five years, and sometimes even longer, the "gang" provides almost all the rules of what we can and cannot do and what we *absolutely have to do and will die if we don't do.* When I was in high school, my life couldn't have been more controlled if I had been in a Marine boot camp. The clothes I wore, the music I listened to, the opinions I expressed on life, parents, school, girls, and even food came from the IL-IM-IC's of my gang.

When I reached adulthood, I moved away from the gang

and became "my own person" with my own opinions, tastes, and decisions. At least that's what I thought. It took me an embarrassingly long time to realize I was no more free than I had been in childhood under my parents or in my teens with the gang. I simply had a new crew of jailers.

Jailers can go by many titles: boss, friend, co-worker, spouse, son, daughter, IRS agent, neighbor, doctor, landlord, minister, president of the country club, principal of my children's school, and just about anyone else I permit to get a foot in the door (and there are scores of people waiting to get their foot in the door).

THE JAILER'S MOTIVE

Today's newspaper has a headline on the women's page: "Paris designers dictate shorter skirts." Do you like the word "dictate"? I don't like to be dictated to by *anyone*—and that includes fashion designers. But I suppose there are some people who don't find being dictated to particularly unpleasant. So a group of French couturiers who know how to turn a profit become their jailers.

At least with the designers, you can figure out what they have to gain. But what of your brother-in-law who tries so hard to become your authority? What does he hope to gain for all his effort? Being a jailer can, after all, take a great deal of effort. No one takes on the job of jailer unless they hope to get something from it. In my community, the voters recently voted on a zoning ordinance. The proponents told me I had to vote for the measure if I had a concern for my neighbors, the ecology, and "the future of your city." The opponents told me I had to vote against it if I wanted to protect property values, keep taxes down, and insure "the future of your city." On both sides, working very hard to sell me on these opposing IM's, were public-spirited civic leaders. It may seem a bit cynical of me, but I suspect those on each side had a personal stock financially in the outcome. So long as they stay within the law, I find nothing wrong with these public-spirited civic leaders looking out for their own bank accounts. At the same time, truthfulness is not a virtue I generally expect from politicians. The "civic-minded, concerned" statements of such politicians are taken with the same grain of salt with which I take the sales pitch of a patent medicine peddler. But I must admit, I am not always immune. I do have something of an IL that says "a good citizen shows concern for the future of his community," and here were these would-be authorities trying to give me conflicting IM's as to how I should demonstrate my good citizenship. Only if I could be free of their IM's—on both sides—could I vote on the basis of what personal stock *I* had in the outcome.

What of those friendly IM's we are handed by neighbors, friends, relatives, and even total strangers? My neighbor tells me I should weather-strip my house. Since I have not asked his advice on the matter, he is gratuitously trying to give me an IM. If I accept it, he may gain something: maybe the feeling of being a good guy, maybe the feeling he is smarter than his neighbor, or maybe my expression of gratitude next winter. But of all the possible rewards which motivate people to try to be the jailers of others, at the top of the list are *power* and *control.*

For many people, power is the ultimate ego trip. The reason might be stated as an IL: "If I have power over this person, it is because I am smarter, better, or more capable than he is." If I can get my friend to accept my view of the world, or buy a CB radio because I tell him he ought to, or give up his plan for making a killing on the horses when I tell him it can't be done, I have effectively exercised power. He undoubtedly holds a high opinion of me to give me this much authority/power. And my self-esteem may take a jump. Esteem comes from power, and power is really the measure to which I can get other people to *do* what I tell them and *think* what I tell them. Control also comes from power, and if I can gain control over someone, I can get that individual to serve my needs and desires to the extent of my control. This may be the dream of every parent. How wonderful it would be to tell Junior to do something just once and see him spring into action. But not being robots, our children seldom give us that much control. If we climb high enough in the business world, we may have better luck with our employees. A business executive may claim he doesn't want a staff of "yes men," but I find it hard to believe. Some people like to be told what to do, of course, but they certainly aren't the better for it.

The rigid moralist wants to control your sexual behavior. The temperance leader wants to control your drinking. Your doctor wants to control your smoking. Your clergyman wants to control your religious practices. Your mother wants to control your diet. Your children want to control your time and money. Your neighbor wants to control your politics. Your boss wants to control your business practices. Your spouse wants to control your love life.

And what can you do to counter these efforts to imprison you? If you are like the rest of us, you have probably struggled from time to time to reach independence, often in childish and fruitless acts of rebellion. One psychiatrist told a story of a henpecked husband, who, when his wife left on a trip, celebrated his independence by urinating into her kitchen sink! There are usually a lot of little ways in which we try to fight back. Some of them are effective, some not. Recently, classes in "assertiveness training" have gained popularity. The classes have recognized a need: There are many people who feel they are the sort who invite others to crowd in front of them in the supermarket line, and they have been stymied by not knowing what to do about it. In class, they hope to learn how to assert themselves without ending up with a broken nose. Most of the time, however, we don't counterattack through assertion. We do it by attempting to control those who are attempting to control us. We try to put our jailers in prison. And before you say, "Not me! I don't want to control *anybody,*" consider how many times in the past week you may have attempted to persuade those people who were trying so hard to control you to accept IL-IC-IM's which would give you control over them. My children spend time and effort attempting to manipulate their father, and I must admit, they are often frustratingly successful. But in the name of "good advice" and "parental direction," I spend more than a comparable amount of time and effort trying to control them (though with notably less success).

There was recently a debate before the school board of a Midwestern high school. On the one side, a group of parents and ministers argued for the removal from the school library of a highly acclaimed novel which contained four-letter words and "explicit" sexual material. On the other side, teachers argued for "academic freedom." The group who wished to ban the book were quite obviously opposed to freedom. Not so obvious were the efforts to control freedom being argued by the teachers. If the teachers had won, and in this case they did not, they would have had the "freedom" to assign the novel as "required" reading by the students. Being *required* to read a book—*Mein Kampf, The Bible*, or a highly acclaimed novel—restricts my freedom every bit as much as being forbidden to read said book. Cries of "violation of civil rights" and "restriction of freedom" often come down to a matter of whose ox is gored.

One basic rule applies: *If you want freedom, you must grant freedom*. And there is a corollary to that rule: *You will never enjoy more freedom than you are willing to grant to others*.

In San Francisco, a judge awarded "custody" of five young adults to their parents to undergo thirty days of "de-programming" from their beliefs as members of the Unification Church, the so-called "Moonies." The leaders of the "Moonies," it was claimed, had "brainwashed" these young adults into accepting the teachings of the Unification Church. The parents sought to get them back in order to have the opportunity to "brainwash" them in reverse—back to the parents' belief. The judge, a man who I would assume does not hold freedom in the highest regard, handed down his decision favoring the parents. (The decision was subsequently reversed on appeal.) Had the leaders of the Unification Church really "brainwashed" these young people? Undoubtedly, if by brainwashing we mean any and all means of persuasion found to be effective. Are the parents and their "de-programmers" contending they will use only ineffective means?

A psychiatrist charged with the responsibility of studying American servicemen held captive by the North Koreans during the Korean War spoke of brainwashing. He said the word could mean anything from driving bamboo splints under the captive's fingernails to what you tell your date in a parked car on a Saturday night. The case of the five young "Moonies" is one more example of the tragedy of history: We grant freedom only to those with whom we agree. If these young people had joined the Presbyterian church or been converted to Catholicism, can you imagine the judge handing down such a ruling? But the judge is not free; nor the parents, so they counterattack through attempts to restrict the freedom of others.

We have been shocked by the mass suicides of the followers of Reverend Jim Jones in the jungles of Guyana, and there have been demands for governmental control over such cults and their leaders. Should society assume a role in protecting the gullible, the easily exploitable, and the emotionally vulnerable? Most of us feel children and those who suffer from severe retardation need our protection; but if an adult, who may to us seem quite crazy to follow a guru who leads his followers into a life of severe abnegation, chooses a course of action which seems bizarre, must we —*should* we—intervene to "protect" him? I feel sure there were those who viewed the followers of Moses into the desert as weirdos, those who left their occupations to follow Christ as fanatics, and those who accompanied the Mormon leader Brigham Young over the plains to the Great Salt Lake as gullible. With paternalistic arrogance, there will always be those who say, "We must protect them from their folly."

Always, there is the paradox: The jailer is a prisoner. In one of those easily forgettable movies of the 1930's, a gangster was being taken to the penitentiary by train. He was handcuffed to a police detective. There was a derailment and the detective was injured and knocked unconscious. The gangster took the key from the detective's pocket, unlocked the handcuffs and escaped. Suppose, however, that in the story both men had survived, still handcuffed, but that the detective had lost his identification, and the prisoner claimed to be the detective. Until each could be correctly identified, law enforcement officials would have no choice but to treat both as prisoners. Handcuffed together, they were each both jailer and prisoner. This is the price you and I pay when we exercise control over others. To keep them confined to a cell, we must ourselves stay within prison walls.

I have a friend who told me he had had quite a struggle with this concept of freedom. He said, "I felt that without discipline and control, people would act in a totally irresponsible manner; the world would be in chaos. I didn't mind my life being controlled, so long as I could be sure there were controls over others. It was only when I was able to see myself as a rational and worthwhile person, and to discover that by acting freely I did not act irresponsibly, that I was able no longer to fear the exercise of freedom by others." He told me that out of this he learned an important truth: "All the chaos, the destructiveness, the cruelty, and the unhappiness in this world comes from a lack of freedom. Those IL-IC-IM's are what makes up hell."

He went on to tell me of another reason why the concept of freedom bothered him so much. "I was afraid that if I acted freely, and not in accordance with all those IC's and IM's everyone gave me, I would lose all my friends. But then I realized something: Can they be my friends if they want to put me in a cell? They may not be trying to keep me locked up out of malice. It may only reflect their fears. But to whatever extent they are doing so, they are not acting in my interest. I did lose some 'friends,' but I gained so much freedom in return—including the freedom to make new friends I would not have been free to make before. And with some, but not all, of my old friends, I feel my newfound freedom gave them a measure of freedom. And that, in itself, is a wonderful feeling."

3 Cellmates

I once had a boss who was addicted to long work hours. It wasn't that he was a workaholic, just that he worked long, long hours. His family life was less than a source of joy and he was in no hurry to go home in the evening. His work habits, in turn, presented an IL to the members of his staff. "The dedicated administrator is not a clock watcher," he would say. "He stays at his desk long after the clerical help and others have gone home." His ambitious assistants accepted the IL. And it soon gave rise to an IC: "I can't leave before the boss leaves." Of course his aides were unaware of his reasons for staying late. But they did accept the IL his actions communicated. And the company was able to get an hour or two of additional work out of each of these employees.

Someone may hand you one of their IL's or you may hand them one of yours. Or the two of you may meet and find you already hold the same IL. Since any IL is a statement of "how the world is" (in the perception of the individual holding it), it may seem that those holding a joint IL share their view of reality. But this is not necessarily true. Even when an IL is an apparently simple statement of "fact," the meaning of the statement—the definitions we apply to the words in the statement—may vary greatly.

Let's say the guy who lives next door and I have a joint IL: "I am a man." That sounds simple enough, but without having discussed it with him, I have no idea how he may define "man." If we don't have the same idea of what constitutes "man," this apparently joint IL may generate very different IC's and IM's for the two of us. He may define "man" as a male who is strong, unemotional, aggressive, sports-loving—the John Wayne macho type. I may define a man as responsible, hard-working, compassionate, and gentle. If, then, one day we happen to be talking of the fellow who lives down the block, and I say, "He's a real *man,*" I may get an argument. My neighbor may try to convince me of his IL definition, and I will probably try to persuade him that my definition is correct. If he succeeds in bringing me over to his side, I may feel he has gained control over me. If I persuade him, then I have the upper hand. Not really, of course, but in the way our perceptions take shape. In any case, and regardless of who wins the argument, the result can only be to lock both of us into an IL which is a sexual stereotype. This joint IL control may not seem like much, but wars have been fought over less. If, at some later time, one or the other of us should start questioning the "reality" of our new joint IL, the other one can be expected to fight to maintain it. It is as if the prisoner can't stand the thought of his cellmate escaping.

A twenty-one-year-old college student told me he had sold his shotgun and was giving up duck hunting. I asked him why.

"I just figured it was the right thing to do," he said.

"Right? In what way?"

"Well, guns are dangerous."

"No doubt they can be, but doesn't that depend on how cautious you are?"

"When my Mom found out I was duck hunting, she had a fit," he said.

"Did that have something to do with your giving up hunting?"

"Well, I can't have Mom taking a tranquilizer every time I even mention hunting."

"So it was really your Mom's decision."

"Well, she says she can't even look at a gun. And I guess she's right. Guns are dangerous."

His mother had given him the IL "guns are dangerous," and had told him of her IC: "I can't even look at a gun," and her IM: "I have to take a tranquilizer whenever you talk about hunting." From the same IL, he had generated the IC: "I can't have anything to do with guns," and the IM: "I have to give up hunting." Mom lives in a prison of fear, and she has succeeded in locking her son into a prison. He holds a cornerstone IM, "I must please my mother." Mom's IL about guns, and the IM of pleasing mother he has incorporated, could generate any number of further IC's and IM's. In time, he may forbid his children to play with water pistols because they represent guns and "guns are dangerous." He may restrict their television viewing to shows with no violence because "guns are dangerous." Joint IL's, like other IL's, have a way of snowballing and generating countless IC's and IM's which imprison those who accept them. Mom, of course, had a vested interest in pushing her IL. Once her son had accepted it, she could sit back, relaxed, free of fear that he might shoot himself in the foot. And in pushing her IL, she enlisted the aid of friends, relatives, and the opinions of "experts" to prove her point that yes, in fact, "guns are dangerous."

YOUR REALITY VS. THEIRS

We humans have a need to believe everyone perceives reality exactly the same as we do. Our world is their world; their world is ours. If they don't see things exactly as we do, we suspect they are: 1. crazy, 2. lying, 3. stupid, or 4. evil. I have an IL which says, "cauliflower is awful." Whenever I run into someone who tells me they like cauliflower, I'm tempted to say, "I don't believe you," or "How can you be so dumb?" However, since I feel it is not wise to antagonize crazy people, I usually don't argue with them. Cauliflower *is* awful. That is my perception of cauliflower, as I am sure it is the perception of any sane individual, and I cannot understand how anyone can like something which is in every respect simply awful. To me, the awfulness of cauliflower is an indisputable fact of life.

I have convinced myself that nearly everyone feels as I do towards cauliflower, and that the cauliflower eaters are really oddballs, people with strange tastes who are, by reason of their strange tastes, alienated from the rest of us. Believing this, I don't have to face the possibility that *I* may be the misfit, the only guest at the table who doesn't enjoy cauliflower. Should I entertain such a possibility, I would have to face the question, "Is the world *really* the way I see it?" In matters more serious than cauliflower eating, such a question might cause me to doubt my sanity.

MY CAN'TS ARE YOUR CAN'TS

You may have noticed how often others try to hand you their IC's. Especially their IC's. I think it has to do with the feeling: if I can't eat ice cream, I don't want anyone to enjoy it. When your friend tells you, "You can't find a good auto mechanic these days," he is actually saying, "*I* can't find a good mechanic; therefore you can't, either." Our world is filled with IC's bestowed on us by well-meaning friends, parents, teachers, and others. I recently had a banker tell me why I should not invest in securities. "You know," he said, "you can't make any money in the stock market these days." But since I know there are individuals who are making money on stock investments, and I also know he knows nothing of my knowledge of the stock market, whether negligible or extensive, I can only assume he is saying, "I cannot make money on the stock market; therefore, no one can."

Before Roger Bannister refused to accept the IC that no human could run the mile in under four minutes and went out on the track and broke the "four-minute barrier," there may have been many runners capable of accomplishing the feat had they not been locked in by the IC, "You can't run the mile under four minutes." I can imagine track coaches telling young athletes, "Don't be unrealistic, boy, you can't break four minutes." And since if you don't believe you can do something, you can't, they didn't. I don't believe I can walk on water. And it's true, I can't. Have I tried? Of course not, because I know I can't. Could I if I thought I could? Who knows. I *know* I can't so I don't try. Furthermore, I am surrounded by people who affirm my water-walking IC. Should I take it into my head to stroll across a swimming pool, they will no doubt remind me: "What? Are you crazy? You can't walk on water!" They might even have me locked away for my own protection before I have half a chance to disprove their IC.

The questions of whether we do, in fact, have individual physical limitations or whether there are natural and physical laws which are immutable and which delimit the *possible* and establish the *impossible* are inevitably asked by each of us. A major part of our education, after all, has been aimed at answering these questions. Not always, however, with validity. They were the answers—the limitations—agreed upon by the majority, and those who did not accept them were held up to ridicule. Limitations were generally accepted until a courageous few, acting *as if* they did not exist, refuted them. Few of us may smash the established "truths" as effectively and dramatically as did the Wright brothers, Einstein, and Marconi, but we can approach life with the same skepticism. We can act *as if* there are no limitations. This does not, of course, mean we step from a tenth-story window believing in a superpower to support us, or that we ignore the evidence (e.g., physical "laws" which have been "discovered") which may lead to still greater knowledge. It does mean we hold *all* things as possible.

The fact that two people hold a joint IC does not necessarily mean that their accompanying IL's and IM's are the same. Twelve-year-old Willie and his mother have a joint IC, but very different IL's and IM's:

Willie: "Hey, Mom, the circus is going to be in town next week. Are we going to go?"

Mom: "How long is it going to be here?"

Willie: "Just one day, Saturday."

Mom: "But that's the day you promised your father you'd clean the garage."

Willie: "Ah gee, Mom, I could clean the garage on Sunday."

Mom: "No, I'm afraid we're not going to the circus this year."

Mom's final answer, "We can't go to the circus this year," is their joint IC. Her IL is "Prices are going up all the time, and her IM is "I have to stay within the family budget." Willie, on the other hand, has an IL "Parents never let you do what you want to do" and an IM "I have to spend Saturday cleaning the dumb old garage."

When you and I were kids, we were given a lot of IC's without the explanatory IL's or accompanying IM's. We were just told "You can't," and that was that. We were left to figure out the IL's and IM's for ourselves—and they may not have been the IL's and IM's intended by the adults. Little Penelope watches the astronauts walk on the moon, and decides she will be an astronaut when she grows up. When she mentions it to her father, he discourages her. "Honey, I think you'd better think of something else; you'll never be able to be an astronaut." Daddy may be a male chauvinist of the first order who believes the kitchen is the only suitable environment for a woman and that, as a father, he has an obligation to teach his little daughter what it means to be female. But if his wife walks in before he tells Penelope "why" she can't be an astronaut and he knows his wife does not support his views on women, he may clam up before giving Penelope any further explanation. So Penelope is left to guess why she can never hope to walk on the moon. She searches through what information she has and concludes it is because she is not a good student. So her IC, "I can't be an astronaut," is built upon the IL, "I'm not a good student." The IL daddy wanted her to learn is, "I am female." More than a few parents have told their child, "We're sorry you won't be able to go to college. We don't have the money to send you." The parents might believe, in all good faith, no child can go to college if parents cannot afford to pick up the tab. But the message (and the IL) the child learns is, "I'm not bright enough to get a scholarship or capable enough to work my way through college."

YOU HAVE TO, TOO

Everything said about joint IL's and joint IC's can be said of joint IM's. Since IM's often mean "I have to do such and such and I really don't want to," and there is a little of the "misery loves company" in each of us, if I hold some nasty little IM such as, "I have to spend my weekends doing chores around the house," I may do my best to hand you the same IM. And I may attempt to hand you a guilt-trip if you decline it. If I see you going off to play golf, I may drop in a casual remark about your unmowed lawn or that uncropped tree of yours which is dropping leaves on my property. Children in the same family are often expert at passing along IM's. The parent hands the IM to child one, who in turn hands it to child two, who in turn hands it to child three. If I tell my son Steve he must get at his homework, he may turn to his brother Mike with, "Come on, Mike. You have to do your homework." And Mike may then go in search of sister Mary to pass on the order.

Many of what sound like joint IM's are, in fact, only slightly veiled orders given to you by a "boss." When a general says, "All right men, we have to take that hill at any cost," the infantry private doesn't take the words literally. He doesn't expect to look up and see the general by his side in the bayonet charge. And when I tell my kids "*We* have to clean the garage," they know who's going to get stuck with the job. A true joint IM or IC is binding on both parties. The "we" really means what it says. The remarkable thing is that almost anyone can assume the authority to hand out a joint IC or IM. Even more remarkable is the fact that so many of us readily accept them. The joint IM "We must support the decisions and policies of our President" may be proclaimed by any self-appointed patriot. And the majority may accept it—with sometimes disastrous consequences.

A young businesswoman, after participating in some of our seminars, told me she had kept count of the number of joint IC's and IM's others attempted to give her. In one week, she tallied 37. They came from her sister, her co-workers, two men she was dating, her niece, and several others—including her hairdresser. She smiled when she said, "But now when they say, 'we can't' do something or 'we have to' do this, I can think to myself 'maybe *you* can't or maybe *you* have to but that doesn't apply to me. There isn't *anything* I can't do. And there isn't *anything* I have to do.' "

4 The Incompatibles

The situation gets really sticky when you hold two or more incompatible IL's. Suppose you hold the two IL's:

1. I am Christopher Columbus with a commission from the Queen of Spain to find a sea route to the East Indies, and
2. The world is flat.

You would be in what might be called a classic bind. If you follow the first IL, you go sailing into the sunset in search of the spices of the East Indies filled with great expectations of riches and fame. If you hold the second IL, you jump ship. The problem arises when you hold both IL's at the same time. This occurs more often than you might imagine. Since we learn so many IL's, it is inevitable some will conflict. (In a later chapter I will discuss IL's we are taught as proverbs; they provide a good example of incompatible IL's. For almost every proverb, there is another which says just the opposite. I was taught, for example, "Look before you leap." But I was also taught, "He who hesitates is lost.")

Because of the meanings and definitions we give to our IL's, these incompatibilities, when they occur, can literally tear us apart. I spoke with a minister who felt he could not cope with the conflict of his incompatible IL's.

"I'm married, and I love my wife very much. But I'm

also an ordained minister. The sacrament of matrimony is to be a total commitment. When I married Edith I made a promise before God that I would devote my life to her, that I would love her and cherish her. From the Book of Genesis to the writings of Apostle Paul, we are told that in marriage a man is to leave his father and mother and cleave unto his wife and the two are to become one. And I believe that. That's what marriage is. I promised Edith she would come before everything and everyone. But when I was ordained I also made a commitment, a total commitment, to God and to His people entrusted to my spiritual care. So tell me what I am to do when it's 10:00 P.M. and I get a call from a parishioner who needs my help at a time when I know that Edith also needs me? I have a total commitment to both of them."

As he saw it, resolving these incompatible IL's would call for choosing between abandoning his ministry or abandoning his marriage. Or re-defining one or both of his IL's. The simplest solution might have been for him either to get a divorce or resign his ministry, but he did not want to do either. In order to resolve the conflict, he had to first free himself of a cornerstone IL: "I have no life of my own." Once he was able to break out of the restrictions of that cornerstone IL, he found the IL's of total commitment to his wife versus total commitment to his flock could be redefined.

When I first met him, Phil was a middle-management executive with an electronics manufacturing company. He had several supervisors under him with whom he met once a week to discuss policy and go over progress reports. Phil's immediate superior at that time was the vice-president in charge of production. Frequently, he would sit in on Phil's weekly staff meetings. The evening we met, Phil told me: "I really get uptight when he's there. I know it isn't him. I can feel perfectly relaxed when it's just the two of us, but when I'm there with my own men, I just don't know how to act. I feel I have to maintain a certain image of authority with my employees. After all, they have to know

I'm the boss. But when he comes to the meetings, I'm caught in a very uncomfortable situation. He never just sits there and listens. He offers suggestions and asks questions, and the next thing I know, I've lost control. He's taken over the meeting. I know he doesn't intend to. It just happens. As soon as he opens his mouth, I almost automatically move into second chair. I don't know how to be both boss and underling at the same time."

Phil's IL's were:

1. I am a boss.
2. I am an underling.

Needless to say, these IL's generate very different and opposing IC's and IM's. The incompatibility, however, did not arise out of the fact that Phil felt he had to play two roles rather than just one. In his daily life Phil was called upon to play more than a single role. We all are. I am a psychologist, a writer, a husband, a father, and the person who unplugged the stopped-up toilet yesterday. Ordinarily, I don't feel any role conflict. But I probably would if I defined my roles in such a way that they were in conflict with each other.

This sort of bind can arise quite easily. Since any of us can have more than one jailer at a time, and since our jailers may not all view the world in the same way (it would be unusual if they did), we may have accepted a number of IL's which do not agree with one another. You may find you're holding on to an IL which was taught to you as "appropriate" at an earlier time in your life, but which now is in conflict with an IL that has resulted from significant changes in your life and your relationships. Like most IL problems, the difficulty comes with the definitions. What do you mean when you use words like boss, father, Christian, lover, employee, student? If you combine two of them, and attempt to play both roles, the meanings you have attached to one could conflict with the meanings you have attached to the other.

After less than two years of marriage, Charlotte found two incompatible IL's that were leading her to a divorce court:

1. I am a daughter.
2. I am a wife.

The definition she had been given by her mother for the IL *I am a daughter* virtually locked her into childhood, in which all direction comes from mother. Her IM's included, "I must consult mother before making a decision," "I must put my mother's desires before those of my husband," and "I must go along with whatever mother wants."

As you might expect, these IM's conflicted with her husband's expectations. She became painfully aware of this. She had opposing IM's and IC's based on her IL of being a wife. Sometimes these would win over her role of daughter; and sometimes they wouldn't. Either her mother was satisfied or her husband was, but seldom both. She found herself increasingly pulled from both sides. Her mother and her husband demanded that she make a choice: "Prove that I am the most important one in your life." Ironically, they were both attempting to give her the IM, "You have to choose one of us over the other; you can't love us both." Fortunately, as Charlotte's self-esteem grew, she discovered she did not have to choose between the two of them, she did not have to reject one or the other, she did not have to reject both of them, and, in fact, she didn't have to love either or both of them. The options were entirely her own.

CONFLICTING IC'S AND IM'S

You may also hold IC's and IM's which are incompatible. Let's say you hold an IL: "Typing is essential to my job." If you have convinced yourself, however, that you have twelve thumbs on each hand and do not have the coordination necessary to scratch your head, you may have an IC which says, "I can't learn typing," and the conflicting IM which says, "I have to learn to type." Most of us hold some conflicting IC's and IM's. They all take the form of: "I have to, and I can't." This type of bind is generally immobilizing. Caught in such a bind, one does nothing except feel frustrated and miserable. If either the IC or the IM can be refuted, the bind dissolves and there is a resulting freedom. Again, it is ironic that frequently such conflicting IC's and IM's have been taught to us by the same person. The same people who taught me I had no aptitude for mathematics (another way of saying, "you can't learn math") also emphasized "you have to learn mathematics." About the same time I broke free of the IC and was able to say, "I can learn mathematics," I also found I was able to say, "and I don't have to learn mathematics." Wonder of wonders, I found myself learning mathematics.

A MULTIPLICITY OF CELLS

You don't live in just a single cell. No one does. Unless you're absolutely and totally free, and I have yet to meet such a person, you live within a jail which has a number of cells. You may break free of one to find yourself locked within another. When the prison con, as played by Burt Lancaster, plans his escape, he first figures out how to get out of his cell. But his planning can't stop there, or he is no better off than before. Once out of his individual cell, he has to get through the door to the cell block. From there, he must get to the prison yard, and then over the wall. Even then, he has to make good his getaway or end up back in the cell again.

In escaping and reaching true freedom, you break out of one cell at a time. But before you decide that you live in a jail with 739 cells and that it would take a lifetime to break free of them, let me throw in a couple of encouraging points: Through the V.I.F. (which will be introduced in a moment), you can soon become very adept at lock-picking. Once you learn the technique of breaking out of two or three cells, you become a skilled escape artist. Not only that, freedom has a way of generalizing. When you break out of one cell, you find two or three others crumbling. If I have a fear of women, and I break out and date a redhead, I am going to be free to date blondes and brunettes as well. Furthermore, the fear of freedom quickly vanishes after you break out of a few cells. One further point: Since one IL can generate several IC's and IM's, when a major IL falls, especially a cornerstone IL, it can crumble a number of IC's and IM's. In fact, the entire jail system may fall.

Your many-celled prison presents a unique problem. While we ordinarily expect a prison to look like a prison—stone walls, bars and all—prisons don't have to look like that. Imagine you awoke this morning to find yourself in one room of a 100-room mansion located on a 1,000-acre estate. You might wander from room to room marveling at the luxury of your new home and then stroll about the grounds for hours and even days before discovering the estate was enclosed by a 20-foot wall. That it was, in fact, a prison.

Most of us live in prisons which are comfortable enough to conceal the fact that they deprive us of freedom. A business manager in his late thirties spoke with me. He told me he had no problems other than high blood pressure and chronic colitis. He was married, the father of three, with a bedroom for each in a home in the suburbs. He said he had a marriage "with no problems." "I figure I've got it made," he told me, and "all I'd like to do is get rid of the physical problems I have. But I don't see that they have anything to do with any lack of freedom." He told me he played golf on Saturday morning and was gradually reducing his score. He never had more than two drinks a day, headed his church's building committee, and had the money to send his wife on a vacation to her parents every year. Almost every sentence describing his life described another jail cell. Finally, I interrupted him.

Quoting his statements back to him, I tried to give him a view of some of his cells and the IL's on which they were based. He stopped me with, "All right, maybe I'm not entirely free, but what's wrong with staying in what you call a jail if you're happy there?'' I told him I don't find anything ''wrong'' with staying imprisoned; I just don't think it the most fulfilling way to live. I don't believe someone locked in a cell is really *living;* he seems closer to the patient who is tied to the life support system of intravenous feedings, respirators, and heart stimulators. As for being happy locked in prison, that claim strikes me as being absurd, somewhat like the time-worn IL: Ignorance is bliss.

A prison is a prison, and ignorance is only ignorance, nothing more. Prisons don't lead to happiness and ignorance does not lead to bliss. Both result only in misery. I have observed one thing which I feel argues strongly against the question, ''But what if you're happy in prison?'' It is this: I have never met a man or woman who has found freedom who expressed any desire to return to prison. I have concluded that the only person who could speak of being happy locked up is one who has never experienced the exhilaration of freedom.

There are, of course, those who seek to ''escape'' from freedom by turning over their choices, even their thought processes, to others. One may be ''freed'' from the responsibilities of making moral choices, deciding on the direction of one's life, and even of coping with money matters by turning over everything to a cult leader. But it is a sad perversion of logic and semantics to call blind following ''freedom.''

5 V.I.F.: The Formula for Freedom

While people and things have a lot to do with the construction of your jail, it is important to remember that your jails are not constructed of people and things. They are built of *words*. The three walls—IL-IC-IM—are built of sentences you have been taught. It would not be strictly true, therefore, to say people are keeping you locked up. What they have told you, and what you have come to believe and to fear, are what keep you in prison. But as we all know, there is no such thing as an escape-proof prison. Desperate men and women have scaled the Berlin Wall. Alcatraz was vulnerable. So was Devil's Island.

Your jailers have to rely on the power of two things in order to keep you locked up: unquestioning acceptance of what they teach you, and fear of the consequences should you try to escape. If you don't accept what they tell you, you're out of the prison. What can be learned can be unlearned. What was once accepted can be rejected.

When I was a child, my friends may have told me the symbol H_2O is the code name of a spy, but one lecture in elementary chemistry would be enough to unlearn the belief. I once had a strong IC: "I can't swim more than fifteen or twenty feet. I flail around in a struggling, gasping, combination breaststroke and dog paddle; I'm not strong enough to swim further." Then came the day when I joined the Navy. To my horror, all recruits were required to pass a swimming test. I was faced with swimming the length of a 55-meter pool. I felt I might be able to swim the width (with some effort), but the length? Never! The military, however, has some unsympathetic means of getting you to do what they want you to do. So into the water I jumped, and began paddling down the center lane of the pool in a struggling attempt to swim. By the time I reached what I was sure was the absolute limit of my stamina, the point beyond which I knew I could not swim another stroke, I found I was somewhere in the middle. And I was looking down into 14 feet of water. Self-preservation overcame my IC.

The IC's and IM's, being the weakest walls, are the logical ones to attack. It's simply a matter of learning how. My IC of not being able to swim more than 20 feet was easy to escape: all I had to do was find myself in deep water with more than 20 feet farther to swim. But to get into that deep water, I had to be "pushed." If I have to be pushed to get out of each and every prison (an IM), and I feel I can't break out without someone's assistance (an IC), then I will be locked in a cell for a long, long time. Could I have escaped that prison alone? No, not as long as I held the IC "I can't swim over twenty feet." The power of any IC lies in such unquestioning acceptance. If I have been taught *all* snakes are dangerous and therefore to be avoided, I'm not likely to voluntarily disprove this IC by playing with harmless snakes.

Counseling and psychotherapy are aimed at assisting the patient or client in ridding himself of IC's (fears, phobias, anxiety, inhibitions), IM's (compulsions, depressions, guilt), and IL's (negative self-image, obsessions), or learning to cope with them, even if this means only resignation to what is inevitable. Therapeutic methods have usually included one or more of the following:

1. Identification of the antecedent conditions under which the IL-IC-IM was learned.
2. "Reliving" (emotionally) the traumatic events under which the learning occurred.

3. Moral suasion to believe in a different (moral or social) value system, one sanctioned by the therapist.
4. Analysis of the patient's irrational beliefs, and encouragement to change behavior in accordance with a more rational belief system.
5. Behavior, under the direction of the therapist, designed to desensitize the patient from the feared stimuli (*e.g.*, gradually going in the water in order to overcome a fear of swimming).
6. Expressing strongly felt emotions (catharsis) in a permissive (and therefore "therapeutic") environment.

In the counseling role, the therapist plays the role of:

1. Accepting parent
2. Demanding teacher
3. Moral judge
4. Logician
5. Healer
6. Confessor

All such traditional methods to varying degrees are based upon one or more of the following (depending upon the school of therapy and the personality of the therapist):

1. The patient's or client's admission he is incapable of effecting positive change in his life without help.
2. The patient's acceptance of an inferior role in relationship to the therapist (who is seen as more knowledgeable, insightful, mature, and "well adjusted").
3. The agreed-upon premise that the patient is suffering from a "condition" (emotional problem, "block," mental illness) which, if treated successfully, can be relieved.
4. Acceptance that "therapy" is a long, difficult, painful process.

In recent years, a number of psychologists and psychiatrists have experimented with the use of visual images in psychotherapy. Essentially the techniques involve teaching the client to conjure up a visual image of himself performing actions which he may previously have felt incapable of performing. Seeing himself, in imagery, performing the feat, he finds himself "in reality" able to do so. Applying the technique to therapy, reliance shifts from therapist to client. The image is the creation of the client rather than that of the therapist.

The effectiveness of visual images is not a recent discovery. "As you believe yourself to be, so you are" is a truth which has long been known. The patient's belief in his ability to cure himself is fundamental to the curative powers of medicine. If he can "see" himself gaining recovery, he has taken the first steps toward health. If he cannot do so—or will not do so—he stands little chance of regaining his health. Visual imagery may be related to self-hypnosis, but there are important differences. While many people view self-hypnosis as an induced altered state of consciousness (which it is probably not, at least in its shallower stages), the visual imagery employed in the method we have used is in no way an "altered" state of consciousness. It in no way alters my consciousness if I use my imagination to plan and anticipate my future. In my childhood it was called daydreaming, and teachers and parents frowned upon it. Perhaps we would have been better off had they encouraged it. In daydreaming, we create a visual image of ourselves engaged in a pleasurable activity, usually one in which we are achieving or experiencing the rewards of achievement.

Industrialist Henry J. Kaiser once said "you can imagine your future," and he believed much of his success was due to his use of daydreams. A number of famous sports figures have made similar use of daydreams. Golfer Jack Nicklaus uses visual imagery in making his phenomenal putts: "[It] gives me a line to the cup just as clearly as if it's been tattooed on my brain." O. J. Simpson has said that on the way to the stadium he will strive to "see" himself running plays. The great Russian weightlifter Vasily Alexeev pauses before attempting a lift; he has said he pictures in his mind the weight being lifted over his head, his elbows locking in a successful lift. Only if he can create such a visual image, he claims, does he feel he can succeed. Thomas Edison, when confronted with the most vexing problems, made a practice of relaxing and permitting daydreams to take over his mind. Dostoevsky relied heavily on daydreams. Brahms found he could best create when stimulated by a state of daydreaming.

Until recently, however, the potential of visual imagery has received little attention in Western medicine and psychology. Suggestion of its potential has more often been met with skepticism, even open attack, than with consideration as a possible "working hypothesis."

Work in the area of localization of brain function, especially research with the so-called "split brain" in study of the left and right hemispheres of the human cortex and the function of the corpus callosum, a neural cable link between the two hemispheres, may lead to a greater understanding of visual imagery, insight, and how we can utilize the complementary functions of the two hemispheres of the cerebral cortex. Since the latter part of the last century, we have known the right and left sides of the brain serve somewhat different functions. The initial observations showed that the right side of the brain controls functioning of the left side of the body and vice versa. Thus, in handedness, the right-handed person would be left-brain dominant in this motor skill. Later, other differences were observed in cerebral dominance. The left hemisphere is involved in language—reading, writing, speaking, arithmetic, the processing of sequential information, and "logic," rationality, and "common sense." The right hemisphere is our "intuitive" brain. It is through our right hemisphere that we experience the "aha!" phenomena, the description of insight given by psychologists. Three-dimensional vision, pattern recognition, musical ability, and holistic reasoning also reside in the right hemisphere.

It has been suggested that the left hemisphere acts to inhibit the right—a suggestion which parallels what we have said of those "practical, down-to-earth" IL-IC-IM's we are given. Our educations have been overwhelmingly left-hemisphere dominant. Dreaming "impossible" dreams is right hemisphere.

The answer, in terms of human happiness (*i.e.*, freedom), cannot be found in becoming either "left" or "right," but in developing the ability to fully utilize—and value—both. "I think the most significant creative activities of our or any other human culture—legal and ethical systems, art and music, science and technology—were made possible only through the collaborative work of the left and right cerebral hemispheres," says Dr. Carl Sagan. "These creative acts, even if engaged in rarely or only by a few, have changed us and the world. We might say that human culture is the function of the corpus callosum." *

It is possible the method we are about to describe, the Visual Image Formula (V.I.F.), acts to open the right hemisphere and/or counteract the inhibitory action of the left hemisphere. It cannot, however, create information, logical analysis, or specific skills. If I hold the belief "I can't learn to dance" (IC) because "I don't have natural rhythm" (IL), the formula may rid me of the belief which blocks me from taking that first dance step, but it will not *implant* a knowledge of dancing into my head and feet. Impossible dreams may take on life at the time of their conception in our right hemisphere, but we still must nurture them through their gestation and labor to give them birth.

In developing a technique which we believe to be most effective in employing visual imagery, we found the following elements to be essential:

1. Acceptance, at least as a "working hypothesis," of one's potentially limitless personal power.
2. Images must be of achievement events in one's life in which there is a strong element of personal power.
3. There must be such a clear visual image of the event that one can "see" the event clearly.

* Dr. Carl Sagan, *The Dragons of Eden* (New York, Random House; Ballantine Books, pap. edn., 1977).

4. The description of the image event must be in one's own voice.

These elements all underscore the repeatedly supported conclusion that change must come from personal desire and effort without "direction" of a parent/therapist. Significant change cannot occur in an atmosphere of impotence in which there is reliance upon someone else. Positive change occurs only if the individual confirms his or her ability to function with autonomy—and to function with omnipotence.

The first step in the technique is in identification of IC's and IM's. Don't try to identify all of them; simply jot down a sampling of your IC's and IM's. You are going to test the Visual Image Formula (V.I.F.) for yourself. After you have jotted down a few IC's and IM's, you can select one or two for your test. Do not, however, add any reasons why you can't do what you say you cannot do. This is very important. You see, the minute you say, "I can't because . . . ," the *because* jumps you immediately to your IL. And as soon as you reach your IL, you have what passes for a sensible rationale for your IC—and then you quit searching for an escape. You will have merely convinced yourself, once again, that in fact, you *can't*.

Avoiding this temptation to jump to your IL may not be easy. Most of us do not like to announce an IC without explaining an IL upon which it is based. Next time a friend tells you one of his IC's, try ignoring his IL; it will drive him crazy.

"I can't ride a bicycle."

"Really? I'm very sorry."

"Do you know why?"

"No, but I'm sure you have a good reason. By the way, do you still spend your vacations in Montana?"

"Huh? Are you saying you don't want to know?"

"Know what?"

"Why I can't ride a bicycle."

We like to believe all our actions have an explanation. Only a child is satisfied with "just because" as a reason for his or her actions. We feel somehow compelled to justify our actions to others. It provides what psychologists call "closure." But for this initial step, don't think of why you can't do what you believe you can't do or why you must do what you believe you must do. A little later I will expand upon why this is important.

Be expansive in listing your IC's and IM's. Again, you may find it tempting to censor out some before you write them because they are "obviously too far out," that is, they are IC's you are sure you really "can't" or IM's you feel you really "must." For now, suspend judgment. Just assume you can do absolutely anything and there is nothing, absolutely nothing, you have to do. When Wilbur and Orville Wright were repairing bicycles, the commonly accepted IC was, "If God had intended man to fly, he would have given him wings; everyone knows man cannot fly." Obviously the brothers Wright didn't buy the IC. They may have taken note of it, but my guess is they simply ignored it, and went about disproving it.

Ask yourself: "What do I really want?" Suspend judgment on whether you can or cannot get it since your answer may only repeat long-standing IC's and IM's. If you cannot immediately think of anything you may want (and many people have told us they have this problem), try approaching from the opposite direction. Ask, "What do I *not* want (physically, financially, in my love life)?" The answers may tell you what you do want.

I suggest you include some of your social IC's and IM's. There are a lot of prison cells contained in those dictates saying, "You just don't do such things in 'polite' society," and "It is one of those things you are expected to do when you're out to dinner." Don't forget also to include IC's and IM's tied to your roles as parent, employee, spouse, son or daughter, neighbor, student, club president, hostess, or whatever else is your thing. In the chapters to follow, I'll give a brief tour down the cell block of a few of these common areas.

Once you have a short list of IC's and IM's, go a step further—and this is a tricky one, for it demands monumental honesty: jot down some things you have not done because you feel you simply don't want to. Most of us have some of these "I can do it, but I just don't want to" explanations to cover activities we feel we can't engage in. Often, these are activities we are frightened to try (IC's) or feel coerced into doing.

A middle-aged businessman who could easily afford to fly and who took frequent business trips, had never been in an airplane.

"I always drive or take a bus, even on long trips," he said.

"That must be pretty inconvenient and uncomfortable. Why don't you fly?"

"I just don't like to. I'd rather ride a bus."

"Are you afraid of flying?"

"Of course not. I could fly if I wanted to. It's just that, well, what's wrong with liking to go by bus?"

Obviously nothing is wrong with preferring a bus to a plane; however, I suspect an IC. I use a simple test to pick up my concealed IC's and IM's: If it is an available activity which many others engage in by choice and which they claim to find enjoyable, my claim of simply not wanting to may hide an IC I don't care to admit. And if there is an activity I do "by choice," claiming I do it "simply because I want to," but one which I would be hard put to justify if someone asked me why I would want to, then I'm probably holding an IM.

"Why do we always have to invite Uncle George for Christmas dinner?"

"Who says we have to?"

"Well, I'm not the one who invites him; you are."

"That doesn't mean I feel I have to. It's just that I want to."

"I can't understand why. You say you can't stand his loud mouth, that he drives you up a wall."

"So what? I can still *want* to invite him. It doesn't have anything to do with feeling I *have* to."

You are not going to escape an IL-IC-IM prison if you believe your jailers are in the best position to know whether or not you should stay locked up. To escape, you have to believe you are at least as good, as wise, and as worthwhile as those who are trying to give you those IL-IC-IM's—and those who gave them to you in the past. Believing in your own great value is not something which can be achieved by accumulating "evidence," accepting somebody else's word for it, or "thinking it through rationally."

In the early days of computing, imaginative writers referred to the new electronic marvels as electronic "brains." Soon, they said, these machines with their flickering lights and spinning tape reels will be making many of our decisions for us. The big boxes will be thinking on their own. It made exciting newspaper copy, and inspired more than a few science-fiction movies. But it expressed an appalling ignorance of computers. Knowledgeable computer scientists have never claimed their sophisticated hardware is capable of thinking, or ever will be. All the computer can do is regurgitate what it is fed. The computer scientists have an acronym to express it: GIGO—garbage in, garbage out.

Part of the human mind is like a computer. Part of it—the part that makes us human—is not. The human part is our thinking, reasoning, evaluating, choice-making mind. It is our *conscious* mind, and it is the tip of the iceberg. The bulk of the iceberg, beneath the surface where we cannot easily get at it (as any psychoanalyst can tell you), is our *unconscious*. And the unconscious has much in common with the computer—garbage in, garbage out. Unfortunately, the decision-making part of our mind frequently gets short-circuited by the regurgitated garbage from our unconscious.

Our computer-like unconscious stores whatever it is fed. It doesn't evaluate the "input." It doesn't reason. It has no common sense. It has no conscience. It has no source of information except what it gets through the *conscious*.

And how does the conscious get the information it feeds into the unconscious? From the world in which we live. From events, experiences, and most of all, from what we are taught by the people around us.

Through our senses, we gather information about our

world. The information may be accurate or inaccurate, true, partially true, or false. The information then passes through the conscious to the unconscious. It is there, in the unconscious, that it is stored. It is not lost, simply stored. It remains accessible. From time to time, it will be "retrieved" into our consciousness, sometimes when we want it least. Remember I told you when I was nine years old I was taught I had no aptitude for mathematics? That message registered on my consciousness and was then filed away in my unconscious. There it remained effectively to block my education in mathematics for many years. All I had to do was see an algebraic equation and the message would crop up out of my unconscious to short-circuit my learning abilities. You can't, you can't, you can't. The IC was a broken record. So why didn't my conscious mind take a second look at it and say, "Hey, I'm not so sure that message is true. Maybe you *can* learn math if you put some effort into it?" Why? Because I don't have a mechanism for reevaluating all that data stored in the unconscious. No one does. Right or wrong, true or false, the messages pile up in little storage bins in the unconscious.

Throughout your life you have been told, "You can't" and "You have to." Without your being aware of it, all those IC's and IM's ended up in your unconscious. In time, those IC's and IM's shape the way you see yourself: as someone who can't do a lot of things others seem able to do, and who must do a lot of things others seem not to have to do. From there, it is only one short step to the conclusion, "I am inadequate." The same thing has happened to all of us.

Years ago, I thought there must be somebody somewhere out there who grew up feeling totally adequate to cope with anything—a person who reached adulthood with it "all together." In my high school, there was a small clique of kids who seemed blessed by the gods. They never had pimples. They always wore the right clothes. They never had trouble finding dates. They were disgustingly popular, totally self-assured. I'd like to think they ended up terribly obese and on welfare. By now I have concluded "no one grows up with it all together." We all acquire too many IC's and IM's in childhood. Those IC's and IM's form our self-images—for better or (more probably) worse.

But what can be learned can be unlearned. In the case of these negative IC's and IM's you can do better than unlearning them. And you can do it much quicker. Since the unconscious doesn't operate rationally, to unlearn an IC by reasoning you would have to retrieve each IC and, in your conscious mind, go through a tedious process of logic. Even then it might not work. Instead of going through a process of unlearning each and every IC and IM one by one, visual imagery permits you to bury them with positive messages which you send to your unconscious.

Keep in mind these two points: *reality is what you perceive it to be,* and *much of what was fed into your unconscious was garbage.* Don't waste time trying to reason out whether those negative IC's and IM's were "true." They were "true" to the extent you accepted them, to the extent you did not have sufficient positive messages to overcome them, and to the extent they affected your behavior.

The basic purpose of the V.I.F. is to send positive messages to overcome the garbage stored in the unconscious. Please note, however, this is not the "every day in every way I am getting better and better" notion for self-improvement. That seldom helps if in your reality you don't have a good opinion of yourself. Fortunately, the V.I.F. does not call for feeding in more positive messages than the number of negative IC's and IM's you have stored. For most of us that might take a lifetime. A relatively small number of positive messages can overcome a multitude of negative ones. Don't ask me why. Perhaps it is because we are apt to repeat and nurture messages which make us feel better rather than worse. Those who have employed the V.I.F. have discovered that these positive messages, when applied within the context of the V.I.F., have fantastic power to overcome garbage.

In case you should ask, "But what if I don't have anything good to tell my unconscious about myself?,'' let me reassure you: I think there are many, many good things you might tell your unconscious about you. And remember what I said about the unconscious: it doesn't know whether what it is told is true or false, real or unreal, roses or thorns. So you might as well tell it whatever will make you feel good.

THE VISUAL IMAGE FORMULA (V.I.F.)

Step 1: Recall the memory of a time in your life when you felt the exhilaration of accomplishment. This is not to be a "period" in your life, just a point in time. Usually it will span only a matter of minutes. It should be a high point, one which produced the thrill of accomplishment. Try to recall what you were wearing, who was there, the surrounding scene, everything that was said. Bring back as many visual details as you can. Try to make it as vivid as a color motion picture you are viewing. If you cannot recall specific details, create them from your imagination. It might be the time you won the 50-yard dash in high school or the time your boss praised your work in front of the other employees, or the time the soufflé you attempted came out perfect. Do not include anything which gives you negative feelings. If the memory was of an achievement which was for you a peak experience, you should feel the exhilaration returning as you recall it. Write out this visual memory in as much detail as you can. But be sure to write it in the present tense—as if you are describing a peak experience you are currently going through. Once you have it in writing, check to be sure the experience is totally positive and *in the present tense*.

Step 2: Conclude your written description of the achievement experience with the words "I can do anything, absolutely anything." And follow with the words "I am now . . ."

Step 3: Then go on to describe *in the present tense* a visual image of yourself enjoying the rewards and satisfaction of having achieved what you previously doubted that you could achieve. Be sure it is *your* achievement, not something attained through "luck" or bestowed upon you by someone else, and not the result of any "team" effort. Write it in such a way that you can see yourself savoring the satisfaction and rewards of your achievement. Describe the scene in sufficient detail to make it real to you. Do not describe it in the future tense. It is not something to tell yourself you hope to do or plan to do. In your description of it, *you are doing it right now.*

Step 4: You now have the two visual images written out in detail with the words "I can do anything I want to do—absolutely anything." Now, make a tape recording of your voice reading the material you have written. When you read, try to give your words enthusiasm and authority. Your unconscious needs to get the message loud and clear. If they are truly delightful images, it should not be hard to read them with joy in your voice.

You now have heard your voice—and will hear it again —sending a positive and power-filled message to your unconscious. This, plus the words "I can do anything I want to do, absolutely anything," is the key to the success of the V.I.F. Consider this: Of all the voices you listen to, the most influential by far is your own. You might have a friend or adviser whose judgment you value highly, but if his or her words conflict with those coming from your unconscious, you will ignore that voice and listen to your own. In committing the images and affirmation of independence and freedom to a tape recording and listening to the sound of your own voice saying the words, you will acquire an "authority" strong enough to overcome the IL-IC-IM authorities you have listened to for so long. Reading the words will help, but hearing them on a tape recording is far, far better —and necessary for maximum effectiveness.

This raises the question of investment in a cassette tape recorder, and whether tapes are essential. We have experimented with the V.I.F. and other methods of visual imagery without tapes (what some have called "head" tapes). We have attempted to analyze why their effectiveness is significantly less than the V.I.F. when tapes are employed. Since our analysis has led only to conjecture, however, we will say only that the employment of tape recordings of one's own voice in the V.I.F. is virtually essential. In a word, investment in a cassette recorder and a few blank tapes may be the best investment the reader has made in many years. In many households, including my own, each family member has purchased a small portable recorder. Personally, I carry mine (and play it) on the way to work, while I'm shaving, during the commercial breaks of a television program, and on a weekend vacation.

ELIMINATING AN IC

A friend of mine, I'll call him Henry, is a thirty-four-year-old father of three. He worked at what he considered a dead-end job while he dreamed of opening his own dog-grooming business. Henry felt, however, his dreams would have to stay just dreams. He didn't have much money, and he felt that even if he did start such a business, it would take a long time to get established. He also doubted that his wife would support his ambitions. He was willing, however, to give the V.I.F. a try. Here in brief outline, is how Henry employed it:

Step 1: Several years ago, Henry had appeared before his city's planning commission to argue for the installation of a badly needed streetlight on the block on which he lived. He had carefully prepared his arguments and, although he was nervous speaking in public, he fielded the questions of the board members well. The streetlight was approved. The following evening his neighbors stopped over at his house to give him a surprise party. The feelings Henry experienced at that time formed his first image.

Step 2: After clearly describing his remembered image, Henry enthusiastically said the words, "I can do anything I want to do—absolutely anything."

Step 3: Henry continued with his second image. Starting with the words, "I am now the owner of my own dog-grooming business," Henry described his feelings.* In his descriptions, visually creating an image, he created a reality. In both the first and second image, he provides a detail in the present tense, which makes them "real." Here is the completed transcript which Henry put on tape, with, to use his words, "all the enthusiasm a pretty hesitant guy could muster":

> "I am standing at the front door. Sid is standing there with a big grin on his face, and right behind him I see Phyllis and Bill and the others. Clare comes up behind me and snaps on the porch light and says, 'Hey, don't make everybody stand there; invite them in.' Bill is holding out a bottle of champagne toward me, and they are all offering congratulations. It takes me a minute to catch on. They are all telling me what a great job I did at the Commission meeting, how I had the members eating out of my hand, and how no one else could have done it. Clare kisses me on the ear and tells me she is proud of me. *I can do anything I want to do—absolutely anything!* And I am now the owner of my own dog-grooming business. I'm pulling my car up to the curb, and as I glance up I can see the sign, 'Mr. Henry—Dog Grooming.' It's a great-looking sign, expensive and exclusive looking. There is a beautiful lawn in front, and there are broad trees. Now I am walking up to the front door. I'm taking out my key. It's my key. And my own business. And it is going to be one hell of a success!"

* Actually, Henry made several second images in progressive tapes as he took the steps toward his ultimate goal of owning his dog-grooming business. He had a tape on securing adequate financing, convincing the bank loan officer of the potential of the proposed business, and a tape on finding a suitable location. The above, however, was what might be called his "sustaining" tape, the one which represented the fulfillment of his dream.

ELIMINATING THE IM

Essentially this involves the same three steps. The visual image in Step 1 should be a point in time when you felt the greatest freedom, a time when you felt you didn't really have to do something you didn't want to do. It might be the same memory of a point in time that you recorded in your first image (Step 1) in breaking out of an IC, or it may be another memory. When you have described in writing that visual image in detail (and remember, fill in all the details you can), say, "I can do anything I want to do. Absolutely anything!" When you say them on tape, try to say the words as if you mean them. At Step 2, say "I am now . . ." and visualize yourself doing something you *want* to do rather than whatever it is you have in the past told yourself you *have* to do. Describe and write that visual image in detail. And, Step 3, read and record it with enthusiasm.

About now you may say, "Okay, I can understand what you're suggesting so far. But then, how do you go about planning how you are going to accomplish your second image? Obviously Henry had to figure out how he could save money to open his shop, how and when he could afford to quit his job, and perhaps how he could talk his wife into going along with his ideas. That must be the next step."

Definitely *not*. It will defeat the V.I.F. If you merely give yourself a pep talk and then start planning, you are saying to your unconscious, "Being free to do what I want to do is my goal." That tells your unconscious it is not your present reality. And since your unconscious will believe anything you tell it, what you would then be telling your unconscious is, "I'd really like to be free, but I'm not free now; I'm a prisoner." Your unconscious stores simple messages only. It can't deal with a lot of qualifications and explanations which began with, "Yes, but what I really mean is . . ." All your unconscious would hear is, "I'm a prisoner." Furthermore, your unconscious deals only with the present; it doesn't operate on future tense.

Planning how to achieve your goals will be little more than an exercise in futility unless and until you see yourself as the sort of person who has already achieved these goals. If you do presently see yourself as a person who has achieved the goals, then you don't need to plan how to become such a person: you *are* that person. If my friend Henry is already a dog groomer, he does not have to plan how to become what he already is. Any of his actions in opening a dog-grooming shop will simply follow "as a matter of course." Use the V.I.F., and the planning will somehow take care of itself.

This may seem to contradict what was said about Henry making several intermediary-step tapes on the way toward acquiring his business. A distinction can, however, be made between the mental "planning" which says, "I am not a business owner; therefore I am going to have to find out what I might do if I ever hope to be," and the establishment of a second image which tells your unconscious, "I am a successful businessman, and as such I will, of course, take the necessary steps in opening a new shop." The distinction may seem very subtle, but it is very real and very important. Any second image should be designed to enable you to see yourself enjoying the rewards of your "I wants."

Another thing you and I have been told, over and over again, is that everything comes with a price. And that, presumably, would include breaking free of IC's and IM's. "Everything has a price" is about as universally accepted an IL as you are apt to find. The consequence of refuting an IC or IM generally takes the form of "Because . . ." (the IL) followed by, "and if I did, then . . ." (the price tag).

IC: "I can't take trips with my husband."
IM: "I must stay home with the children."
IL: "Because I am a mother."

Price tag: "And if I did, something would happen to the children."
"And if I did, my mother would think I'm a terrible mother."
"And if I did, the children would hate me."
"And if I did, I would worry all the time."
"And if I did, the children might find they don't need me."
"And if I did, my husband might get the idea I'll go along with anything he says."

It is seldom wise to consider the possible price of freedom. First of all, we seldom can know with any certainty what price might be demanded for our exercise of freedom, but there is an even more important reason why asking the price tag makes no sense. The answer you come up with will always be a reflection of your self-image. If you don't think much of yourself, you will always anticipate an exorbitant price tag. Some people attach a price tag that looks like the national debt to any and all freedoms. I call it the my-world-will-come-to-an-end price tag. If Henry had applied it to his IL-IC-IM, it might have been expressed as follows:

1. "I hate this dead-end job of mine, but I've got to stay here" (IM).
2. "What I'd really like to do is to start a dog-grooming business, but I can't" (IC).
3. "After all, I do have responsibilities, a wife and three kids" (IL). If the business didn't make it, what then? I'd be out of a job, we'd have no savings left, we could lose the house and be out on the street, and I don't want to end up on welfare with my kids going hungry" (the price).

These fantasized my-world-will-come-to-an-end price tags go beyond any reasonable answer to the question, "What price tag could you reasonably expect to pay for this freedom?" They frequently go beyond the question, "What is the worst thing that can happen?" They are simply unbelievable. "I'm twenty-one years old, and I'd like to be able to have a drink in a bar, but I'd better stay away from the stuff because if I take that first drink, and I like it, I could become an alcoholic, and then my family would disown me, my friends would no longer have anything to do with me, I wouldn't be able to keep a job, and I would end up dead from cirrhosis of the liver in some skid-row gutter before I reach twenty-five." If you hold the IL, "I'm a natural-born loser," you have a bushel basket full of IC's. You obviously can't take risks. You are certain to lose. Why? Because you are "a natural-born loser." But if you believe you can do anything you want to, you'll no longer be a loser. Then you can take risks, because for you, they will not be risks.

The way to deal with questions of price tag is therefore quite simple: Don't ask the questions! Stuff your unconscious with positive messages and don't spend time and energy on those "Yes, but what ifs?"

In our seminars we have found questions of price tag to be among those most often asked. Most people don't discourage too easily when their treasured IL's are challenged. But the idea of stepping off a cliff (which is what most people foresee happening if they fail to evaluate price tags) seems totally and absolutely crazy. I usually suggest, therefore, that if the price tag is too frightening a prospect for them to ignore, and is preventing them from testing the V.I.F., that they try it out on an IC for which the price tag can in no way be "disastrous." Personally, I don't like to see people edge into things with that much caution. I may feel they have nothing to fear, but if they are hanging on to such fearful IL's that they feel they cannot jump right in, they would be better to start cautiously than not to start at all.

Ranked right behind questions of price tag are questions involving the rights of others and concern for the feelings of others. These are questions of justice, fairness, kindness, and loving. When we were young, we were taught freedom is a dangerous thing, and that if we exercise our freedoms we will do dreadful, awful, despicable things. We were taught we are by nature biting, clawing, scratching, thoroughly despicable creatures. And we cannot be allowed to act freely or we will run amok. These questions, then, frequently take the form, "But if I have that kind of freedom, what's to prevent me from stepping all over other people?" Our answer is: "It doesn't happen." If I am free, I have discovered the value of freedom. Valuing freedom, I will not want to deny it to anyone. This I would be attempting if I were to disregard the rights of others in pursuit of what I might call "personal freedom." Infringement on the rights of others is not an exercise in freedom; it is an attempt to enslave.

If I play my stereo full volume at 2:00 A.M. while my neighbor is trying to sleep, I am not exercising freedom; I am practicing tyranny. The individual who is most adamant in demanding his "rights," and most aggressively protective of his "freedoms," is often the one who runs roughshod over the rights and freedom of others. There is a big difference between defending one's rights and being defensive. And the difference stems, once again, from one's self-image.

I once had a difficult neighbor I'll call Clyde. Clyde held a cornerstone IL "Given half a chance, people will walk all over you." With this IL, Clyde behaved in a most paranoid manner. His IL generated IC's, such as, "I can't get friendly with the guy next door or he'll want to borrow my lawnmower and never return it." And IM's such as, "I have to holler at the newspaper boy if he misses the front porch or next thing he'll be putting the paper on the roof." Clyde had a lousy opinion of himself. He saw himself as less successful, less educated, less capable, less everything than just about everybody. So he felt he had to defend himself against a world which was, in his opinion, populated by people who could walk all over him. In "defending" himself, he advocated restricting the freedoms of everyone else. One of his favorite declarations was, "There ought to be a law against . . ." And he included just about everything with which he disagreed.

With a better self-image, all this would change. It is not that the free individual, once again, *restricts* his or her freedom out of regard for the rights of others. I cannot *restrict* a freedom for myself which has never existed. The free individual never feels his freedom is limited by the rights of others. In honoring and protecting their rights, he is protecting his own—and strongly affirming his own freedom.

These, however, are questions only of justice. There remain those questions of concern for others, kindness, and loving. These are questions involving what we choose to give to others. And the key word, of course, is "give." If you feel obligated to send a dozen roses to Aunt Martha on her birthday, that's an IM, and you lack freedom. The dozen roses is not a gift (regardless of how Aunt Martha might choose to interpret it). To qualify as a gift, it would have to be a freely chosen act. Once you have refuted that IM, you will no longer feel any obligation to send roses. And you will also no longer feel like a hypocrite. I am not, however, suggesting that people who are free of IL-IC-IM prisons are uncaring, ungenerous, unloving people. Far from it! In fact, only free individuals can be caring, generous and loving. If someone puts a gun to my head and demands my money, I am not free to hand it over to him. I cannot be giving. I have no choice. Free of those IL-IC-IM's, would you ever send roses to Aunt Martha? Possibly. But if you did, it would be because of what you anticipate you may get out of it; not because you feel you have to.

Freely *giving* to someone makes you feel good. You cannot, under any circumstances, get the same good feelings in meeting an obligation. When you are paying a moral debt, and "giving" out of obligation, you are likely to resent the one to whom you are "giving." I once worked with an organization in which the practice was to take up a collection for a going-away "gift" when an employee retired. One of the men would come around to collect. "I guess you know Frank is retiring. We're taking donations for a going-away gift. Your share is five dollars." Donation, hell! It was an assessment. And I found myself resenting not only the policy but old Frank. I could only get rid of my resentment of old Frank by ridding myself of the IM "I have to kick in five dollars for old Frank."

SOME QUESTIONS ABOUT THE V.I.F.

Following are questions commonly asked by those setting out to write images for the first time:

"I've never had anything really big and important happen to me. I've never achieved much of anything. What memory do I use for my first image?"

The *event* you remember is not what is important; it is the *feeling* which is. It might have been the moment when the examiner told you you passed your driving test. It might be the time you filled in all the squares in a crossword puzzle. It is any time you really had a great feeling about yourself and what you could do. But keep in mind that the second image as well as the first must narrate achievement. It is something you have accomplished, not merely a happy occurrence.

"I've written out a couple of first images, but I find that I don't feel any good feelings about myself when I listen to them. Can you suggest a reason?"

You may be selecting a memory for your image which is not entirely positive. It may be that there are some pieces of your memory which "taint" it, or that you are including in it events which occurred either before or after the "point in time" which were not particularly pleasant.

Many individuals have said they had to rewrite or re-record the first and/or second images two or three times before they could get to the description which was totally capable of generating *exhilaration*. This is not to say, however, that the images must be models of perfection in order to be effective. If they contain the essentials of workable images—rewarding feelings for personal achievement, visual imagery, present tense—they will be effective. Few of us are professional actors.

"I have so many IL-IC-IM's, I don't know where to begin. Can you work on more than one at a time?"

Sure. But generally, people find it easier to work on no more than three or four at a time, especially when first using the formula. Personally, I seldom work on more than one or two visual image sets at any one period of time, although I frequently write new descriptions and make new tapes. There is a fallout effect which most people experience in using the V.I.F. Great things start happening in many areas of one's life.

"If I can do anything I want to do by using the formula, how come I can't get my husband to be more romantic?"

Because you cannot acquire freedom while attempting to deprive someone else of freedom. You are, in effect, saying, "I can't give my husband the IM I want him to have." If your husband is free of IM's, good for him! If his choices do not coincide with yours, use the V.I.F. to free yourself of any IM's which say, "I have to depend upon my husband for my satisfaction." There is a basic rule that no one can write a second image for someone else. What I *can* do, however, is write a second image in which I have succeeded in changing the manner in which I approach and interact with others. I may then find their reactions are changing.

"Should I have a different first image for each IC or IM I want to lose? And should my first image somehow tie in with my second image, that is, should the two be related to the same class of events?"

You're not obliged either to use a different one for each IC and IM or to try to select images which tie in. You can, in fact, use the same first image in ridding yourself of any and all IC's and IM's. It is the feeling in the first image which is important. It should be a feeling of "I have the world on a string." That is the important thing to keep in mind. The first image acts as an emotional springboard for the second.

"Will it do any good to play my tapes when I'm feeling depressed or discouraged?"

That is an especially good time to play your tapes. Your unconscious isn't going to know what mood you're in when you send it good news. And even if the good news does not result in immediate positive feelings, it will at least counter any negative IC's and IM's you might be tempted to dump into your unconscious. In those depressed times, it often helps to replay your tape several times.

"I have a first image of myself getting admiration from a room full of men for my glamorous, sexy appearance, but I don't seem to get any feelings of omnipotence from it. Why not?"

I don't believe you can elicit feelings of power with the memory of an event which is, in fact, not a personal achievement. A sexy appearance may be little more than the product of an inflatable bra and greasy lipstick. It has nothing to do with being able to do anything (except buy bras and lipstick). Select a memory in which you did something and achieved something.

"In my second image I have been promoted to senior engineer. I am working at the plant in a new office making $2,000 a year more. But somehow I have a hard time feeling omnipotent."

There are three possible reasons to account for this. The job of senior engineer may not be what you really want. It could even be an IM ("I have to get a promotion because I need more money to support my family"). Also, the job of senior engineer may be nothing more than an expected step up the ladder, something you already anticipate, and no big deal. Perhaps most significant, the job itself may not be very rewarding; few jobs are. The additional money might provide rewards but in your image you see yourself doing the job rather than enjoying the rewards provided by the added money. You might try a second image such as, "I am now on vacation from my job as senior engineer sitting on the balcony of my hotel room in Acapulco." Why not be expansive in your second image? When you dream, dream big. Remember, you can do *anything*.

"After all has been said and done, however, isn't faith the key to whether or not the V.I.F. will work?"

This question is asked over and over again. The answer is: definitely not! When anyone tells me they believe something "on faith," I know they are telling me one of their IL's. The V.I.F. does not have to be accepted on faith. It does not have to be accepted at all. The V.I.F. should be viewed as an "empirical question." It can be tested, and the results can be evaluated. And they should. Your unconscious doesn't give a damn whether you believe in the V.I.F. or not. In fact, your unconscious will never know.

FIRST HAPPENINGS

You can expect several reactions—all of them good—almost immediately after you begin using the V.I.F. I won't pretend to know why some of them happen; your guess is as good as mine. The following are the most commonly reported reactions:

Euphoria—Feelings of intense exhilaration, a bubbling-over sensation, a feeling of walking on air.

Humor—As one woman said, "Suddenly I find a lot to laugh at. I can laugh at all the trivial little things I used to take so seriously, including myself. My friends can't understand it. So many of them see the world going to the dogs. I'm driving them crazy—and that's also hilarious."

Efficiency—This is one of the most surprising. Almost everyone who has tried the V.I.F. has reported a new-found ability to be incredibly productive with no apparent effort. One woman said, "Work which used to take me all day is now done by ten in the morning, and I'm not even aware of doing it."

Lack of Fatigue—Most people report sleeping less, seldom tiring, and arising in the morning feeling full of pep.

Flood of Ideas—It is as if the creative part of the mind has been dammed up, and now the floodgates are opened and ideas and concepts pour out.

Timelessness—This is a strange one, and again I have no

explanation for it. It is the sensation that time stands still. As one man told me, "It's as if clocks no longer matter. I'm constantly checking to see if my watch has stopped. What seems like three hours of pleasure can occur in a period of twenty minutes."

Insight and Self-Awareness—A greatly increased understanding of the causes of one's unhappiness and frustration—the present IL-IC-IM's.

Sensory Acuity—Another surprising one. Many, but not all, have reported colors, sounds, and odors are more vivid. "It's as if everything has been faded before; now it's a world of color. The sky is bluer than I've seen before, and I have become aware of how many songbirds I have around my apartment," was the way a young woman reported the change.

Loss of Guilt Feelings—Most people report an almost immediate loss of guilt feelings, even those which are not associated with the subject they are describing. They become capable of acting responsibly, but without guilt.

THE NOT-SO-LONG RANGE

If the immediate happenings were the only payoffs in using the V.I.F., it would be more than worth the time spent in preparing and listening to the tapes. The ultimate reward, however, is in being able to take control of your destiny and get what you want from life. The eventual results, then, are:

Total Freedom—Liberation from all those IL-IC-IM prisons, and immunity from all the IL-IC-IM prisons in which others would confine you.

Achievement—The ability to achieve your every dream and desire—no limits—without having to work your head off to do so.

Living—A continuous savoring of life to the fullest.

Self-Worth—The firm conviction that you are a truly remarkable, wonderful human being, and the most important person in the world.

SO WHY THE HOLDOUTS?

It never fails. I can present the principles of personal freedom to a group, describe the V.I.F. in detail, and talk of the benefits to be expected, but there will be some members who will turn off my words and never put it to the test. I have tried to discover why. Some have said, "I don't have the time, but I do hope to get around to it." Others have written off the concept as foolishness without giving it a chance. Some have dismissed it as just another pep talk, as a variation on the "power of positive thinking," or psycho-cybernetics, or a modern-day version of faith healing. It isn't any of these, and I can explain the differences, but with those who turn off to it at once, I seldom have the opportunity.

The reasons, as best I can determine, why some individuals avoid trying the method, include the following:

Doubt It Will Work—It might seem the argument, "I just can't believe it will work," could be answered by pointing out that since the method calls for little time and effort, and is not in the least bit painful, "What have you got to lose?" But for an individual who holds the IC, "I can't take disappointments," even a guarantee of the effectiveness of the V.I.F. may not suffice. The skeptics will answer, "I hear what you are saying, but I don't see how it could work for me. It would be just one more let-down."

Denial of IC's and IM's—I could hardly believe it the first time someone told me they had no IC's or IM's. "You're putting me on," I said. But they weren't. Some people, it seems, develop a "block" against recognition of IC's and IM's. It protects them against the pain of frustration—"If I don't think about all those things I can't do, I won't become unhappy." Now the protection, of course, may break down from time to time, but they persist in denying their prison walls. These denials, it seems, are most frequently expressed by individuals with strong feelings of inadequacy.

Fear of Impulses—This is the common fear that one may be overcome by "hidden" impulses. "If I were totally free, I would probably commit irresponsible, cruel, depraved acts." Some believe they have a nature so bad and so dangerous they should be locked up for their own protection as well as that of others.

Fear of the Price—Since we were taught: "You don't get something for nothing," it is normal to be suspicious of anything which offers as much as the V.I.F. seems to. "What price freedom?" is a question which has frightened many people into a passive acceptance of enslavement.

Freeing Others—This is the fear that my freedom will encourage freedom in others, and I'm not sure others will exercise freedom in the ways I want them to. It is also the feeling that while *I* can handle freedom with responsibility, I'm not at all sure others can.

If you find yourself reluctant to test the V.I.F., you might question whether your reasons include one or more of the above. Freedom is so foreign to most of us, even the concept is poorly understood. One misunderstanding I've heard expressed a number of times is the belief that if you get rid of an IC, you must replace it with an IM. Or if you get rid of an IM, you must substitute an IC for it. So, supposedly, when you free yourself from that IM, "I must phone Aunt Martha," you feel compelled to replace it with, "I can't phone Aunt Martha." That's trading one jail for another.

I feel sure there are other reasons people may have for not giving the V.I.F. a trial, not the least significant of which is that it doesn't on the face of it make sense. This is a reason I feel I can understand. It still doesn't "make sense" to me. Even the concept of *freedom* and all it implies is beyond my comprehension. More than a few times I have felt I am not ready to direct my own destiny—if, in fact, I can ever achieve freedom on any permanent basis. We have theorized about the V.I.F., but when people have challenged our theories, we have had to admit the theories are really nothing more than our attempt to make sense out of what works but does not conform to everything we have been taught about the capabilities and limitations of human beings. I console myself with the knowledge that we still do not fully understand the workings of the heart, or even why it should start beating prior to birth and continue for, hopefully, several decades. I am only grateful that such is the case. I therefore can only implore the reader to give the V.I.F. a trial. Despite fears of disappointment, fears of impulses and price, or reluctance to grant similar freedom to others, we have nothing to lose but our jail cells.

Sidney R. had been using the V.I.F. for eight or nine months when I met him and he told me his story. "You are looking at a former stereotype," he said. "I was a cliché; a mother-dominated, self-hating, anxiety-ridden, thirty-four-year-old University of Chicago-educated sociologist. I was twice married, making a lousy salary, and striking out every time I tried to establish what I used to call a 'meaningful relationship.' Believe me, I was the kind of klutz you'd expect your sister to hang up on. I wasn't a loser; I was worse than that. I was the kind that never had what it takes to even get in the game."

"The V.I.F. made a difference?" I asked.

"More than a difference. It made a new me."

"Don't you mean it helped you change yourself? I don't believe the tapes change people. People change themselves."

"O.K., I changed myself, but I did it with the V.I.F. Say, are you recording this?"

"Do you mind? I'll turn it off if you like."

"No, I don't mind. I've already told my story to all my friends."

"How did you start with the V.I.F.?"

"A friend of mine told me about it. He spent a whole evening on it. You would have thought he was trying to convert me to a religion. I thought he had gone bonkers. But a few days later, I decided, 'What the hell. I'll give it a try.' "

"Do you remember the first image you used?"

"Oh sure. Would you believe I had to go back twelve or thirteen years to come up with one? It was during a time I was working for a vending-machine company. I needed some extra money, and I had this friend of mine who used to cater private parties. He asked me if I could tend bar for this wedding party. I told him sure I could, even though I really had never mixed anything more complicated than a Scotch and water. I spent a couple of evenings going through a bartender's guide, and I not only carried the whole thing off, the father of the bride told my friend I was one hell of a bartender."

"What about your second image?" I asked.

"The first one I put on tape? I tried it to get rid of a tennis elbow."

"And it worked?"

"I couldn't believe it. I wrote a second image in which the pain had left. It had just flowed out of my body, and I could feel the warmth going down my arm. In about three days it was all gone. And my arm had been hurting for about a year and a half."

"I think most of us have had trouble believing it at first. Where did you go from there with the V.I.F.?"

"I'm not sure how I used it next. I think it had to do with interviewing for my present job. I was locked in to a job with a computer services company that was going down the tubes. I knew I had to get out or go down with them, but I had this IL saying, 'I don't have anything to sell, so how can I expect to get a really good job?' I managed to line up this interview, however, despite my feelings that I would probably blow it, and I figured I might as well give the tapes a try on it. I did, played the livin' hell out of it for about three days and, well, you can figure the results: I got the job. What's more, my income has more than doubled since then. I'm getting to where I have tax problems, but I figure I'll make a tape on that, too."

"I assume the V.I.F. has had an effect on your self-esteem. Have you anything to say about that?" I asked.

"I don't know how to answer that. It's been total, really total. I have really learned to value myself. I don't even like the way that sounds. I mean, what does it mean to value yourself? I guess I mean I now believe I've got a lot to offer."

"You claim you have gotten certain things you've wanted through use of the V.I.F., and that you intend to go on using it. That raises a couple of questions we have frequently been asked. I wonder what you might answer to someone who asks if you are not concerned about becoming dependent upon the V.I.F., and also to the person who asks when you expect to reach the point when you feel you can give up the V.I.F.?"

"I've already been asked those questions. All I can say is I'm certainly not worried about getting 'hooked' on my tapes. If anything, I was hooked before the V.I.F. on a whole lot of negative things I was telling myself about myself. And with all the negative people in this world who want to put you on a downer, I'd have to be a fool to ever give up the V.I.F. Believe me, if I don't play my tapes for a day or two, I notice it. By the third day, my wife will begin to notice it."

"If you had to boil down to a sentence or two what has changed for you since you took up the V.I.F., what could you say?"

"That's a hard one. I've used the V.I.F. on more 'I wants' than you could ever believe. For example, I had the IC, 'I can't communicate with my kids,' so I made three or four tapes on having a successful talk with one or another of my three kids. The same with my wife. She used to be on my case about half the time, just like my mother, so I made tapes on being assertive and letting her know what I wanted. And they worked. Boy, did they work. For the first time, I think, we began to listen to each other. I can't tell you how many tapes I have made. I have gotten over my hang-up about being a sociologist who wasn't earning a living as a sociologist—you know, the trip about 'wasting your education.' According to my wife, I've even become one hell of a lover. What can I tell you? The V.I.F. works."

About four months following our conversation, I got a phone call from Sidney's wife. She told me Sidney had resigned from his job and they had moved to Phoenix where they have gone into business together. "We're having so much fun," she said. "We have each tried so many new things. We're like a couple of kids. We now have a lot of new friends we have turned on to the V.I.F. But you know what I think has been the biggest change for us since we started using it? We have each discovered a lot of things we really didn't want. I had a lot of things I always said I wanted which I have found I don't want at all. They were nothing more than IM's."

FIRST IMAGES

Occasionally, someone will tell us they cannot recall any experiences which might serve as first images. We believe this is often a result of a self-image which is so negative it will not permit past achievements to enter consciousness. Other times, the individual may be too selective in searching for a first image. A first image certainly does not have to be "the day I won the Nobel Prize" or the "afternoon I shot par golf." One of my own favorite first images recreates a time I built a shelf under the kitchen sink while we were living in married student housing. (I had held the IC "I can't even drive a nail straight.") Lois has one of the time she turned out a "perfect" strawberry mousse. The following are examples of first images. Once the V.I.F. starts working, you will find yourself enjoying experiences of power and achievement which will provide material for countless first images.

By a businesswoman, single, mid-thirties:

> "I am playing first base on a girl's softball team. While I am a pretty good hitter, I have a reputation for

being poor at fielding. It's the bottom of the ninth and a crucial game. The stands are filled. My team is ahead by one run. There's only one out, and they have a runner at first and second. Their best hitter is at bat. My mouth is dry and I'm sweating even though the day is not very warm. The runner at first has taken a long lead off base. She knows the pitcher probably won't chance throwing the ball to me. I can feel my heart pounding. The girl at the plate takes the first two pitches. And the third pitch, she swings. The ball is a hard, high, line drive over my head and a little to my right. I move quickly, then up in the air. I feel the ball hit my mitt hard. I've caught it. I can hear the crowd screaming. Almost without thinking, I run toward first base. The first-base runner was so sure I wouldn't catch it she is more than halfway down to second. When my foot touches the bag, I hear the screams. I've done it. An unassisted double play. My teammates are running toward me. We've won the game. I've won the game. I can do anything I want to do—absolutely anything."

By a housewife, mother of three, forty:

"I have been cast in the lead in the Junior play in high school and it is the night of the performance. I have this really great scene in the final act. It didn't go so well this afternoon at dress rehearsal, but then nothing in the play went too well. My drama teacher said we were 'wooden,' and I wonder if I'm going to make a fool of myself this evening. The auditorium is filled. My parents are sitting in about the sixth row, and the boy I'm going steady with is right down in front. I don't want to do lousy in front of my folks or him and this afternoon I even had thoughts of what I might do if I screwed it up. I wouldn't want to face any of them again. But so far at least I haven't forgotten any of my lines. Now we are in the final scene, and I can feel I am the girl who's part I am playing. My nervousness has gone away and

I am really acting—feeling all the emotion of the scene. I know I can do it. It's as if I am standing back watching myself, and my performance is flawless. I feel I can go on forever. Then the curtain falls, and the applause is fantastic. I take several bows. I'm sure my mother has tears in her eyes. My drama teacher presents me with a bunch of red roses and says, 'You have a career ahead of you on the stage if you really want it.' I can do anything I want to do—absolutely anything."

By a junior engineer of a manufacturing firm, single, twenty-three:

"My boss has asked me to take his place at a meeting with several department heads to discuss the project we are jointly working on. The project is behind schedule and is fouled up all along the line. I'm just supposed to read a progress report of our department. We are actually involved in a minor part of the project so what I have to report isn't too important. I am sitting here at the end of this long table. All the others at the table are department heads. I read my short report and the project director says thanks, but nobody pays much attention to it. They start discussing what they think is going wrong with the project. I don't say anything until at one point it occurs to me they are all overlooking something obvious. It has to do with the flow of the project going to this one department before it goes to this other one and if they simply reverse the procedure, it might unsnarl things. I find myself speaking and making this suggestion. Suddenly, all these big brass are talking about it. One of them calls it 'absolutely brilliant.' They decide to put it into effect, and when the meeting breaks up, the project director walks out with me. He has his arm over my shoulder. My boss meets us in the hall and the project director says, 'Say, you've got one hell of a bright boy here. Look out, I may try to steal him away from you.' I can do anything I want to do—absolutely anything."

The following first image is one of the most lengthy I have heard. Personally, I prefer to keep my first images to a length which will consume no more than two or three minutes of reading or listening time on the tape. If it runs much longer than that, I find myself soon becoming impatient; I want to get on to the second image. I also find, due to time limitations, I do not play the tape as frequently. I prefer one I can play in the length of time it takes me to shave: usually three to five minutes. I decided to include this first image, however, because it is a superb example of the re-creation of a visual image of the event. I believe the reader will agree that "Campbell" (not his real name) makes us "see" what he describes.

By an executive with an electronics firm, married, four children, forty:

> "It's confining here in the cockpit. It's hot. I'm tense, nervous. This parachute seems heavy. This is the day. Just a few minutes ago, it seems, my instructor said, 'Campbell, this morning you're going formation—solo.' 'Yes, sir.' 'You'll be number two.' 'Number two, sir?' 'Yeah. You've been flying formation well. Normally we don't do it this way. There's been a change in schedule. We don't have another number-two man, so I can make you lead; you'll be number two. We've never done it this way before, but I have confidence in you. You're also, by the way, the first one in your class to solo. Don't bust the bird.' 'No, sir.' I hope I spoke confidently to him, but in any event, here I am in the cockpit. I can see the dew on the wings. The canopy is in the open and upright position. I can see rivulets of dew that's run off in sheets from the humidity that spreads up the air. It's clear out, no breeze. I see a few birds flying overhead. It's very early in the morning. It's about six forty-five. Yeah. The sun is a ball, red, orb. I can see it in some trees out there in the distance. It's very serene. But it's getting noisy. I can hear other aircraft starting up. I can see my other student friend

there in the front part of the cockpit in the aircraft beside me and the instructor. We've gone through our preflight preparation and the aircraft both look good. The crew chief has pulled away the ladder. The power's on the aircraft right now. Checked out all the lights and switches and everything seems to be O.K. We're full of fuel. I'm nervous. But I know it'll work out. I'll give her a damn good try. There's the starting power sign. O.K. Low whine. I can hear it building, coming up. O.K. Ignition start. There's the rumble, rumble through the aircraft. I can feel it through the seat. Engine start. O.K., all the gauges are moving. The oil pressure's coming up, generator's coming up, exhaust gas temperature's coming up. Rolling up, coming, easy. O.K., there it is: forty percent. Power stabilized. O.K., signal the crew chief. Let's get the auxiliary power cable out. Go to main power. There. We're in good shape. Look through the aircraft. Is everything clean? O.K., yep. Nothing popped; all the lights are green. O.K., his power's O.K. He's giving me the thumbs-up sign. I give him the thumbs-up sign. Yeah, he needs to be checking with the tower. Yeah, there it is. Kilo flight to taxi. Yeah, that's us. My instructors say, 'Yeah, think! Think! Think as a formation.' O.K., let's pull this off, Campbell. Go, Don! There it is. Kilo flight, let's taxi. O.K., let's go. He's rolling out. O.K., bring the throttle up. Release the brakes. Give her a little burst of power to get her going, O.K., then back on the power. All right, let him go first. Let him roll out. Rolling, rolling. Get in behind him. Here we go. Stay pretty close. I can see the heat waves shimmering off his aircraft. I can see him looking around. The canopies are still up. Taxiing out. Seeing the birds rise in the marsh. We're thinking formation. Think formation, Don, all the time, think formation. Still and comfortable. The breeze feels kind of good. Gauges all green. Everything looking good. Forward. Keep your position, keep right in there with him. O.K. Still see the heat waves coming off his aircraft. Smell the kerosene—nauseating, but exciting. There's his canopy going down. Get yours down. O.K., coming down. Watch your fingers. It's down. Lock it. Lights out. Everything's clean. Looking good. Flight control check-out. That looks pretty good. On down. Pulling up to the runway. There's tower clearance to get on. He's swinging wide, rolling onto the runway. Swing there kind of tight. Stay in there, stay behind him, a little to his right. O.K., he's slowing down. Stay with him. Brakes, brakes. In position. There. We're stopped. O.K., everything is fine. All right, we're in position. God! look at that runway! It goes out to infinity. It's like a highway. There's a mirage out there. I see water on it. Goes out there forever. It's flat as can be. It's calling me. It really is. O.K., time to go. He's bringing his power up. Bring mine up. Bring her up to eighty percent. Check it out. Everything's looking good. Keep the brakes, don't let it crawl. Full brakes. Keep the brakes on it! Looking good. The aircraft's shaking, trembling. His is too. There's his fist sign. Full power. Roll up to a hundred percent. Easy, coming up. Shaking. Both aircraft shaking. Looking good. He's looking at me. Thumbs-up sign. Looking good. Instructor's looking at me. O.K., this is the time, Don. We're going to do it. It's coming up. There's the signal. Let's roll! Rolling. Here we go. Rolling forward. Rolling down the runway. Stay close to him. Don't worry about the grass. He isn't going to lead you into the grass. Just stay five feet away. Stay by him. Bring up the power, little bit, bring it back, jockey, keep in position. Keep in position; think formation. Rolling down the runway, faster, faster. The runway's rushing by. Aircraft's shaking, nosewheel's pounding a little bit, aft stick a little more, get the weight off the nose. His nosewheel is coming up. Roll yours up, Don, a little bit more. There. Faster. O.K., rudder is taking control now. Must be eighty knots now. Coming up. Feels good. Rolling down. Looking good. There, he's rotating. Rotate,

Don, keep it in there. Rotating, up, up. O.K.! We're clear! We're off the runway. And there we go. Looking fine. I'm right in position. Coming up, climbing. There's his gear. Get your gear up, Don. See his gear folding into the aircraft, wheels still spinning, doors coming shut. Clean. Up we go. Clear. Rising. I can see my shadow on his plane. My head. I can see my head on his tip tank. Five feet away. Keep it going. Passing two hundred miles an hour. Going. Up we go. Up higher, higher, climbing more. Acceleration's pushing me back in the seat. Stay in there. Be close. Rolling, climbing. Up we go. Higher. Passing four hundred. We're on our way. We're there. The hard part's over. Up we go. Stay right in there. Stay as one. Up we go, higher, the ground is far away. We're climbing into the sun, up there, higher, in position. By God, I've done it! The first take-off. The first takeoff—solo. Wingman! Don, I've done it! The first one in the class! I've done it! I didn't think I could, but I've done it! I have power. I'm hollering into my face mask. Yeehee! I'm singing to myself. I've got the world by the balls! I can do anything I want to do—absolutely anything."

SECOND IMAGES

In the chapters to follow, there are examples of second images which have worked well for people who have generously shared them with us. The most effective second images have been found to be those which aim at a change in total life-style, habits, or relationships, rather than those which are intended to refute only a single, and limited, IC or IM.

Those who have, from their own reports and what I have had the opportunity to observe in their lives, benefited most from the V.I.F. have been those who are "committed" to freedom. For many, this is not an easy commitment to make. None of us who embark on such an undertaking can be unaware of the friends, relatives, fellow employees, and even total strangers who will strive to keep us in the prison cells in which they find themselves—or in which they find it to their advantage to keep themselves. For this reason, and the fact that lack of freedom may be hard to recognize, I have attempted to raise questions which, it is hoped, may help you identify some IC's and IM's of which you may be only dimly aware.

6 V.I.F. As a Life-Style

"Getting that first tape to where it really worked, with a first and second image that turned me on, and the right amount of enthusiasm in my voice, was one of the hardest things I've ever done," said one man. "But once I got it right, my life turned around." He said he has since made a number of tapes. I have found this to be common. Just writing a first and second image, or just another second image, is a turn-on, and this may be one reason why most people add to their "collection" over a period of time. There are two additional reasons: Living a life of freedom is "addictive." It is always exhilarating to uncover another area of freedom. And, since you want to be good to yourself at all times, you can always discover additional "I wants."

Contrary to what we expected when we first introduced the V.I.F., very few individuals report becoming bored with a tape they have played over and over again, sometimes several times each day. "Good news" seldom gets to be "old hat." Most people say they make additional tapes because of the good feelings they find in making and listening to them, for variety, or because of a specific IC or IM (*e.g.*, weight loss) they want to attack. A salesman told me he has a collection of tapes, most of them employing the same first image, which he carries in his car. He has them filed under topic headings. One he plays on the way to his office if he is going to have a meeting with his boss, another is designed to give him a lift before he keeps an appointment with a client, and one prepares him to greet his teenage sons when he arrives home. He gives the tape for meeting with his clients credit for doubling his income in less than a year. I asked him if he had recorded a new first image. "No," he said, "I still have the same one. It's of a time I won a speech contest in the tenth grade. I guess it has been so good to me I don't want to give it up."

Others have told us they have used a new first image each time they have recorded a new second image. After employing the tapes successfully for a time, most people experience achievements from which can be formed new first images, but in the beginning, as I mentioned previously, coming up with a workable first image may be the most difficult hurdle. "I just can't think of a single time in my life when I felt any exhilaration of achievement; my life has been pretty much humdrum" is a common complaint. I advise such people to take their time and not push it. Within a week they will usually remember an event. If you try to come up with one under pressure, you will be likely to recall an event which, although it was an achievement and was probably recognized as such by your family and friends, did not give you what one woman aptly termed a "rush," that overall thrill of power and satisfaction.

In order to achieve the desired effect, that is, to bring about change in your life, the second image must embody "achievement" and the feeling of power. It must be an image of *reward* for that achievement. Effective second images, therefore, are always "after the fact" with a "flashback" describing the achievement. For example, "I am now sitting on my patio with a glass of wine in my hand, feeling completely relaxed and happy with myself" (reward) "because today I presented my new ideas on how to increase sales of the widgit to Mr. Shangfiester, and I did one hell of a job of it! I handled it in a way that I know the points I had to get across came through. From now on, I'm on top of the world; I know how it should be done, and I can communicate it to others."

Frequently, when individuals have brought us their written descriptions and tapes for an opinion, we have been able to point to a lack of achievement in the second image. To obtain the desired results, your second image should contain:

1. *Singular Achievement.* Not an achievement event which is a "team" effort or something you are doing with your spouse. It should be a mountain you climb strictly on your own.
2. *Autonomy.* Embodying a freedom from others, a lack of dependence—physically, emotionally, and financially—on anyone else.
3. *Power.* Most, but not all, achievement carries an element of power to get what you want *from* others or *despite* others. A second image of losing weight might not have this element, but one of obtaining the best table in a posh restaurant certainly would. To be free and (ultimately powerful) omnipotent means to be able to say, "Step aside world; I'm coming through."
4. *Desire.* The second image has to be something *you* want for *you*. If you create a second image which you feel you should want because others have told you you should, you put yourself into another jail. A second image should never be an IM.
5. *Reward.* The second image should always contain the element of reward for achievement, not merely achievement itself. It may be the new sports car you bought when you got the promotion, or the slinky new dress when you lost the twenty pounds.

I have been asked how long one should continue to employ the V.I.F. The answer, of course, is use it as long as you want to. Those who have turned-on to the V.I.F. have seldom given it up. It tends to become as much a part of your life-style as brushing your teeth.

"Isn't there a danger of the V.I.F. becoming a crutch?" This is the question we asked Sidney earlier. It strikes me as similar to asking, "Isn't there a danger that in using the formula you may develop a habit of self-reliance?'' since the ''crutch'' you ''lean'' upon is your own voice—it's *you!* You may, of course, use people as crutches. Some husbands and wives continually use each other in this way. Their relationship is neurotically symbiotic. Some psychotherapists encourage dependency in their patients, the therapist assuming a directive, parental role. Astrologers, ministers, and gurus of various persuasions provide crutches for the insecure masses. The V.I.F., we feel, is the most potent weapon against crutches. In employing it, you are saying to yourself and to the world at large, ''I am in charge of my own destiny; I don't need any support; I can stand on my own feet.''

It is important, therefore, that you decide whether standing on your own feet is really what you want. For many people, it is not. They may pay a price in self-esteem, but it is a price they seem willing to pay. The motivation to be a free, autonomous, self-sufficient human being, capable of doing anything you want to do, get anything you want to get, and not feel forced to lead your life under the direction of others, is, paradoxically, a *negative* motivation. It is knowing what you do *not* want, even if you can't say what it is you *do* want. In this respect it is what psychologists refer to as ''negative reinforcement.'' That is, it is a desire to avoid an undesirable situation that motivates the individual (as distinguished from an attraction to a desirable one). An insightful woman expressed it well when she said, ''All these years I've been supported by my husband, financially and in every other way, and I haven't rocked the boat by saying what I wanted because I haven't wanted to give up my security blanket. Well, I'm sick of it, and sick of myself. I don't know what I want in my life from here on, but I damn well know what I don't want: I don't want to go on being a whore.'' Her statement expresses the motivation to be free. Not the freedom to do a particular thing (since she admitted she did not know what she wanted to do in the future), but a freedom from the IL-IC-IM's which had ruled her life. This may actually be the only genuine motivation toward freedom. The prison inmate who thirsts for freedom does not ask, "Where will I go once I am over the wall?" He makes his escape if he can, then faces the question.

For some, knowledge of "what I *don't* want" without knowledge of "what I *do* want" leads to creation of second images of total escape, a walking away from everything in one's present life. Does it lead to an actual walkout? It may or may not. I think we must each choose to be totally free before we are able to make individual choices of commitments and actions. Only if I feel I am free to leave spouse, family, friends, and job can I make specific choices to stay.

One man played his tape for me. This was his second image:

> "It is a bright, sunny day. I am walking out the front door of the house. My Yamaha motorcycle is sitting in the driveway. The sun is shining on the chrome handlebars and pipes. I am carrying a bedroll. I tie it on the bike and I swing my leg over. As I fire it up, I glance back at the house for the last time. I slip the bike into gear and roll down the driveway onto the street. A few blocks and I turn onto the highway. It's clear ahead, and I'm finally free."

I don't know if today, somewhere, he is riding his motorcycle into the sunset. If that is what he needed for freedom, I hope so.

But there was a complacency in his voice when he described his life. As in every area of life, self-deception can creep in. There is a big difference between a second image which is an expression of something you really want and will go after if and when you break out of the IC or IM, and a second image which is a "Walter Mitty" daydream. When I was a child, I did a lot of daydreaming. I would stare out the classroom window at the clouds, and daydream I was a test pilot or the captain of a submarine. Much as I enjoyed my daydreams, however, I never thought of them as anything other than daydreams. I never had the goal of being a pilot or a submariner. My friend with the image of the motorcycle may or may not crave freedom. His second image may be only a pleasant daydream, the reality of which would be thoroughly undesirable.

This problem arises frequently when we speak with groups of housewives. A woman may not be happy with her husband, marriage, and homelife. She may come up with a second image of herself sitting at poolside in Hawaii, flirting with beachboys, but it is a paid vacation trip she is enjoying, and when the two-week vacation is over, she will return to the comfort of her suburban home. There is no power and no autonomy in her image. Her daydream does nothing to change her unhappy life. The tip-off that such a second image is only a daydream often comes when we ask her how she got to Hawaii, and who is paying for the vacation. If it has not been by any achievement of hers and she still sees herself as dependent on her husband, there is no power in the image, and no freedom.

Another potential problem stems from relationships in which both parties have previously lived in mutual jails and now one of them, but not the other, has determined to be free. What happens to such a relationship? Usually it is unpredictable. How such an individual may react to freedom in others will depend in a large part on how he or she believes they may be affected by the freedom. If I am living in a prison of IC's and IM's in a relationship, and the woman I am living with liberates herself so that she is no longer bound to me by her own IC's and IM's, she may no longer choose to stay with me. Of course, I may then react to such a threat by attempting to force her back into the prison. Or I may begin to reevaluate my own lack of freedom and decide to explore the freedom she has found.

Soon after I first presented the V.I.F. to a group (about forty, with an almost equal number of males and females), I was struck by the unpredictability of what might follow. Within two weeks, over half the participants had experimented with it. About a third of those who had made descriptions and tapes were still struggling to try to get "workable" images, and within a short time they did. Of the less than half who had not, for whatever reasons, experimented with the V.I.F., the majority had spouses who had developed workable images. Needless to say, I was curious to find out what might happen to these relationships. I was also interested in what the spouses using the V.I.F. anticipated. Typical was the response of one woman. I asked her if she had considered the possibility that now that she was rapidly becoming free and totally capable, her marriage might go on the rocks. "Certainly I've thought of it," she said, "but if that is what happens, well, it will be all for the best, I'm sure." She was not saying, "I don't care about my husband." She was saying, "I do care about myself, and I am confident that no matter what happens I will come through with flying colors."

I predicted that the spouse not using the V.I.F. would be disturbed by the exercise of freedom of the other spouse. This prediction seemed to hold true in about half the cases. For the other half, for every husband or wife who saw the spouse's freedom as a threat, there was one who reacted with relief. "She has now begun to depend on herself rather than calling on me for every little thing. She's off my back," was the reaction of a husband who said he "wanted no part" of the V.I.F.

I also predicted adverse reactions when friends heard of the V.I.F. After all, freedom is an understandable threat to anyone raised to believe in the basic "virtues" we were all told would be found in self-control, unquestioning obedience to authority, and conformity. But most people who have employed the V.I.F. have reported surprisingly little opposition from friends. In retrospect, I might say I should have known better. Individuals who are free of IC's and IM's are the most genuinely nicc people one will find. They have no need to attack, defend, or even proselytize. It is understandable, therefore, that they would encounter little opposition to their views. They may not convert their friends to a life of freedom. But neither do they have many bricks thrown at them. Parents of growing children, rather than meeting resistance, discovered a positive fallout from use of the V.I.F. The behavior of the kids improved immeasurably. Some have turned their children on to it. With others, it has been a matter of the children responding positively to a parent who is less uptight, more cheerful, and much more self-confident.

The degree of "generalization of effect" in use of the V.I.F. has come as a surprise to many. One may create a second image designed to increase income, help control temper when dealing with children, shoot golf in the nineties, or reduce the waistline, only to find that just about everything improves. The effect generalizes. For this reason, many have found IC's and IM's dropping like autumn leaves when they begin using the V.I.F. each day. They even discover IC's and IM's they had not been conscious of holding—which vanish almost as soon as they become aware of them.

For many of us, the V.I.F. becomes a way of life. The lift which comes from using the V.I.F. is so great you don't want to go without it. Those who have employed the V.I.F. have found nothing to replace it. "I need to go play my tape" becomes the answer to any frustrations which come along. Everyone who has developed a working tape has found playing it can eliminate or reduce feelings of frustration or depression. When you are feeling out of sorts, the tape will bring you out of it, but it may not lift you all the way up the first time you play it. So, as many have found, it may be wise to press the rewind button as soon as you play it through the first time and replay it. On a particularly rough day, you may play your tape three times in a row to bring yourself up.

Many have also found it beneficial to play a tape before facing what could be a tension-producing situation. When I have received a phone call which I knew would probably be a hassle, I have at times told the caller I would return the call. I then took a break to play my tape. When I did, the hassle invariably failed to develop. I have also found the tape to be a wonder-worker before giving a lecture or doing a television talk show. College students play their tapes before an exam. A woman told me she plays her tape whenever she knows her husband (who does not use the V.I.F.) has asked his parents to drop by. Another told me she plays hers before each shopping trip. If only Nixon had used the V.I.F. and played *his* tape instead of taping everybody else!

THEME AND VARIATIONS

It was inevitable that once turned-on to the V.I.F. people would start experimenting with variations and improvements. What they have come up with has consistently added to the scope of the V.I.F. Here are a few of the innovations people have tried with good results.

The Feeling Good Tape—This is a tape which does not attempt to refute any specific IC or IM. There is achievement in the second image, as there always must be, but the emphasis of the image is on reward for achievement, and it has as its purpose to give you good feelings about yourself and the knowledge that you can do anything you choose to do—without specifying any particular thing. I have a tape in which my second image has me on the island of Moorea in French Polynesia. It isn't a Walter Mitty daydream because I am very aware of the achievements which put me there. But I don't have to describe them. The tape simply gives me great feelings about myself. It fills me with ambition and self-confidence. I can't tell you if it is an IC tape or an IM tape. It is probably a combination of the two. The important thing is it gives me feelings of both power and freedom. This is my Moorea second image:

> "I am now sitting on the porch of my *farea* on Moorea, out on stilts above the water. I am sipping on a gin and tonic, watching the sunset and the clear, blue-green water below. The sky is turning from orange and pink to red and purple. There is a wonderful, almost musical, stillness. Out on the lagoon there are a couple of laugh-

ing, golden, Polynesian children in an outrigger. I feel like I am floating on a cloud of happiness and self-satisfaction. I have earned this vacation. These last few months I have made everything go right for me—financially, socially, and in every other way. I have taken complete control of my life. I have proven to myself what power I have. I really can achieve anything I want to, and knowing that fills me with even more power and ambition. The world is mine in every way I want it to be. I am totally free to enjoy it."

The Double Second Image—When I was first asked if you could add a second image following the initial one, I said I did not know how well it would work. My personal feeling was that since I enjoy savoring the feelings generated by my second image, to go on immediately with another "second" image would cut short this "afterglow." Others tried it before I did and reported good results. Finally, I tried it myself, and I found they were right. Just as the first image acts as a springboard of positive feelings for the second image, the second image acts as a further springboard for another "second" image. So you might, for example, have a second image of yourself burning up calories and twenty pounds lighter followed by another image of yourself graduating from college with honors. The only thing I am sure would not work in using more than one "second" image would be to select two which cancel each other out because of their incompatibility. In other words, don't try to tack an image of leading a more active social life onto an image of achieving in medical school.

The Well-Being Tape—This is another tape which does not attempt to refute a specific IC or IM. It is designed to maintain rather than regain physical health. It is a good one to play first thing in the morning—or even read, if that is the only possibility—and perhaps at the end of the workday prior to spending an enjoyable evening. On the tape (following, of course, your first image and the words of the affirmation), you tell yourself how great you feel, how rested and full of pep, how exuberant, good health flows through your body. One man who works at a particularly strenuous job told me, "Since I've been using my 'well-being' tape, I feel better and more energetic at seven o'clock in the evening than I used to feel at seven o'clock in the morning, and as for sex, I'm doing it better and more often than I did twenty years ago."

His second image, as well as I can recall it, was as follows:

> "I am now sitting at the kitchen table working on my ship model. Here it is ten o'clock in the evening, but I feel great. I have worked today with a lot of energy, and I have accomplished everything I set out to accomplish, but at the same time I feel rested and full of strength and pep. Each time I take a deep breath I feel health and power flow into my body. I can see the blood pushing through my veins and arteries, fighting off any possible disease. I have never felt better in my life, and I am ready for a long, long, evening with Cindy."

The Parents' Tape—This seems to be a successful exception to the rule that the second image should be an individual achievement rather than a joint cooperative achievement. In this tape, developed by a husband and wife who had previously worked successfully with their personal tapes, both parents contributed (alternating in talking on a tape). The second image related to their children, and stressed the closeness of their "united front" approach and their mutual satisfaction in their roles as parents. Using this technique, another couple described a second image of a successful camping trip, and another of their parental handling of homework versus television watching. Another couple taped a second image of the two of them selling their house, packing the car, and leaving for another part of the country, far away from their adult children, grandchildren, and relatives. The two of them sounded like twenty-year-olds off on a honeymoon, a good description of self-determining, beautiful, people.

The Child's Tape—Initially, we did not know how the V.I.F. would work with children. Children are, after all, dependent, and their dependency severely limits them. As parents, we preach a lot of IC's and IM's. Hence, there seemed to be no way they could be told, "Yes, you can do anything you want to do, and you don't have to do anything you don't want to do." But other parents beat me to the punch in introducing their children to the V.I.F. (obviously I had an IC in there somewhere). What they discovered is that children are remarkably receptive to the V.I.F. Given encouragement, they can easily recall a first image, and given assurance they do not have to reveal their second image to anyone, they can produce very effective tapes and written descriptions. Having done so, they are often eager to play their tapes for their parents (although this should never be urged; it should always be at the child's instigation). What parents have discovered is that, no, a child is not going to create a second image of overthrowing the parental establishment. Thirteen-year-old Willie didn't make a second image of himself riding a motorcycle cross-country, and fourteen-year-old Sue didn't create one of herself dropping out of school and going to Hollywood to become an actress. They created images of making "A's" in their classes, hitting home runs, and being popular.

The results of children using the V.I.F. have been remarkable. The usual squabbles between children within the family are greatly reduced, and resistance to the direction of the parents is replaced not only by cooperation, but by voluntary efforts to help. "It's as if the kids all matured ten years in a week," said one father. "I can't believe it," a mother of three told me. "Breakfast, even when we're all late and trying to find a misplaced book or shoe, is actually pleasant."

There are now teachers who have introduced the V.I.F. to elementary and high school classes. It is still too early to report on the results, but they look promising.

All evidence so far points to one thing: We have only scratched the surface in application of the V.I.F. Men and women who have used it seem to acquire a drive to apply it in every area of their lives. There are those who are experimenting with it in "team" projects in business, in individual as well as team sports, in the practice of law, medicine, and dentistry, and even in politics. While the results have been very promising, we do not yet have sufficient data to draw firm conclusions. I am sure some adaptations will be more effective than others.

Our own children have a practice of making a tape when they have a test coming up or when they are going to make a presentation in class. There have been tapes made on finding an after-school job, completing a science project, and getting a date for a school dance. They have each made tapes on having a successful, hassle-free, winter vacation, and on earning the money for a second high school V.I.F. seminar.

7 Emotions

There is an old song which goes:

Sometimes I'm happy
Sometimes I'm blue
My disposition depends on you

We have so many emotional jails we take them for granted. We assume they go with human relationships. The closer the relationship, the more secure the jail. How many times have you said such things as: "You made me angry," "You turned me off," "You put me in a bad mood," "You make me uptight," "You make me nervous"?

If someone—anyone—has the power to make you angry, jealous, sad, nervous, fearful, or to trigger any emotional response in you that you would not freely choose, he has you imprisoned.

I spoke with a husband and wife who had developed elaborate techniques of mutual imprisonment. "He hums while he reads the paper. It drives me up the wall and he knows it," she said.

"So maybe I do. But she makes me so darn mad. She knows I like my eggs over easy, and she always fries them so they're hard as a rock. She knows all sorts of ways to get to me, and she uses every one of them."

"He's a fine one to talk. Nobody could live with a man with so many annoying habits."

They are both inmates and jailers. They have traded their

emotional freedoms for what they hope to get from being jailers. Since this seems like such a poor trade, however, we might ask why anyone would choose it.

The answer is the same as in many of our prison situations: They don't know any other way to live.

During childhood, someone was always manipulating our emotions. Anyone who could say "yes" and "no" to what we wanted could control our reactions (that might have included older brothers and sisters, babysitters, teachers, grandparents, and others as well as our parents). They could frustrate us. As children, we had only one reaction to frustration: rage. Later on, we learned other reactions. We may have learned to cope. Then again, we may not have. We may even have learned how to prevent our "buttons" being pushed. If not, others could put us in jail. They could cause us to react.

Who are these others? Just about anyone you give the power to control you. But the major jailers are the IL's you may have about your emotions.

We were taught emotion is one thing, reason is another, and never the twain shall meet. Or almost never. There is a school of thought which holds that we are not responsible for them (emotions or feelings), and can do nothing to change them. It is expressed in IL's such as the following:

I'm only human.
I'm a woman, so of course I'm emotional.
I'm a man, so naturally I'm not as emotional.
I'm just the emotional type.
I'm easily hurt.
I'm Italian (or Irish, Spanish, etc.).
I'm the temperamental sort.

I sat in on a "self-discovery" group for married couples. The leader preached the gospel of *emotions-are-beyond-our-control-and-we-should-not-try-to-hold-them-in.* After a couple of hours of group discussion, the group took a break to give husbands and wives the opportunity to "express your inner feelings." And express they did. By the end of the day, every participant had taken the leader's words to heart and emoted all over their partner. One woman said, "It was wonderful. I told my husband everything I had bottled up for years. I let him know every one of my complaints, all the little things he does which bug me. He had to agree to keep his mouth shut no matter what I said because they were my feelings I was expressing and you can't argue with feelings. I swore at him; called him a lot of names. It was a very liberating experience. I even told him what I didn't like about him physically—have you noticed those ugly big pores on his nose?—and the way he bores me when he talks about his job." Had she tried to temper what she said out of concern for her husband's feelings? "I think I did at first, but we were told we should be completely open, and once I started I found myself getting more and more angry; my emotions just seemed to get in high gear. It felt good." But not for her husband, of course. I asked him how he had felt "openly" expressing his feelings. "I never got a chance," he said. "She wasn't finished telling me what she thought of me when the time was up." Was he looking forward to telling her what he felt? "An hour ago I would have said yes, but now I don't think so. What's the use? Since she feels the way she does toward me, what I feel isn't going to make any difference. I'd rather get drunk and forget I ever came to this crazy group session. I don't need to spend a day being told what a son-of-a-bitch I am. That much I already know."

I don't believe anyone should spend time being put down. Most of us do enough of that to ourselves as it is. Even if these "get in touch with your feelings" techniques of "therapy" don't turn into regressive and vicious sessions of verbal mayhem, they still teach that emotions are something which happen to us, like being caught in an unpredicted rainstorm. That we are prey to them, overcome by them, and controlled by them. Sometimes we may enjoy them; often we may not. But they say there is nothing we can do about them.

The IL's which these views generate are ghastly distortions of what we humans are and what we can become. If you have no control over your emotions, you have no control over your life. You are not just a prisoner, you are a puppet whose strings can be pulled by everybody and anybody.

When I was a child, I believed I had a guardian angel sitting on my right shoulder and a little devil sitting on my left, each of them whispering in my ear, telling me what to do. If I picked a fight with my sister, it was because the devil won out. If I said, "I'm sorry," it was because my guardian angel won (or because I was made to apologize). At the end of a day, the score was often devil 9, angel 0. When I grew up, "The devil made me do it" became "My emotions got the better of me."

SELF-SENTENCES

I learned my emotions form the worst IL-IC-IM prisons of all. I also learned emotions and reasoning are *not* separate. Emotional responses, we might say, are the result of reasoning and assumptions. As I am walking around my backyard, I glance down to see a snake at my feet. My heart jumps into my mouth. My pulse raises. My palms sweat. Fear! But it isn't the snake I fear. It is what I tell myself about the snake: "A rattler! Set to strike! Poison! Deadly!" But the "rattler" might be a piece of rope or garden hose. If so, my fear may dissipate as soon as I discover the truth about my "snake."

Psychologist Albert Ellis calls these self-sentences "verbal mediations." It isn't the "snake" (stimulus) which triggers the fear (response). The "snake" triggers fear words in my unconscious, and my unconscious sets off those physical responses.

You probably seldom come upon a snake, however, so let's talk about situations more commonly a source of anxiety. You may get nervous when you walk into a room of strangers. You may say, "Strangers make me nervous." But it wouldn't be true. What you *tell* yourself about a room full of strangers is what makes you nervous. Perhaps something like this: "I don't know any of these people. They probably all know one another. They may resent an outsider. They'll probably all stare at me. What will I say to them? What if I'm not dressed right? They may snub me. I'll probably feel like a fool. Is my fly zipped?" The conversation in your head can have you in a cold sweat before you cross the threshold.

A similar thing occurs when someone "makes" you angry. What makes you angry is not the person, but what you tell yourself about the situation ("He's attacking me; I have to defend myself," "He won't do what I want him to do," "He keeps doing what I don't want him to do."). Anger is a result of frustration, "I can't do what I want to do because others won't let me," and "I have to do what I don't want to do because others make me." In one form or another, these IC's and IM's are anchored in the IL: "I am inadequate; I am at the mercy of others."

There is nothing even remotely rational about emotional jails. A young man with a history of breaking up furniture and pounding on his wife said, "I can't control my temper; that's just the way I am." Curious about his IL, I asked him why. "I'm a typical redhead," he answered, "and my name is Mike." I couldn't believe he was serious, so I suggested if he shaved his head and changed his name the problem would be solved. He got angry.

Any emotional IC or IM statement I may make is a statement of belief in my own inferiority. Take each of the following IC's and add to them the IL, "because I am inadequate and vulnerable to others."

I can't control my temper.
I can't keep from crying.
I can't help being deeply hurt when I am rejected, put down, ridiculed, criticized.
I can't bring myself out of a blue mood.
I can't predict how I will feel.
I can't be rational.
I can't express my emotions.

The IC's can be summed up: "I can't keep others from pressing my buttons," or, "I can't express my feelings" (or allow myself to feel anything). And the IL supports all of them. In fact, it is the only IL which *could* support them. Now try the same IL on the following IM's.

I have to get things out of my system even when it gets me in trouble.
I have to live with my mood swings.
I have to defend myself when I feel I'm being put down.
I have to keep my feelings bottled up.
I have to keep my mouth shut.
I have to let people dump on me.

If others can put you into these emotional boxes, they *must* be superior to you. And you *must*, somehow, be inadequate. It follows; and it is a cornerstone IL.

ANXIETY

Anxiety has been defined as a feeling of impending doom. It differs from fear in one respect: Fear has an identifiable stimulus. If you barely miss colliding with a truck in an intersection, you have an almost immediate fear reaction. As soon as you become aware you are safe, however, the reaction begins to subside. Your self-sentence is, "That was a close call; I almost got hit, but now I am safe and I can turn off the fear." With anxiety, on the other hand, there is no truck. The same feelings are there, but you cannot identify what it is that is evoking them.

In fear or anxiety, there is an IL present (another word for what Albert Ellis calls "self-sentences"). The IL (*e.g.*, "You never know; a disaster may be just around the corner"), firmly ensconced in the unconscious, triggers the system which controls our emotional response: the *autonomic nervous system* (ANS). The ANS impulses increase the heart rate, constrict the peripheral blood supply, increase the flow of hydrochloric acid into the stomach, increase the blood pressure, activate the sweat glands, and, in general, add to the body's muscular tension. These are primitive responses, more adaptable perhaps when man was living in caves. They prepare the body for "flight or fight."

But today, when we are not faced with the alternatives of fighting or fleeing from a saber-toothed tiger, these reactions often serve only to make us miserable and physically ill. Dr. David A. Hamburg of Stanford University College of Medicine has said, "The contemporary human organism frequently gets mobilized for exertion but ends up doing little or nothing—preparation for action, without action." A critical note from your boss may raise your anxiety level with all its accompanying physiological reactions, but it is unlikely that you will be free to either run from the building or punch him in the nose. His note triggers IL's and IC's. "I need this job." "I can't displease the boss." Within moments, you experience that hollow feeling in the pit of the stomach which signals anxiety.

Anxiety breeds anxiety since the IC, "I can't do anything to control this situation" (or, "I can't do anything to please the boss—and I have to") results in further feelings of impotence which, in turn, leave you feeling vulnerable to additional threats. You become, therefore, susceptible to increasingly frequent anxiety attacks. In time, the condition may become chronic.

In anxiety, the IC is often linked with an incompatible IM: "I can't do it; but I have to." These classic-bind IC-IM's result in the worst feelings of helplessness (and, ultimately, depression). If either the IC or IM is refuted, the entire IL-IC-IM crumbles. Many of our recurring and identifiable sources of anxiety and depression are of this IC-IM–bind variety. Take the monthly bills. How many of us have gone through an every-thirty-day anxiety bind: "I have to make more money, but I can't."

If these IC's and IM's can be identified, you can prepare tapes to break out of them. This can be done either by refuting the "reality" ("I have to make more money/I can't make more money") or by refuting the unpleasant emotional reaction to the perception of reality. You might, for example, write a second image in which you refute the IM, "I have to make more money." Why do you have to make more money? Is it because of financial IM's given you by spouse, family, parents, or keeping up with the Joneses? Is it because of IM's having to do with what is called the "work ethic"? Or your image of masculinity? You might decide you are personally getting little satisfaction from what you are doing with the money you are earning so why bother to make more? You might do a second image in which you have changed your financial standard of living to one which gives you satisfaction without the monthly pressures brought about by the "responsibilities" imposed upon you by others. You also might write a second image in which you can make more money, one in which you have the power to make as much as you desire—and without pressure.

Refuting the emotional reaction (anxiety) is applicable in a situation in which you do not want to refute the "reality" (*e.g.*, the fact that you have children or a job you don't want to give up) but you do want to get rid of the anxiety associated with it. The second image does not refute the present situation. You do not, for example, write a second image in which you have disposed of the children or quit your job. The second image actually "creates" the situation which has triggered the anxiety (or, to be more accurate, the self-sentence which ignited it), but with no anxiety reaction. Following is the second image of a sales manager of a pharmaceutical company who had experienced severe anxiety when called upon to present an annual report to the board of directors:

> "I am now sitting by the wall in the boardroom in a leather chair. Mr. Michelson is droning on with his F.D.A. progress reports and other bullshit. From where I sit, I can see out the window. It is a beautiful spring day. There is a chestnut tree outside and the leaves are moving in the breeze. The sky is a mixture of gray and

blue. I feel very relaxed, completely at peace. I've done a good job on the report and I'm running my operation as smooth as silk. It is almost as if I feel a kind of inner laughter. Mr. Michelson has finished his report and is answering questions. Now they are calling for my report. I walk over and sit down in the chair next to Farley. God! I feel good. My pulse is slow and steady. There is no tenseness anywhere in my body. It is almost funny. All these uptight characters sitting around the table, and I could not be looser. I'm smiling as I start to read the report, and as I go on, it is apparent my enthusiasm is infectious. I've got them all right in the palm of my hand. I can feel the self-assurance and power surging through my entire being. I am the coolest dude in town!"

Following is the second image of a woman with a longstanding fear of flying:

"I am now sitting beside the window in a 707. The plane is taxiing down the runway. It is a beautiful plane, and as I lean back in the seat, I think of the vacation I have ahead. In just a few minutes I will be flying out over the Pacific on my way to Hawaii. The sky is blue and I will be able to look down at the deep blue water with its little white lines of waves, sipping my drink, reading a magazine, and thinking nothing except happy thoughts of anticipation. My beautiful 707 has now made the turn and is ready for takeoff. It is moving down the runway, gathering speed. The runway markers are rushing past. I am smiling as I look out at the broad wing and the power engines. I am like those engines: efficient and powerful. I am completely relaxed and self-confident. Not the slightest worry or anxiety. This is my airplane, and that's my world out there. I feel fantastic. There I go, yawning again. Maybe I'll take a short nap before they come around to serve drinks. Then I'll be wide awake when the movie comes on."

DEPRESSION

We have found common, so-called neurotic, depression to be almost invariably associated with a self-imposed IM. There may admittedly be physiological factors involved with some severe depressions, but even these conditions may themselves be the result of IC's and IM's. Most frequently, however, the IM-triggered feelings of depression can be identified.

The mechanism of the IM/depression is not fully understood. We have only theories. Acting on the demands of a self-imposed IM is probably the most destructive thing we can do to our self-esteem. This is because there is seemingly no escape from it. If someone else tells you you must do something, you *may* feel free to refuse, or they *may* rescind the order. If, however, you have incorporated the IM so that it is now you giving the command to yourself, you seemingly have no way out but to follow it.

A woman in her forties told me she had been depressed for two weeks. I asked her if she could identify what it was she was doing in her life that she did not want to do. She spoke without hesitation:

"I've been preparing for a dinner party I'm giving for friends."

"And you don't want to give the party?"

"I dread it."

"Then why are you doing it?"

"I don't feel I have a choice. They had us to dinner a few months ago, and if I don't repay them, I'll feel really rotten." Freud wrote of the "tyrannical superego," the overly restrictive code of ethics and obligations which acts to control and compel nearly all actions. Such "conscience" can become the strongest jailer of all. It was not the friends who demanded the dinner party. It was this unhappy woman's IM of what was "right."

Since every IM is accompanied by one or more IC's, a great number of these strong IM's will result in the feeling, "I can't do anything I might like to do." This is a condition in which many mothers find themselves. If they have incorporated the IM: "I must devote my life to my husband and children," they will develop the IC, "I can't spend any time pleasing myself." These women, and you may be among them (or married to one), live with cyclical depressions. And understandably so. If you believe you have no right to seek your own goals and pleasures, but must live your life for others (who are, by inference, entitled to your services), you will, inevitably, conclude you have nothing (for yourself) to live for.

Effective "anti-depression" tapes are often general refutations of any and all IM's. They are tapes which give the unconscious the message, "To hell with messages saying 'You must do all these things you don't want to do—all in the name of responsibility.' " Here is the second image of a young mother of two children:

> "I am now lounging on the couch. The kids are down for their nap. I'm looking at travel brochures, trying to decide where I would like to spend the summer vacation. This summer I am not going to spend it visiting relatives—neither Al's relatives nor my own—and I am going to take a vacation from the children. I've told Al, and I have also told him he can make his own decision as to how he wants to spend his vacation. Sure, I'd like to have him spend it with me, but I am free of any obligation to go along with where he may want to go, and for the first time in five years I will be making my own choice of where to go and what to do. My life is mine to do with as I wish, and I can fulfill all my obligations to my children without turning over my life completely to them, regardless of what Al and my parents say. And I feel great. The depression has lifted like a morning fog. I feel powerful. I am my own person. I am me. And that's special. I deserve the best."

Here is one employed by a twenty-three-year-old man, a college student, living with his parents:

> "I am now getting dressed for my first day on the job. I am now a park ranger. I've left college, and I am free to do what I want to do, to work in the out-of-doors. I know how I want to live my life, and I know I cannot like myself if I am doing something to please others which isn't what I want to do, so I've told Dad going on with college isn't for me, and engineering isn't my thing. For the first time I told him and Mom my views on life and what I believe in. I told them I respect their views, their values, and their way of life, but that I am an individual in my own right and an adult. I will no longer have to seem to accept values I cannot accept and play the role of dutiful son. I look at myself in the mirror in my park ranger uniform. I look great, and I feel great. I am free! Totally at peace with myself, and happier than I have ever been."

Correct identification of the IM is crucial to preparation of a written description or a tape which will lift depression. If it is the first tape the individual prepares, this may be difficult. We generally take for granted so many of those self-imposed "responsibility" IM's we have a hard time seeing them for the jails they are. I feel it is advisable, therefore, to prepare one or two written descriptions and tapes refuting more obvious IC's before making an anti-depression tape. Once you have a couple of them working well, identifying an IM which is triggering a depression will be much easier.

ANGER

There are four principal reactions to frustration: Hostility (rage), perseverance (repeating the same actions—*e.g.*, rattling the doorknob when the door is jammed—even though they do not unblock the frustrating impediment), withdrawal (giving up), and coping. The only one we don't have to learn is hostility (rage). If you restrain the hands of an infant, it will go into a rage. The restraint creates an IC: "I can't move my hands." Frustration is a reaction to an IC ("I can't do what I want to do, and it's your fault"); and anger is a reaction to frustration.

Anger is destructive to self-esteem for two reasons: It often doesn't work; that is, it doesn't relieve the frustration. This results in even stronger feelings of powerlessness. And, since we were taught as children that anger was "bad," it can raise painful guilt feelings. There is even a possible third reason. We may have been taught "losing" one's temper is childish. I spoke with a man who told me that any time he expressed anger, his wife would accuse him of having a temper tantrum and tell him to grow up. "It's not just when I get angry at her or the kids," he said. "This morning I read something in the paper about a law which will increase my property taxes. I said something like, 'the miserable sons of bitches,' and she said I was acting like a child and should stop the temper tantrums."

There are times when anger—real or feigned—can be effective. Skilled trial lawyers learn to display anger for the benefit of a witness or jury. Those of us who have practiced parenthood may choose to show anger in our effort to control children—at times with good result. When we feel that anger is not within our control, however, we are living in an emotional jail. And the feelings are nothing less than rotten.

Any use of the formula designed to control anger is aimed at refuting the IL: "My emotional reactions are under the control of others." Ability to control emotions is one of the most important abilities one can possess—perhaps the greatest power. It has nothing to do with suppressing emotions. It is the ability to make a conscious choice of what emotion to experience, and to what degree or intensity. The frustration which leads to anger *always* represents an IC saying: "I can't get what I want for myself. I am dependent upon others to meet my needs and desires, and if they don't, I will be left frustrated and angry." If I can't prepare a meal, not even as much as frying a hamburger, and my wife does not fix dinner for me, I will go hungry. I am thus a prime candidate for frustration. She can drive me up a wall any time she is late shopping and I'm starving.

Any use of the formula to bring your emotion of anger under *your* control must, therefore, free you of dependence upon others for your satisfactions. Some years ago, I was conducting research in certain functions of the brain. The research called for the use of very elaborate electronic instruments, several of which had to be specially designed and constructed for the project. I am not an electronics engineer. As research psychologist, I was principal investigator on the studies, but the electronics had to be turned over to two skilled engineers. Progress, both in getting the project off the ground and in collecting data, was dependent on their skills and efforts. They would report to me on how they were coming along, but since I literally didn't speak their language, I could do little more than tell them, "Do your best to get it going as soon as possible." I was powerless, and I was frustrated. I resolved, then and there, never to paint myself into such a corner again. It was not worth the ulcers.

Following are some second images which men and women have employed to break out of the IL-IC-IM/frustration jails of anger. First, the second image of a mother of two teenage sons who couldn't "get them to do their chores, keep their rooms clean, or even come when they were called to meals":

> "I am now relaxing in the living room. I am leaning my head back against the cushions of the sofa. My eyes are shut. I am listening to Debussy's *La Mer* on the stereo. It is as if the warm waves of the music are washing over me, removing every last trace of tension. I feel absolutely great. I am in control of my world. No one can get to me. I am untouchable. I can make my own choices about what I will permit to annoy me. If Terry and Dan don't choose to do what I ask them to do, it is their choice. I have told them, calmly and clearly, what I want them to do and what I expect of them as mem-

bers of the family. And I have told them the privileges which follow if they assume these responsibilities as well as what they will miss out on if they don't. They can't make me mad, no matter what. Their rooms are a mess. O.K. That won't press my buttons. I don't have to sleep in the rooms. I don't even have to look in them. If they don't come to dinner when I call them, well, I've told them they won't be served. And I don't feel guilty about it. They won't starve. And if they don't do their chores, they won't get any of the things they ask us for, and that is considerable. Even their fights can't press my buttons. I don't have any mother's obligation to step in when they start shouting at one another. I may tell them to knock it off if it disturbs me, but if they don't, I will simply banish them to their rooms. And without any guilt. I am also worthwhile. I do not need to rely upon my husband and sons to prove how much they love me by doing what I want them to do. I am calm, relaxed, and powerful. No one can turn on my emotions except me. Absolutely no one. And right now I choose to let Debussy pleasure me. Nothing else can touch me."

This is the second image of a husband in his twenties, married three years:

"I am now writing a letter to Edith telling her what I would like to have in terms of our relationship. I am telling her that I consider both of us completely independent persons, not reliant upon one another for emotional support. Edith may or may not agree with my opinions. It doesn't make any difference. My opinions are my opinions. They do not need support from anyone else. I am telling her my independence is total. I don't need her for anything, and it is only by not needing her for anything that I can love her and be comfortable with her. And I don't need her to be dependent upon me for anything. I can do anything I choose to do.

> I can think anything I choose to think. And Edith cannot frustrate me by her criticism or rejection. My emotions, my thoughts, and my actions are mine, and they are mine alone."

After writing and recording this image, he played it three times. He told me he then asked his wife to listen to it. "I sat there while she listened to it feeling freer than I have ever felt in my life. We talked for almost four hours afterwards. The next day, she made a tape which said almost the same thing. I listened to it, and it was as if I watched the handcuffs drop off both of us."

The following second image is by a woman in her forties, an executive with a real estate development firm, who commutes by automobile during rush-hour traffic an hour each afternoon:

> "I am now turning onto the Bayshore. As I swing off the on-ramp, I see ahead of me the long line of cars. They are coming to a stop. The traffic is very heavy. It almost always is. But that's all right. I glance over at the cars on either side of me. Who are they, I wonder. I hope the drivers are as relaxed as I am. It's a beautiful day. It is always a beautiful day driving home from the city. So filled with variety and challenge. Sometimes bright sunlight. Sometimes fog. Sometimes rain. The moods of weather change, but my mood never changes during this drive home. It's my time to be alone, to people-watch, to collect my thoughts, and to dream. The traffic has come to a stop. It moves just a little bit at a time. I used to get uptight when this happened. Now I almost welcome it. It gives me a feeling of power to know that cars, and other drivers, and slow traffic can't push my buttons, and that I will arrive home relaxed and happy and ready for a fun evening."

Second images which will free you of the tyranny of emotions and put you in control of your feelings, rather than vice versa, generally must create the situation which formerly elicited the undesired response. This would seem to be a contradiction to the rule that says, "Never include anything negative in either your first or second image," but in these cases, it is necessary to include the situation in order to describe the reaction which is now positive. In so doing, the second image does create positive reactions; you do feel power and the exhilaration of achievement.

I have given examples of anxiety, depression, and anger. There are others which are "themes and variations" on these three: envy, rejection, jealousy, despair. Workable second images for each of these involves essentially the same ground rules: Develop a second image in which you are in a situation where you have previously experienced the negative emotion. In your image, assert your independence of the person(s) or situation which has previously triggered the undesirable reaction, and describe your newfound positive reaction and the feeling of power it gives you. Tapes which give you control over your emotional responses will be the most powerful in your collection. More than all others, they will give you the confidence that *you are in control of your world.*

8 V.I.F. and Work

Not long ago, a young man came up with an idea while drinking beer in a friendly tavern. He would sell rocks, *pet* rocks. He boxed the individual rocks very cleverly, enclosed a small booklet on the care and training of a pet rock, and within a short time made over a million dollars. In doing so, he disproved the IL: "You have to work hard for anything you get in life."

We were raised to believe the only people who make a lot of money with very little effort or talent are politicians, rock musicians, and crooks. But you and I have to earn our daily bread by the sweat of our brows. Right? One of the synonyms my dictionary gives for the word "work" is "toil." Being curious, I looked up the word "toil" in *Roget's Thesaurus:* "toil: labor, drudge, travail, strain, sweat, struggle." Toil, in other words, is a thoroughly disagreeable way in which to spend one's life.

Built on top of this IL is a whole pyramid of IC's and IM's. Unless you rid yourself of them they can make you miserable. These work IC's and IM's all sound logical. They aren't!

When I was young, going to school and hating every minute of it, I was told, "You have to get an education." Since arguing with adults was seldom prudent, I didn't dispute this IM. If I had, the argument might have gone something like this:

"You have to get a good education."

"Why?"

"You can't get a decent job without it."

"What if I don't want a decent job?"

"If you don't, you may end up a ditch digger."

"But what if I don't want to work at all?"

"It doesn't make any difference whether you want to work or not. You're going to have to work when you grow up."

"Does that mean you can't have any fun at all?"

"Of course it doesn't mean that. But fun is something you do in your spare time—if you have any. Believe me, work isn't fun."

"Well, I think it could be. I'm going to be a race driver."

"I know. I wanted to be a circus clown when I was a kid. But you'll learn that you can't do just what you want to do. Take my word for it, unless you knuckle down in your schoolwork, you'll never amount to anything."

The IL-IC-IM of the messages was:

IL: Work is drudgery.
IM: You have to work at something you hate.
IC: You can't spend eight hours a day enjoying yourself.

The IL is so well ingrained that if you do find an occupation you enjoy, you're likely to feel guilty or try to talk yourself out of enjoying it. Everyone expects you to dislike your work and complain about it. If you don't, your co-workers may hate you. Television star Carol Burnett spoke on a talk show of how much she enjoyed show business. Ms. Burnett said she becomes annoyed when she listens to members of her profession talk about how they hate performing, how hard they work. But the actor or actress who gripes about the rigors of their job may be expressing an awareness of the public. What if they enthused about how much fun they were having in acting? Some guy out there in the audience who detests his job might throw a shoe at his television set. On a level a little closer to most of us, how would the average wife react if her husband came home from work each day bubbling with enthusiasm over his job? She might let the clod know what a backbreaking day she put in, and in the strongest terms.

Through the V.I.F., you can rid yourself of the IL-IC-IM's of work just as you can be free of your other jails. There are three major IC's having to do with work:

"I can't quit my job [or work]."
"I can't get a job [or the job I want]."
"I can't enjoy the job I have [or any job]."

These IC's are based on a variety of IL's. Some of the IL's may seem more logical than others, but since any IL is only your perception of reality as you define it, the IC's don't "follow logically" from the IL unless there is an "essential truth" in the IL as it is defined. And there never is or you wouldn't be locked in. Here is a sampling of some of the more common IL's tied to the three IC's above.

"I CAN'T QUIT MY JOB"

"*I have fifteen years invested in this job.*" This is as logical as saying, "I can't order fish for lunch because I've always ordered steak." The "years invested" argument is often supported by talk of tenure, seniority, retirement and profit-sharing benefits, job stability. None of these arguments makes sense unless:

1. You believe you must live your life for others, but never for yourself (which is, itself, a crazy IL), or
2. You believe you have a guarantee you will live long enough to enjoy whatever benefits you hope to reap when you are finally released from your jail by retirement.

Can you imagine an inmate sitting in a cell at San Quentin who, when offered his release from prison, says, "But I can't walk out of here; I've got fifteen years invested in my sentence."

"*I have responsibilities.*" This IL stands on the shoulders of another: "I really don't have much to offer, and I'm lucky to have any job at all, and if I quit this job I would probably never be able to get another, and then I wouldn't be able to meet my responsibilities, and my family would end up on the streets." In other words, it is based on a put-down of oneself. A few years ago a psychologist, Jess Lair, authored a self-help book titled, *I Ain't Much, Baby —But I'm All I Got*. Without evaluating the content, I would say the title is apt to persuade the reader to hang on to all the negative IL's which make him discontented enough to purchase such a book. Nonsense! You are much, the most important person walking the face of this earth; and you *can* achieve anything you desire.

"*There's a lot of unemployment.*" This one stands on the same negative IL. There might be an unemployment rate as high as that during the great Depression, but so what? Even if there is a 50 percent unemployment rate, with affirmation and the V.I.F., you and I will always be working at employment we enjoy—if we want to.

"*My wife would raise hell.*" We'll be taking a look at some of the marriage jails in another chapter, but for now, consider this: if you hold a job you don't like throughout your employment years, by the time you retire at age sixty-five, you will have served almost fifteen years of your life, awake and asleep, in prison. If you drop dead on the day you retire, you will have spent almost a fourth of your life locked up. Are you willing to do that just in order to please someone else? Especially if the someone else is the sort of person who would demand it of you?

"*I had a hard enough time getting the job I have.*" That one probably isn't even true. If you applied to fifty different places before you were accepted, did you have a hard time getting the job? Not really. Remember, it's always the matter of your own perception. If that fiftieth place had been your first choice in applying, then getting the job would have seemed easy. And another thing: once you have your head together and your potential is unlimited, what makes you think your job-hunting experience will be any problem next time?

"I CAN'T GET THE JOB I WANT"

"*This job is all I know how to do.*" There are at least two holes in this one. First, you *can* do more than one thing. Almost every job calls for a number of skills, not just a single one. The experienced engineer has learned something of marketing, personnel management, cost accounting, psychology, and a half dozen allied fields. If you are like most, you have also probably worked at different jobs along the way. They may have been part-time or summer jobs while you were in school, but they constitute valuable (and marketable) experience. If someone with a less narrow image of you prepared your resumé, you might be surprised at all the things you can do.

The second hole in this one stems from the fact that you may not learn to do anything else if you stay locked in the job you hold. Stick it out at most jobs for twenty years, and you won't gain twenty years' experience; you will gain six months' experience repeated 39 times. The average worker comes home from work having learned nothing that day. With an evening of tasteless food and tasteless television added on, the brain can gradually atrophy. One of the best ways I've found to continue growing is to quit a job shortly after I've learned it, and to go on to another job where I can learn something new. One wise friend of mine contends we should each shift careers every five or six years. I think it's a great idea. Look around. Perhaps there's something you'd rather be doing. If so, go do it. And don't ask the price.

"*I'd have to go back to school.*" This has become almost an old saw. I've talked with countless men and women who have given up any hopes of changing careers, "because it would mean going back to school and starting all over again." It is a carryover from the IL which says, "You have to have an education in order to get a job." We learn to equate education with formal schooling. We hang on to the notion despite evidence to the contrary. I have a friend who has been remarkably successful at four successive careers, moving on each time he became bored. In each situation, he began with no experience or formal education in the field. He simply walked into the office of the prospective employer, told the person behind the desk he was sure he could do the job, and offered to work for one month without salary to prove it. And each time he proved what he said. It's not surprising. Let's face it: one can learn most jobs enough to "pay your own way" in a month. In six months, you can become an expert.

"*The field is overcrowded.*" A field is never overcrowded except to the individual who fails to get a foot in the door. You are not a statistic. You are you. Even if the field you're interested in has forty people lined up at the gates for every opening, with the help of the V.I.F. you'll be the one to get through. There is a name for people who throw in the towel because they have been told the odds are long: Losers. They leave the way open for you and me.

"*It takes connections.*" "Connections," as we employ the word, means you must know the person who may hire you before he can hire you. If he has never heard of you one way or another, he can't offer you a job. So, obviously, if you want him to hire you, you must make some connection with him. You can, of course, wait for him to find you, but if you do, it would be wise to question whether, in fact, you want the job. High achievers make connections which serve their purposes. The individual who *knows* he can achieve anything and wants to write for television packs up his or her suitcase and heads for Hollywood. The individual who might like to write for television but who is locked into the "connections" IL is working right now in a hardware store in Ogden, Utah, saying, "Yes, but it takes connections."

Some years ago, when I landed my first professional job, I was given some rare and valuable advice by one of the older employees. "Don't ever forget," he said, "you were looking for a job when you came here. Never stop looking." I learned from experience the wisdom of his words. I've never changed careers or quit a job without coming out the better for it. And I have made a number of such changes. The changes were not the result of "opportunity knocking." I simply got tired, or bored, or frustrated doing what I was doing, and began to feel locked in. So I would quit. I resigned from one position some said offered a "promising future" five days after I got married. Did I have another job offer? No. Did my family suffer financially? Not at all. By the end of the first month at the new job, I found that I made more money than I would have had I not quit. Quitting a job can actually be a lot of fun. It opens up new horizons, new possibilities, and can even provide an extra vacation.

As far as those IC's of "I can't get a job" or "I can't get the job I want," like most IC's, they can easily become self-fulfilling prophecies. From time to time, I have had the responsibility of hiring people. There are some who walk in to apply for a job who you know you will never employ. I have not always known why, but I have known that I would not employ them. Something about them communicates the IC: "I can't get this job." Perhaps I am somewhat susceptible to their IC because they *don't* get the job. The power of the IL-IC-IM's you have stored in your unconscious is absolute. If you believe you lack the strength to pick up a pencil, you will be unable to pick it up. The most valid statement is: *Wherever you are right now in your life, you have achieved the goals you set out to achieve, and the goals you believed you were capable of achieving*. Luck played no part in it. Those IL's which stand for what you believe about yourself did. If there is a job you want, you can get it—once you break out of your jail. If you don't take the step to break out, perhaps you should ask yourself the question, "Is it really what I want, or am I merely saying it is what I want because of what others expect of me?"

"AFTER ALL, YOU GOTTA WORK"

There are a few great big IM's which were handed to you early in life. A major one was enshrined as the Work Ethic.

The IM was expressed, "I have to be productive." The IL on which it stood was: "We each must contribute our efforts to the society." If it has the faint ring of the ethic of a fascist state, it is because the two are very similar. It says, "You, the individual, have no importance except as a contributing member of the larger society." In other words, one more put-down. It is foisted on us as a virtue. But such "virtue" you can well do without.

Needless to say, there are many men and women who find satisfaction in freely giving of their time and talents in the service of others. Their contributions, it is important to note, however, are motivated by the personal satisfaction they find in the "giving," not feelings of "obligation."

The so-called "idle rich" we heard about when we were kids were looked upon as sinners. If you were born a Rockefeller, you could supposedly redeem yourself for the sin of being born "with a silver spoon in your mouth" only by devoting your life to "public service." Frankly, I have a hard time understanding such self-punitive nonsense. If I am able to live a life of comfort without working, and I am not demanding that someone else support me, why should I go out to take a job I don't like? Perhaps I prefer beachcombing. Or going to bullfights. Must I do something else if I can afford not to? This IM is an outgrowth of a miserable self-image, one which says, "I'm really no damn good, and I probably don't deserve to live—unless I contribute enough sweat and strain in the service of others that I can earn my right not to be killed."

I can hear some self-righteous Calvinist out there right now saying, "But someone has to work. Where would we be if everyone felt as you do? Wouldn't you feel guilty if you were a millionaire just sitting around enjoying yourself while someone else was breaking his back hauling away the trash, checking your water meter, and sweeping your street? Someone has to do those jobs, don't they?" My answer is: "Well, my righteous friend, I have no fear. Someone undoubtedly will do those jobs. Don't worry, you've taught enough of them to think of themselves as no damn good that they'll be out there joining you hauling trash while I'm sitting by my pool with a drink in my hand. And please be reassured, I wouldn't dream of restricting their freedom to choose to work if that's their thing. I wouldn't even dream of attempting to stop you from preaching your negative nonsense. As long as children are being raised with your sort of guilt-trip and work-ethic IM, there will always be 'virtuous' individuals like yourself.'' Does this mean I am a hedonist? Probably. If by ''hedonist'' is meant someone devoted to being good to themselves. To me, hedonism makes more sense than masochism.

Not long ago I talked to a young nurse. She admitted to me she did not like nursing and she had skills which would enable her to earn more money doing something else. Yet she stuck to nursing because, as she said, ''It makes me feel I am contributing something to my fellowman.''

''Do you get a kick out of contributing to your fellowman?'' I asked.

''It's not that I get a kick out of it. But I feel we each have an obligation to give to other human beings.''

''Why?''

''Because we all live on the same earth,'' she said.

''That seems an accident of geography. How did it give rise to an obligation?''

''Because there are unfortunate people in the world.''

''So?''

''So I feel an obligation to help.''

She has built her life around such IL's. Her IL's do not contribute to her happiness—and other people do not contribute to her happiness. She goes on contributing and contributing. What does she get out of it? Only the limited satisfaction that martyrs find in martyrdom.

Earning money can be a lot of fun. It does not need to be hard work. It does not need to be exhausting. It never needs to be unpleasant. There are baseball players earning seven-figure incomes having a lot of fun on a baseball field; standup comics having a lot of laughs making other people laugh. There are even people making a lot of money doing in bed what others are paying a psychoanalyst to help them do in bed.

Since most of us were raised to view work strictly as an IL—"I have to work for a living"—you may have never thought to ask yourself, "What do I think would be fun to do that would make money?" It is an approach which makes a lot of sense. If you have a choice between two or more jobs, one of which would be fun, why not go for the fun job? Do you have such a choice? Almost certainly. How do you discover a job which is fun? It calls for freeing your mind to allow dreams, ideas, and creativity to arise and take roots. As you may recall, one of the immediate results of the V.I.F. is an "undamming" of ideas and creativity. One fellow quit a teaching job to conduct scuba diving groups in the Cayman Islands—and at more money. Another fellow resigned his position as a stockbroker and signed on as the athletic director on a cruise ship in the Caribbean. A woman in her thirties quit her job as a department manager in a clothing store to refinish furniture—and found she not only had more fun, she made more money.

Most housewives have more than their share of IM's: "I have to get the laundry caught up today." "I have to keep my house cleaned up or it will be a mess." "I have to serve nutritious meals to my family." For them, being a wife and mother means never getting to say you're free. They live in elaborate IL-IC-IM prisons. The good news is that through the V.I.F. they don't have to.

I recently spoke with a woman who is the mother of several children. She told me she had for years felt her life was a continual contest with the housework. If she didn't keep things picked up and cleaned, the house would be a shambles in no time. I suggested she plug in the V.I.F. to rid herself of those IM's. She did. A week later, she told me she had spent the most delightful week of her married life. She had rid herself of her housework IM. Miraculously, however, the housework got done. "I don't know who has been keeping my house so clean," she said. "Perhaps there are little elves or something." Her husband said, "The house has never been cleaner."

One of the immediate results from the use of the V.I.F., you may recall, is an incredible increase in productivity with no apparent effort. This may have accounted for that woman's "miracle." Another result is "timelessness." This may also have contributed. She said she would find herself busy and completing certain activities at 8:00 A.M. that previously had taken her until mid-afternoon. But whatever brought about the result, she was freer—and happier—than ever before.

Getting rid of work IC's and IM's is no harder than getting rid of those in other areas of one's existence, but many people seem to have a resistance to trying the V.I.F. where work is concerned. There are those cornerstone IL's, "man works by the sweat of his brow," which stand in the way. Think about it for a moment: What if you didn't have to work? What if you wanted to work and could work doing exactly what you like to do? What if you could acquire as much money as you wanted without having to put in long hours? Or without having to do anything unpleasant? What if you could take vacations when you wanted to rather than when some boss permitted you to? And what if you could quit your job whenever you decided you would rather do something else? What would it all mean? One thing: those IL's would crumble. They would burst like so many soap bubbles. Please, before you start answering with a lot of "Yes, buts . . .", list your work IC's and IM's. Do not, repeat, do not, add the IL's. If you do, you may never use the V.I.F. to get rid of the IC's and IM's. Then take one or two of your work IC's and IM's, plug in the V.I.F., and see what happens.

I have a friend I'll call Sam. Sam had been employed for fourteen years by a soft drink bottler. He had risen up the ladder to quality-control supervisor. But Sam didn't find much satisfaction in his job. It was the same routine day after day. Not hard work, but tedious. Sam, however, had never thought of quitting. Sam has a wife, Betsy, and he has three children who were then eight, ten, and eleven.

"I told myself it was a good job as jobs go and I had no sufficient reason to quit," he told me.

Then Sam decided to at least give the V.I.F. a try. He didn't start by attempting to rid himself of any great and monumental IC's and IM's. He began with a few small ones, found he could break loose from them, and went on from there. Not long after, Sam quit his job. With the money from the sale of his home, the funds from the company pension plan, what money he had in his savings account, and what additional money he could borrow on his life insurance, Sam figured he could "retire" for at least a year and a half. By some budgeting, he might even stretch it to two years. "I figured I might be retiring for good," he said, "because, who knows, none of us has any guarantee of living forever. And I want to live now, not gamble on a tomorrow."

He traded his two cars for a motorhome. For fifteen months, Sam and his family traveled the United States. They crossed over to Canada, and drove down the Baja Peninsula of Mexico. Betsy stocked the motorhome with schoolbooks and taught the children on the road. The most important things the children learned, however, did not come from schoolbooks. They learned what Sam and Betsy also learned: how to live fully. They ate fresh trout for breakfast pulled from a stream a dozen feet from their front door. They stayed on a cattle ranch in Mexico. They visited the United Nations in New York City, and the Capitol in Washington, D.C. They watched the Rose Parade in Pasadena, and the Mardi Gras parade in New Orleans, the assembly of cars in Detroit, and the birth of a buffalo in South Dakota.

Sam never returned to his job at the soft drink company. He met a man while surf fishing in Southern California. Over two or three days of fishing and beer drinking, the two men came up with an idea to make money. Starting on a very small scale, they packaged and sold an inexpensive, but very useful, gadget for fishermen. It was adapted from something Sam had seen Mexican boys using in La Paz.

The business took off. Sam and his new partner added

other items to their line, and within a year, Sam was making a lot more money than he had been earning at the soft drink company. When I last saw Sam, he was once again planning on selling everything and retiring, "at least for two or three years—Betsy and I have been reading about some of the smaller islands in the Pacific."

If you don't decide to "retire" as Sam did, you might still find a way to set your own hours, decide what you want to do and when you want to do it, and determine how much each year you want to work. And how much you want to earn. You can contract *by the job*. This, of course, is already common in many occupations.

I may for example, hire a secretary to handle my mail and type the final draft of this manuscript. But then I will have to pay all those annoying employer taxes as well as the secretary's salary even when I may not have enough to keep him or her busy. Instead, I contract with a competent person at an agreed price per page typed and I am free. The secretary is free, too—to set hours, working conditions, etc. I don't have to provide space, a desk, or a typewriter.

In the case of typing, this is, of course, a common practice. It can be adapted, however, to many more jobs, perhaps even the one you now hold. In recent years, many employees, in a variety of industries, have found that they can quit their jobs, then be rehired by their former employers on a per-job contract or as a consultant. The company may have IL's called "company policies" against such a practice, but they may not want to lose the talents of a valued employee. "Company policies" are seldom chiseled in stone. This is also an ideal arrangement for mothers of small children who want to tailor their working hours to the schedule of their families. With the move toward equality in careers of husband and wife, such an arrangement also offers a possible means by which both can pursue careers and share the responsibilities of home and children.

If you currently hold a desk job, you might consider something: you perhaps already bring work home from time to time. If so, you'll have already proven you can do your job at home perhaps as well as in a stuffy office. Maybe even better. So if you prefer to stay home, why not? If you do the job you're being paid for, how can your boss complain?

Since most of us work to earn money (in addition to some other reasons, some sensible, some not), perhaps we should take a look at those scraps of paper and those little pieces of metal for which we work. After all, as they say, it's only money, whatever that is.

I must admit when I hear economists talk about "real" money versus currency, "hard" money versus "soft," and other such things, they lose me. All I know is that when it comes to the things I want in life, they are either free, or someone has given them to me, or I have paid for them. Additionally, I've always thought that old saying, "The best things in life are free," was rather stupid. "Best" for what, and to whom? If I want to drive the "best" automobile, I will acquire it either as a gift or by purchasing it. I handed over a very large bundle of francs for the "best" meal I've ever eaten. A sunset may be free, but if I want to enjoy the spectacular sunsets of the southern beaches of Mexico or those from the peak of Penang Island in Malaysia, I'm going to have to spend money getting there.

So let's not talk about money not being important. I think it is unimportant only to those who have given up all hope of ever getting it or to a small group of confirmed masochists. The things I want, those things which give me pleasure, are important because *I* am important. Some of them cost money, and therefore money is important. At least to me. But its importance is only in relationship to the contribution it makes to the "good life."

You may have some IM's having to do with spending your money. Some people spend almost no money which is not in response to an IM. All their money goes for things or for services they feel they have to pay for but from which they get no personal pleasure. There are, for example, thousands of violin teachers giving lessons to children who hate practicing. The teachers are paid by parents who hate listening to the practicing. Score one for the teachers, zero for the kids and parents.

Spend a few minutes thinking. Do you have any IM's in the spending of money? How about gifts? Every year I expect to listen to people tell me how they go broke and crazy at Christmastime buying cards and gifts for others, not because they want to and get pleasure from it, but because they feel obligated to do so. One woman told me it usually takes her and her husband six months or more to pay off the bills they run up at Christmas buying gifts for relatives. I asked her why they spend their money that way.

"I don't know, we just always have," she said. "Everyone in the family does. We know we will be getting gifts from them."

"Do you really care for them enough to put yourself in debt every year?"

"I can't say that. Some of them—like my sister-in-law's kids—we've never even met. We just don't know how to get out of the gift-buying thing without alienating the whole family."

I asked her for some figures. We concluded that in fourteen years of marriage, they had paid almost a year's income trying to avoid alienating a group of relatives. If they had gone ahead and "alienated" all of them, they might have the memories of a dozen or more luxury vacations.

"Donations" are another one of those money IM's. As I previously mentioned, the going-away "gift" collection for old Frank was actually an assessment. When that nice lady who lives in the next block rings your doorbell collecting for "Save the Aardvarks," what do you do? Make out a check for what you consider an appropriate amount? Tell her you gave at the office? Or tell her you don't wish to spend your money that way? If my neighbors want to take care of the aardvarks, fine. But aardvarks don't happen to be my thing. And since I am almost totally free (thanks to the V.I.F.), I don't have to do anything I don't want to do. And that includes spending my money saving aardvarks. I may find a charity or two to which I wish to donate, but then again, I may not. If I am going to *give* to charity, I am going to make sure it is a *gift*—not extortion.

Tips are also something that I refuse to treat as an IM. If there is a service charge added to my bill, as is common practice in many countries, and it is just that, a service charge, I consider it part of the total price for my meal or hotel accommodations. But a "tip" is a tip. As far as I'm concerned, it is a gratuity, a gift, given by choice in recognition of exceptionally good service. For services no better than ordinary, I leave no tip. In my rather scattered past, I've worked for tips, and I have listened to the argument that a tip should be left even if the service is only so-so, "because the person is working for tips and gets only a small salary." I don't buy the argument. If he is working for tips, let him earn the tips. He may then find me a big tipper. He may even get what I save up from not tipping his smug co-workers who don't earn a tip.

Social approval, whether sought through charitable "contributions," gifts to remote relatives, or tips, motivates a lot of IC's and IM's. Although no one admits to spending money "keeping up with the Joneses," we all know all our neighbors do it. The IL which compels you (by an IM) to spend money impressing your friends is almost universal. You were taught it almost before you cut your milk teeth.

There is a kitchen device which has recently taken the home-cooking market by storm—the food processor. It does a truly marvelous job of chopping and slicing. Experts like Julia Child swear by it. Stores haven't been able to keep it in stock despite the fact that the appliance costs more than most electric mixers. Housewives who want to be the first on their block (or at least not the last on their block) to own the latest gadget have gone after the things like King Arthur's knights pursuing the Holy Grail. For most of these women, the food processor now sits like a trophy on the shelf. To quote one distributor for a manufacturer of food processors, "They sell to women who use them twice a year to shred cabbage for coleslaw." Such is the price of "keeping up with the Joneses."

Men are no different. They drive expensive sports cars

which give them nothing but status and back trouble. The salesman for one such mechanical marvel told me the automobile was capable of 140 miles per hour. On the freeways of my state, the law limits me to 55 miles per hour and with the crowded conditions that prevail, I'm fortunate if I can exceed 40. Yet if I want to impress my friends and neighbors, I can spend a small fortune on the automobile, park it in front of my house, keep it groomed like a thoroughbred, and brag about its potential speed.

Couples give costly parties for people who bore them, people who leave cigarette burns on their furniture. Parents send their children off to private colleges which charge admissions plus room and board rates of $25,000 or $30,000 for four years of "liberal arts," even though their offspring might receive as good an education at the local public college. They might even receive a better education at the local public library. But such parents have an IM saying, "I have an obligation to send my child to the college of his choice." And parenthetically, "All our friends' children go away to college."

What happens when you get rid of the money IM's? Fred is a twenty-nine-year-old commercial photographer. This is the story he told me:

"It didn't seem to make any difference how much money I made. It was never enough. However, I was making good money. But everything that came in went out again. I wasn't getting anything out of it. The payments on my house, together with taxes, insurance, and utilities, were enough to put most people in the poorhouse. And *I* wasn't getting anything out of it. My friends may have been impressed by my success, but I was beginning to wonder what success was really all about. When I first used the V.I.F., it never occurred to mc that I could be free of my IM's about money. I was so sure I simply had to spend money on all those "necessities" of life. After I had success with my tapes, and only then, it occurred to me that it might work to free me of the IM's of spending money every month on things from which I got no enjoyment. I wrote out new images refuting the IM's about money. And it worked. I still pay the house payments, insurance, taxes and utility bills. But there are a lot of things I used to spend money on which I have dropped. Now I know I can get money if I want it. But the money I get is contributing directly to *my* enjoyment, not toward impressing my friends. And with the money I have saved from not impressing my friends, I have taken four vacations in the last year."

Some money IM's seem unavoidable. Medical expenses are accepted by most people as a part of life. And taxes, as the old saying goes, are as inevitable as death. Neither medical expenses nor taxes, however, seem a desirable way to part with money. Once you escape from your physical jail, you will be able to avoid most of those medical and dental expenses. (In a later chapter we give a brief tour of the physical jail.) As for taxes, you will be able either to avoid them with admirable skill or to earn more than enough money to get what you want even after paying them. The point to keep in mind is this: once you have broken out of your money jail, you will feel none of the limitations imposed by "demand" on how you "must" spend your money. That will include many of these demands which arise out of the IM's of others.

There are a number of joint IM's in money. Most "gift" giving is the result of joint IM's. If I send a Christmas card to 100 people selected at random from the telephone directory, I am sure to receive a surprising number of Christmas cards next year from recipients of my cards. How many times have you heard someone say, "I don't like to have people do things for me, because I don't want to become obligated to them." However, someone may do something for me or spend money on me without it raising any obligation for me to reciprocate. If I do feel an obligation to return the "gift" (and it would not, of course, be a gift if I felt an obligation), then I have acquired their IM. They have given me an IM, but, as always, at the price of their freedom and mine.

A couple in their late fifties told me they had dreamed of retiring early and moving to the mountains but that they now found it impossible. They owned a large home on which the taxes were killing them. They were paying a huge premium on life insurance on each of their lives. They didn't need the large house. Their children were grown, married, and had families of their own. I asked them why they didn't sell the house and cash in a sizable chunk of the life insurance, converting the remainder to paid-up policies.

"We can't get rid of the house," the wife said, "this has been home to the kids. When they come to visit, they expect home to be the same as it always has been."

"As for the life insurance," her husband added, "I don't see how we could cash in those policies. It would leave no estate for the children."

Fortunately, they both learned to use the V.I.F., and a short time later they moved to a cabin in the Sierra Mountains. Sometime later I got a phone call from a woman who identified herself as their daughter. "I want to thank you," she said. "That seminar of yours my folks attended was the best thing that could have happened to my brothers and me. All these years we have felt obligated to make yearly trips home because we knew Dad and Mom were keeping the house for us. It was preserved like a museum. My room was just like it was when I went off to college fifteen years ago. And I don't know how many times they told us about that damn insurance money. So many times I wanted to say, 'Spend the money on yourselves. Don't make me feel indebted to you,' Now that Dad and Mom are free, we can also be free."

Any money IM through which you attempt to obligate someone else to buy friendship is built on an IL which says, "People will never accept or like me for what I am; I have to purchase them." This is not uncommon. In fact, it forms the social fabric of our society. But social relationships between people who carry such negative IL's have a way of becoming little more than mutual obligations played back and forth. If I have the feeling people will never like me unless I do good things for them, I am going to feel compelled to perform these actions if I want people to like me. If they have the same hang-up, they will reciprocate. We don't have to like each other, we only have to have a neurotic need to *be* liked. The late Oscar Levant, pianist-actor-humorist, was reported to have turned to his wife as they were leaving a formal dinner at the White House to remark, "I suppose this will mean we'll have to invite them to dinner now."

Suppose you don't *need* to be liked by people. How much money might you save? You could eliminate Christmas cards. You could stop giving dinners for people who bore you. Or even if they didn't bore you, you wouldn't have to worry about serving the most expensive courses and the vintage wines.

Undoubtedly the number one IC concerning money has to do with not being able to get enough of it. Most people never expect to have much money and they never do. If they come into a bundle of money by holding a winning ticket in the sweepstakes or through the death of a wealthy relative, they will quickly find a way to get back down to a near-poverty level. You may recall what happened to many of the big quiz show winners of some years ago when they were winning over $100,000. Most of them managed, within a few years, to blow all the money they received. They ended up just about where they had started. When they were interviewed by the press, they were bitter. They had no reason to be.

A few years ago, a group of sociologists polled a sample of several thousand men in an attempt to describe the typical American male. One of the questions they asked was, "How much would you like to make?" Note, they did not ask "How much do you think you *will* eventually make?" Only how much they would *like* to make. Less than 1 percent of those questioned answered $50,000 a year or more. The average, in fact, was $15,000. (With inflation, today's sample might average $18,000.) Collectively, these men had the IL, "I am a $15,000 a year man." If you ask one of them, "Why only $15,000; why not $50,000?" he would probably answer with something like, "I am a widgit polisher, and the top widgit polisher never gets more than $15,000 a year."

Quickly, without spending a lot of time to think, what answer would you give to the question? Do you see yourself as a $15,000 a year person or a $500,000 a year person? When you have answered, check yourself honestly. If you have been working steadily for ten years or more at the same job and your income in the last five years has not increased at an average rate of 20 percent or more per year, you have probably leveled off. You have reached your goal. You've reached that point that you see as your financial apex, your financial self-image. The goal you have reached has reflected the price tag you put on yourself. It has nothing to do with recessions, job layoffs, or "the going rate for the job." These facts take away all cop-outs. Whether you are making $5,000 a year or $500,000 a year, your self-esteem, that is, your IL, will be involved in that income figure.

Let's say, however, you have leveled off in your income, but you sincerely would be happier with more money, and you are willing to employ the V.I.F. to earn more. The first question is, "How much more?" I have asked that question of many individuals who have not yet learned to use the V.I.F. The answers given have typically been less than a 50 percent increase over current income. This tells me they feel that aspiring to an income several times what they are presently making would only result in disappointment. Many of us have learned to live with "sour grapes" rationalizations. You know the sort: "I wouldn't want a Cadillac, anyway. They're too hard to park and they consume too much gas." Unless you are free of the money jail, and the IL, "This is what I'm worth, and no more," you will have a difficult time even answering the question, "How much more?"

This IL may also reflect a number of "moral" IL's you've been handed. Do you remember the biblical IL which says, "It is easier for a camel to pass through the eye of a needle than for a rich man to enter the gates of heaven?'' You and I were taught conspicuous wealth was a no-no. It took me many years to figure out why. It comes down to only one reason: Those who have not acquired money envy those who have and then go on to level their moralistic criticisms at those who enjoy it. Those who tell me they would not enjoy wealth are either hung-up on such moralistic IL's or are masochists.

Let's take it a step further. Assuming you have everything "necessary," why would you want to acquire more money? There are two things, it seems to me, tied to money: status and power. Money (and the accompanying status), as I have explained to our seminar groups, means "never having to stand in line." No matter how many people may shrug when they hear this, it is an important element in self-esteem. If I am seated by the maître d'hôtel in the far corner near the kitchen door, I am not going to feel very good about myself. I will leave feeling like a dumb turkey who has been ripped off by the restaurant, a guy who lacked either the status or the assertiveness to get a better table. With money/status/power, I will never be seated in that far corner.

I recognize what I am saying runs counter to the "nice guy" humility most of us were taught in childhood. "Step aside and let the other guy go first" was the rule. But then what does that say about the other guy, and what does it say about me? Obviously, he must be superior to me. I don't like waiting in line. Do you? And I like the best of foods, the best of wines, the most luxurious accommodations. Don't you? And these all can be bought with money. Perhaps most important, MONEY PROVIDES CHOICE. I may feel like dining tonight at a hamburger stand. Well and good. But I don't want to have to dine at the hamburger stand because I can't afford better. Money provides me with choice.

This raises a particular problem if you are dependent on someone else to provide the money. Children are dependent upon parents. Children can, therefore, seldom enjoy as high a level of self-esteem. But children do have, at least, the potential for attainment and self-esteem.

What of the housewife who is totally dependent upon her husband for financial support? How does she feel "I can do anything I want to do?" I have talked with a number of women who have wrestled with this question. Few have resolved it in a manner resulting in self-esteem. I am not convinced a woman cannot develop feelings of tremendous confidence while her husband's name is the only one on the paycheck. I believe it depends upon what job she is doing in the home, how she does it, and how she and her husband view it.

But I must say, somewhat reluctantly, I feel it is an uphill pull. Most women with whom I have talked have felt it was the husband's money and they were being "kept." Even when they were "handling" the finances, they did not feel any self-esteem related to money. Somewhere in the back of their mind the question remained, "Would you be living as well if you were on your own?" Those housewives who had retained a high degree of self-esteem were convinced, either by reason of talents or previous occupational history, they did not need the support of a husband in order to live in their present style. I feel there is a complex interaction of several jails involved here. If a wife feels she "needs" a husband to support her, she is apt to feel she also "needs" a husband for any number of other goods and services. She is, in a word, vulnerable. And vulnerability in relationship to another person structures a jail. Only the self-sufficient woman (or man) can say, "I like myself and I am capable of achieving anything; I can do anything I want to do, and I don't have to do anything I don't want to do."

But then there is the next question, and one asked by both sexes, not just housewives: "How do you acquire money?" Acquiring money is no more difficult than breathing to one who exudes power and achievement, since if you are capable of achieving absolutely anything, you can acquire whatever amount you desire. Whenever I make such a statement to an audience, I am confronted by skeptics: "Okay, wise guy, you tell me how I can get my hands on all that money." When I answer, "I don't know," the doubter leans back in his chair, crosses his arms, and chalks up one for his side. But "I don't know" is the only answer I can give. Where the money comes from and how it is made is something I have never been able to predict even for myself, let alone for anyone else. What I do know from experience is that money has a way of coming to those who want it once they have freed themselves from those IC's that say they can't acquire it. The question "How?" seems irrelevant so long as it is not acquired illegally or in violation of the rights of others.

I know many men and women who have acquired large fortunes in a variety of ways. These have been men and women who started from scratch. They all have had one thing in common: a certain knowledge they would succeed whatever the venture. Their "failures" are only stepping-stones on the road toward success. The V.I.F. leads to acquisition of money in a truly miraculous fashion. And when miracles occur, wise men don't ask why or how. They simply reap the benefits and sit back and enjoy the power. You can be sure of one thing: when you acquire all that money, your friends will attribute it to your dumb luck or dishonesty. But that's their IL. Since you are totally capable, it won't bother you.

SECOND IMAGES

By an employee of a manufacturing company who received a 70 percent increase in salary after asking for it:

> "I am now sitting in my new office. My desk is cleared. Everything is rolling along smoothly under my direction. I'm not only doing the job better than it has been done before, I am doing it in less time. Some days I leave at noon. The high brass are really impressed. They want me to represent the company at several meetings abroad. There will be one soon either in Europe or Japan, and I'll take Marge with me and we'll make it a romantic vacation with time just for ourselves. And the company will pay for it as a sort of bonus. Now I'm leaning back in my chair. It's the end

of the day, and I'm looking over travel brochures. I've got the world by the ass, and I feel it."

By a woman in her late thirties. The mother of three, she subsequently divorced, opened a travel agency, and has purchased a condominium:

"I am now standing in the showroom of an auto agency. The salesman has been showing me models of sports cars. I tell him I have made up my mind. I want that little white M.G. with the dark blue upholstery, and I want to drive it out. He looks at me to say something about my husband coming in, and I laugh. 'If you will give me the total, I'll write you a check,' I tell him. 'And will you have someone fill it with gas? I think I'll take a long drive and get the kinks out of it.' He still has that puzzled look on his face as I put it in gear and drive onto the highway—off and free."

By a highly successful real estate broker who makes up a new tape "tailored" to fit the particular house each time she gets an exclusive listing:

"I am now walking through the Callaghan home showing it to the couple who are going to buy it. I am excited about the house and they pick it up. I point out the built-in chopping block in the kitchen and the large cupboard space. It's a dream kitchen. As we walk into the family room, they are both smiling. The fireplace and maple paneling give the room a warmth, and I know they are both picturing relaxed evenings they will spend there. I know they are going to buy the house. As we move from room to room, I can feel them become more certain, and in just a little while, when we walk out the front door, they will tell me, 'This is it, we want it.' It will sail through escrow, and I will have scored again."

9 The Physical Side

Why did you catch your last nose-stuffed, head-filled, tight-chested, ache-all-over cold?

Illness, you were taught, is something which happens to you. You don't choose to be sick, do you? Or do you? Over forty years ago, modern medicine discovered something which Hippocrates knew centuries before Harvey discovered the principle of blood circulation. It was that physical illness cannot be separated from what is going on in the emotional state of the patient. The one affects the other—without exception.

I spoke to a registered nurse who said, "I can't accept your suggestion that when I get a sore throat or a headache it is because I choose to do so. That seems to deny everything I've learned, even the germ theory." Yet I have worked with pediatricians who have told me, "Ninety percent of our practice comes from ten percent of our patients." Where do their findings fit in with germ theory? Dr. O. Carl Simonton, Director of the Cancer Counseling and Research Center, Fort Worth, Texas, is a radiologist who has treated many, many cancer patients. He has achieved dramatic success through techniques involving "meditation" (imagery) on the normal immune responses of the body (*e.g.*, the white blood cells) attacking the cancerous cells. Simonton does not encourage his patients to abandon accepted medical treatment—surgery, radiation, chemotherapy—but he has accepted in treatment many patients who were "terminal," patients no longer showing progress under acceptable medical treatment. His techniques are similar to the visual imagery we employ in our formula. And Simonton is not alone: Medical scientists throughout the world are recognizing the truth of the "mind-body" interaction; that patients do, in fact, choose to be "sick," even to die.

It was against the resistance of many physicians that modern medicine accepted the reality of psychosomatic illness. Even today, some doctors give it little more than lip service. I have spoken to patients who, under treatment for high blood pressure or colitis for two, three, or more years, have told me their doctors never once asked them about their life, the stresses they might be under, and whether they were happy. Yet even the least knowledgeable layman is aware of the psychological factors in these illnesses. A friend becomes upset in traffic. We tell him to watch his blood pressure. The martinet boss says, "I don't get ulcers; I give them." And the harried housewife complains of her "tension" headache. Physical illnesses are jails in which others imprison you.

How do they do it? The same way they imprison you in other areas of your life: By giving you IL's, IC's, or IM's. I was given a lot of them when I was a child. "If you get your feet wet, you'll catch cold." "If you don't brush your teeth, you'll get cavities." "You have to get eight hours of sleep or your resistance will go down and you'll get sick." "Cold weather causes earaches." "If you eat too much ice cream you'll get a stomachache." (Nobody ever told me I might get sick eating too much cauliflower.) These IL's, like all IL's, may become "incorporated." They may become a part of your belief system. And there is a growing body of evidence that when they do, they become self-fulfilling prophesies. Doctors have long been aware of what they call the "will to live." Somehow, and the physical mechanism is not clearly understood, the patients who want to get well tend to do so; the patients who seemingly want to die or stay sick, or who have given up hope, recover slowly if at all.

We have been conditioned by IL's to view disease as an invading force which attacks our body from without rather than as a potential enemy which is at all times present within our bodies, but which becomes a threat to health only when our psycho-physical defense mechanisms break down. Viewed as an invader, disease is something which happens *to* us, something over which we have little control. If you feel vulnerable, unable to exercise control over your own life and health, and therefore imprisoned, your self-esteem will suffer. Your IL will be "I am inadequate." It is then that the feelings of stress will be felt.

There have been numerous studies showing a correlation between stress and "physical" illness in both animals and man. With increased stress, the body's resistance is diminished and the disease agents are able to take over. Stress, most simply defined, is our reaction to any IL-IC-IM imprisonment. There is sound neurological theory to explain this "mind-body" interaction in "rejecting" or "accepting" disease, but since, as every scientist knows, a theory is never "true" or "false," it is only "useful" to the extent it generates further hypotheses, explains others' findings, and stimulates further research, we don't need to go into how this interaction "works." The interaction is there. It does work for us. And when, as a result of stress, it breaks down, it works against us.

Our IL-IC-IM jails leave us defenseless against the disease. The disease then makes up the IL of another jail. With the IL, "I have the flu," there is the IC, "I can't play golf," and the IM, "I have to stay in bed." The disease is the jailer. When it takes over, you lose your feelings of personal power and self-esteem. You may not be consciously aware of this, but your unconscious gets the message. The illness may require you to seek the help of a physician, and this sets up another jail: "I have to go to the doctor" (IM). "I can't get well by myself" (IC). "I'm sick" (IL). If you have had experience as a patient in a hospital, you will know what I mean when I say hospitalized patients are locked in a maze of jails. Every nurse, technician, and billing office employee can become a jailer.

I have spoken with few people who were able to readily accept the idea they might choose to be ill. I myself have an almost knee-jerk reaction against it. I don't like accepting that I might do anything so utterly stupid as to choose to have a cold, even though all my professional experience, plus the findings of research scientists I respect, tells me this is so. Am I ever conscious of this choice? Almost never. Yet I have found when I have looked back at what was going on in my life just before I became ill, I have been able to identify the stress I was experiencing or the negative feelings I was having toward myself. It is not necessary to recovery, however, that I be able to identify the antecedent factors; it is helpful only in avoiding them in the future.

While in illness your body is your jailer, there may be other jailers playing a major role in bringing on the illness. A spouse, boss, parent, or friend may be the jailer who creates the stress situation which diminishes the effectiveness of your defense system and gives you that case of flu, high blood pressure, or heart attack. As I said previously, people become our jailers by applying for the job and being accepted by us, or by our requesting them to act as jailers. You may have a neighbor who enjoys telling you what you should and should not do in every area of your life. If you permit him in the door (because your self-esteem is too low to close it), he may literally "sicken" you.

When your doctor says your illness is "psychosomatic," he is not implying you are "faking" it. Not only are the symptoms "real," the disease is "real." You can die from a disease which had been identified as "psychosomatic" as easily as from one which has not been so labeled. Many medical researchers object to the dichotomy implied in the word "psychosomatic." You are not a combination of mind and body, spirit and flesh; you are a total human being. Can we identify a "mind," a "soul," a "physical self?" Of course not. But we can identify a brain, liver, pancreas, and the hydrochloric acid which eats an ulcer into your stomach, or the muscle contractions which give you a pain in the neck. Freud was aware of this when he wrote of our employment of somatic symptoms to describe those who frustrate us: "He's a pain in the neck [tension contractions of the neck muscles]," "She's a pain in the ass [hemorrhoids]," "He's a real headache [tension headache]."

In the mid-sixties, Dr. Neil Miller, research psychologist at Rockefeller University, and his associates succeeded in training laboratory animals to control a number of glandular and visceral responses including heart rate, intestinal constrictions, blood pressure, blood flow, kidney function, and brain-wave function. Miller and his associates opened the door to speculation that human beings might be able to develop similar control of their responses. The study of biofeedback—the process whereby you receive information from the organs of your body as to what is taking place—was launched. A number of scientists have employed electronic devices to implement acquisition of this information, but I am using the term in a less restricting sense. If my finger is burned on the stove, a message (pain) is transmitted to my brain which motivates me to seek treatment to relieve the pain. This is an example of biofeedback. I can, and for the sake of my health, should, develop this two-way communication system within my body; what the organs of my body tell me, and what messages I send to the immune system intended to protect my body against disease. As we have found the formula to be effective in combating disease, both directions of communications are given importance, but it is the latter which is employed in the second image.

The work of Simonton and a number of other medical scientists has contributed to our recognition of the importance of a *decision* to get well. If the patient can visualize his body combating the disease process, and if he has the desire to recover, the probability of recovery is greatly increased. In combating disease, we have found the formula to have a two-fold application: To maintain the body's natural immune system in preventing the onset of the illness, and to muster the body's defenses to combat disease should it occur.

It appears that the three most important psychological factors which predispose one to physical illness are stress, despair, and feelings of general impotence. Stress, as I previously stated, is the reaction of frustration felt in the face of any IL-IC-IM. Despair is the loss of hope, the perceived inability to anticipate a fulfilling future. If you feel no exhilaration in dreaming of tomorrow and/or no confidence your dreams can or will come true, you will descend into despair. (Peggy Lee expresses the feeling when she sings, *Is This All There Is?*) Generalized impotence is the feeling that although many things in your world are coming apart, there is nothing you can do about it; you are powerless. These feelings, in combination, are experienced as anxiety and hopelessness. They contribute greatly to lowering the body's defense system. Most of us have experienced coming down with a cold or the flu when things have not been going well at school, work, or home. The V.I.F. combats these feelings of despair, stress, and general impotence, and in so doing apparently affects the cognitive/neurohormonal processes which regulate our natural immune system.

THE "PLACEBO EFFECT"

As one trained in "hardheaded" empirical research, I find our lack of understanding of the mechanisms of how the V.I.F. affects health a frustration. I feel what I am sure must be felt by the aeronautical engineers when confronted with the "fact" that the bumblebee, given its bulk and wingspan, cannot fly—but does. Countless times I have been asked how the V.I.F. can cure or prevent this or that illness. I can only answer, "I don't know." Furthermore, I do not know the limitations, if any, on the power of the V.I.F. in combating disease and maintaining physical health. Only considerable research over many years will provide answers. With the continuing help of medical researchers and clinicians, I hope to have further definitive evidence in the years to come.

At this writing, we have had individuals report success in employment of the V.I.F. in a wide variety of illnesses. They have been most encouraging. These self-reports are not, however, acceptable evidence. Only controlled studies, employing prior medical diagnosis, "double-blind" methodology, and standardized evaluation can supply these answers. Medical scientists are at all times aware of the power of the "placebo effect." If the patient believes the treatment will have an effect, it often will have the expected effect—even if the "drug" is nothing more than sterile water or a sugar pill.

You may recognize the paradox in this. Since a placebo is effective because the patient expects it to be effective, it is, by our definition, an IL. If the patient recovers as a result of changing his IL (whether taking a "drug" he believes in or playing a tape), he might be said to have benefited from a placebo. A physician prescribes a potent drug for two patients suffering from the same illness. One recovers almost at once; the other dies. Did the one who recovered have greater faith in the drug, a greater confidence in his own recuperative powers, or a greater desire to live? The "placebo effect" may be nothing more than evidence of the inseparability of mind and body. To design an experiment which recognizes the psychophysiological aspects of any disease demands a recognition of this fact. It presents problems which can, however, be investigated through hardheaded empirical method. Any therapeutic regime which cannot be so investigated should, in my opinion, be suspect.*

THE PHYSICAL SECOND IMAGE

Common to all physical health second images are the following:

1. Control of one's own physical reactions (including so-called involuntary responses).

* Physicians and medical researchers interested in conducting controlled studies of the application of visual imagery to the treatment of disease and the control of pain are invited to correspond with the authors regarding experimental design and scientific bibliography (see page 238 for mailing address).

2. Power to successfully combat disease through the body's own immune processes, apart from chemical, surgical, etc., intervention (but without rejecting conventional medical treatment).
3. Firm belief in the naturalness of homeostasis—that the natural condition is always health, and that disease is never inevitable.

The V.I.F. may be employed to combat pain, marshal the body's immune reactions to fight a specific disease, maintain health, vitality, and weight control, and overcome "chronic" conditions, aging or supposed physical limitations.

PAIN

Pain is the body's way of telling us something is wrong. It is part of our biofeedback mechanism, and is important in warning us of danger so that we can take the necessary steps to combat the condition of which pain is a symptom. The feedback communication, however, works in both directions. Through our thinking process, our self-sentences, we can induce the pain. We can, for example, *bring on* a severe "tension" headache as well as *experience* a severe headache as a symptom of a subdural hematoma or a tumor. It is obviously important that we receive information indicating a serious illness or injury, but once we have such information and have taken sensible steps in treating it, it makes sense to do whatever can be done to relieve the pain (anything, that is, short of measures which are destructive to the body).

Most of us were taught to view pain as an inevitable consequence of our humanity, an imprisonment imposed upon our "mortal flesh." The pain of labor and delivery is such a learned prison. It is an IL which can be traced to the Old Testament. Hence, some view any refutation of it as a rejection of Holy Scripture. Personally, I feel if a woman can give birth and find it a joyful experience free of pain, God will not be offended. Women have employed second images with success in avoiding discomfort during labor and delivery. Following is the second image of one such woman expecting her first child:

> "I am now feeling the first contractions of labor. The walls of my uterus move in waves of movement urging my baby to come out into a beautiful world. The contraction lasts only a minute or two, then it relaxes. There is no pain. It is more like tightening any other muscles in my body. It is my body, and I feel a power in the strong muscles of my uterus. My baby is beginning to move down, down toward the canal of my vagina through which it will move toward the world, toward joining me and its father. I feel a peace and relaxation sweep through my body. I feel good all over. My body is opening, relaxing, welcoming, expanding to welcome my baby. What I am feeling is tranquil, sensual, and sexual. It is an experience of aliveness. An experience of power. Yes! That's it! I am giving birth. I am in control. Me! I chose impregnation, to have a baby grow and be nurtured inside me, and now I am bringing it into the world. The contraction sweeps through my uterus. I can feel the power. I have a strong uterus. Come on, baby, your mother will move you through into the light. There is a wave of exhilaration sweeping over me. I am opening like a flower. My cervix is expanding and opening a door through which my baby is moving. I feel a power and control I have never felt before. There! There it is, the feeling I have been waiting for. My baby, our child, is comfortably sliding down through my vagina. I feel myself expand. It is a glorious feeling. I am in complete control of my responses. I open! There is no pain, only power. I am able to completely relax when I want to, and to tighten my muscles when I want to. I am floating. And so is my baby. My body feels alive and omnipotent. The joy and sensuality and power overcome any pain. *I* am in control. *I* am. And my baby is flowing through the passages of my body freely, as if flowing down a river, effort-

lessly. And painlessly. And now, the total, sublime, indescribable sweep of pleasure which comes over me as I say, 'Welcome to the world, my baby, let me show you how much fun it can be.' "

She wrote this description and then played this tape two or more times each day during the last trimester of her pregnancy and during the time she was in labor. She requested no anesthesia during her delivery and did not require an episiotomy during delivery.

Following is a second image employed by a forty-two-year-old man with a history of bursitis:

"I am now feeling a health and freedom flowing into my shoulder. There is a pleasant, warm sensation of vitality loosening my shoulder joint. It is like a soothing oil. I feel the pain leaving. It is radiating out from my shoulder, passing like a vapor from my pores. My shoulder is becoming completely, totally, mobile. I can move my arm up and down, stretch it out to the side, now up. I am swinging it freely, around and around. It is free! Completely free! It is like the arm of a child swinging on the rings at a playground. My shoulder joint, my arm, my whole body tingles with health. I feel great! Young! Alive. There is strength flowing in my muscles. No pain. No pain at all. My body is free. It is like running in the sunshine turning cartwheels."

And this one is by a young woman with a history of migraine:

"I am now sitting in the kitchen. It is a clear, sunny day and I am filled with plans for accomplishment and fun. I can see the apricot tree in the backyard. It is in bloom, and the sun is filtering through the branches. I am completely relaxed. Everything is so peaceful. I am aware of good feelings throughout my entire body. The tight feelings I used to have, the irritability, the pressure that used to come inside my head are all a thing of the past. I am totally free of pain, and I have no fear of pain coming since my body functions perfectly. The headaches have vanished. They have passed from my life. I can feel everything in balance. I am light. Soaring. In complete control. My body responds to my wishes. Totally. And I have chosen to be free of all pain, all tension. I feel like singing [humming].''

COMBATING DISEASE

In preparing a second image to combat a specific disease, it is important to create a visual image of a physical process which is actively fighting the sickness. It is not necessary that you have a knowledge of physiology, the immune processes, or pathology in order to do so. Dr. Simonton has found that the most effective imagery is that which is created by the patient, and that this imagery does not necessarily represent any actual physical process. Rather than white blood cells attacking the disease, for example, the patient might create an image of an army of microscopic soldiers doing battle with and defeating the invading enemy. It is important, however, that the image be visual, that you be able to ''see'' the disease being dissolved or defeated and your body being restored to health. It is essential that you experience this as a personal power which you possess.

Following is the second image of a girl in her teens who suffered from severe boils and acne:

''I am now sending out tiny chemicals in my bloodstream to fight the ugly germs attacking my skin. I can see them flowing through my blood vessels and converging on the enemy. There! The chemicals have reached the germs. They are attacking them, devouring them. They are covering the germs all over and dissolving them. The germs are shriveling up and dying. They are powerless. They can't fight my super-chemicals.

The dead germs are turned to something that looks like dirty dishwater and it is washed away—rapidly—in my fresh blood, away from my skin, out of my body. All the redness and the pus is evaporating. All the eruptions are disappearing. My powerful little chemical weapons are cleaning every impurity out of my skin. I can see it changing. And it's beautiful, absolutely beautiful!"

This is the successful second image of a woman in her mid-thirties who suffered from duodenal ulcers:

> "I am now coating the lining of my stomach and intestinal tract with an invisible shield to protect it. The lining is pink and healthy. As I watch, the sores are healing, turning into strong, healthy tissue. Nothing can irritate my strong tissue. It doesn't respond to spicy foods or anything else. It enjoys them and is nourished by them. Those contractions have been completely controlled. They are within my control, and that gives me a feeling of great power. I can relax. I can eat anything I want. I am totally, completely, and wonderfully calm and self-assured. I have two invisible shields: One protects me from all those silly things which used to bother me. Nothing, absolutely nothing, can press my button. I can laugh at my emotions because I am in complete control of them. My other invisible shield protects my stomach and intestines. I can see a coating, somewhat like an acrylic, which resists anything penetrating and irritating my healthy tissue. I can eat what I want, drink what I want, and do what I want. I am strong! Strong! Strong! I can take on the world!"

The following second image was employed by a man under X-ray therapy for cancer of the larynx:

> "I am now watching my anti-cancer cells converging on my vocal cord and attacking the cancer cells. The anti-cancer cells are white, and they pulsate with power. The cancer cells are a dirty gray-black and they

> sprawl out like a group of little funguses. I have sent my strong, white, anti-cancer fighters to eat up the miserable little cancer cells, and they descend upon them eager to destroy them. I can see them moving against the black cells with a vengeance. They suck them in and chew them up. One, two, three, four, five. The black cells are being chewed up. Dozens of them are being eaten up. The black cell area is getting smaller and smaller. The anti-cancer cells I am directing are eliminating them, chewing them up, destroying them, smashing them. My vocal cord is regaining its strength, and all the hoarseness is leaving. I'm destroying the cancer, eating it alive, driving it out of my body for good. Go get 'em, white cells! Chew up the sons-of-bitches! Kill off every one of them!"

Nothing which has been said should, of course, be interpreted as an attack on legitimate medical treatment. Proper medical treatment should always be sought when symptoms warrant it. Holistic medicine, which has in recent years captured the attention of many physicians, stresses the importance of viewing the patient as a total person, an individual capable of exercising great power in the maintenance of his or her health, rather than as a passive machine obeying chemical and physical laws over which he or she has little control. As a tool of holistic medicine, the V.I.F. should be viewed as an important weapon in the armamentarium available to combat disease, but never as a substitute for medical care. Employed to maintain robust health, however, the V.I.F. can reduce significantly the illnesses requiring you to visit your doctor.

Marilou became a grandmother for the first time at forty-three. Looking back on it three years later, she said she felt it was a turning point—for the worse: "I had a lot of IL's about being a grandmother. It seemed to say to me, 'You're now an old woman. You're over the hill. You're no longer attractive, and it's only a matter of time until you start falling apart.' And I didn't have long to wait. The next thing I knew, I had high blood pressure, a recurring bladder infection, and finally, periodontal disease. I was really doing some pretty awful things to myself."

She attended one of our seminars at the suggestion of her doctor, but as she told us the opening evening, "No psychological mumbo-jumbo is going to lower my blood pressure. My doctor has had me on anti-hypertensive drugs for the last year and my blood pressure is still 180 over 115." She did agree to participate in the weekend seminar, however, and to try making tapes. We wrote a second image for her dealing with her blood pressure. After making some changes in visual imagery to make the second image more real to her, she started playing it several times a day. In less than a month her blood pressure was within normal limits and the bladder infection had cleared up. Her periodontal disease, which her dentist had told her would require surgery, took a while longer, but in a few months her dentist was able to tell her surgery would not be necessary. He now routinely recommends the V.I.F. to his patients. "I used the tapes to put myself back together," Marilou told us recently, "and in the process I took ten or fifteen years off my age. I'm a young woman again."

Here is the second image she used in fighting the periodontal disease:

> "I am now smiling at myself in the mirror. It is a wonderful smile, a healthy smile. My gums are pink and firm. Each time I massage them I can feel a tingling of fresh blood flowing into them. It is fighting off the bacteria. My gums are gripping my teeth firmly and tightly, and I can now chew strongly and eat all the foods I enjoy."

It was a short second image—but apparently effective.

THE MAINTENANCE TAPE

Someone during one of our seminars was the first to suggest a "well-being" tape, one designed to enhance vitality, resistance to disease, and a feeling of robust health. The tapes which resulted, of which the following is an example, are designed to recognize and control the essential normality of homeostasis in the machinery of the body. As such, it becomes one of the "core" tapes. It does not refute any specific IC or IM. Rather, it aims at keeping you where you should be—where nature intended you to be—in control of your well-being.

> "I am now climbing out of bed. I feel a surge of power go through me. I run my hands over my body. It is a sound body, a body bursting with health and vitality. I am aware of the messages my body sends to me, the sounds of a perfect motor purring away, functioning without a flaw. And the messages all say everything is great! I walk to the window. It is a dazzling day out there! I am aware of the messages telling me I am hungry, and the messages telling me there is an energy virtually exploding inside me. No illness, no disease, no imperfection can invade me. I am in complete control, and in command of the forces necessary to easily defeat anything which might try to attack me—physically or emotionally. Health is my right, and within my power. I feel it surging through my arms and legs, swelling throughout my body, driving impurities out. Health is mine! I possess it! I control it! And I glory in it. I tighten my muscles, and I can feel it: I'm untouchable!"

WEIGHT CONTROL

We all have three physical IL's: age, sex, and weight. They can each generate countless IC's and IM's. Weight is usually the only one we can change (although sex change operations are becoming increasingly popular). Body weight itself is generally a reflection of an IL, especially if you have held the same weight (even off and on) for some time.

Let's say your "medically ideal" weight (the weight your

doctor advises) is 130 pounds, but you weigh 185 and, except for those times you have gone on the latest diet, you can't seem to get rid of those extra pounds and keep them off, and you *want* to lose those 55 pounds. Your IL is, "I am a 185-pound person," and your IC is, "I can't lose weight without strenuous dieting." If you go on a diet, you may, of course, lose weight, but it will be only by starving yourself. After all, someone who is "normally" 185 pounds just naturally eats more than someone who is "normally" 130. So if you see yourself (your IL) as a 185-pound person, of course you will be starving yourself to get down to 130. Even if you do manage to "starve" yourself down to 130, what happens? Chances are you will gradually edge your way back to 185—your physical self-image, your IL: "I am a 185-pound person."

When employed successfully in reducing weight, the V.I.F. has entailed creation of a new, and more acceptable, IL of body weight. Generally, individuals have found it works best when the second image combines ingestion of fewer calories (in keeping with the new weight IL), loss of appetite, and burning or dissolving of fat cells. Following is an example employed by a woman in her late twenties:

> "I am now standing before my full-length mirror admiring my skinny body. I have been on a very low-calorie diet, but I haven't really been dieting. I am a 130-pound person, and I eat no more and no less than a 130-pound woman would eat. I'm seldom hungry, and I feel more alive than I have ever felt in my life. I am the picture of health. I'm sexy looking, tanned, and oh so slim. I like my body. It's a great body, a body that deserves to be shown off. And I like myself. I can feel any remaining fat deposits in my body dissolving and passing out of my body. My body is freeing itself of all the ugly fat and impurities. I feel lighter all the time. I feel great and I look absolutely fantastic."

Others have found any mention of weight, *per se,* in the second image to be counterproductive. "If I think in terms of weight," one woman told me, "I tend to get into the same old numbers game—the numbers on the scale, the number of calories, the number of ounces of this or that food. I leave any mention of number of pounds out of my second image, and I emphasize appearance. After all, that's what I'm really interested in." She brought us this second image:

> "I am now taking my new powder-blue dress from the closet. I'm going to wear it for the first time this evening. And what an evening it's going to be! The first night of my vacation. What an absolutely gorgeous dress it is—chic and sexy and clingy. I'm slipping it over my head now and over this trim body of mine. As I pull up the zipper, I feel just great. It goes up easily. I knew it would. And I look terrific! Boy! Am I going to turn heads tonight!"

Still others have found second images which create the reality of a reduction in hunger (or hunger for certain fattening foods). Some have combined all three types in a single second image; others have made two or three separate tapes.

AGING

IL's of age, and the IC's and IM's they generate, can be refuted in a similar way. Most of us over thirty have learned self-destructive age prisons. We associate stamina with youth. Hence, when we pass a birthday, be it thirty, forty, or fifty, an IL takes control and we lose the strength and endurance to accomplish what we might like to accomplish.

A man who may have prided himself on his handball game reads the sportswriters who refer to a thirty-nine-year-old as an "old man." If a thirty-nine-year-old baseball player is an old man, and we are impressed that at his advanced age he can make the team, what does it say about an amateur handball player of forty-six? One foot in the grave?

Age IL's, with the limitations they carry with them, are derived from group norms and unsupported beliefs. They have no validity when it comes to any individual. I recently spoke with a man in his mid-forties. He said, "Before I started using the V.I.F., I had taken to reading the obituaries in the paper. Can you believe that? Any morning I came across one on some man my age, it would put a cloud over my whole day. And all those commercials on television cautioning about smoking and exercise and 'moderation' all seemed to be aimed at me, the middle-aged man. My doctor told me at my age I should slow down. He couldn't find anything wrong with me, but he didn't like the number of hours I worked, and he lectured me on the risk of smoking. I actually began to feel old, as if my body machinery was finally just wearing out. And as for my sex life, it was gradually tapering off to once a week, and just about the time my wife was becoming more amorous than ever. Hell! The kids were pretty well grown. Both of them were away at college, and we were free to have a lot more fun together, but I was beginning to feel ready for a rocking chair and a glass of warm milk. I swear this whole crazy society conspires to turn you into an invalid when you pass forty. What bullshit! Do you know what the V.I.F. did for me? My wife and I went on a vacation. We rode horseback, jumped breakers in the ocean, stayed up half the night dancing and boozing, and for two weeks we made love twice a day."

PHYSICAL LIMITATIONS

There are physical IL-IC-IM's which, rather than accepting the inevitability of disease, may restrict your freedom through so-called physical "limitations." When I was young, I was a skinny, sickly shrimp. That was the best that could be said of me. Perhaps I didn't need to have anyone tell me what I could not do because of my physical limitations, but plenty of people did anyway. And from them, I picked up a lot of physical IC's. I was told, and came to believe, I tired easily. The IC was, "I can't engage in strenuous activity,'' with the IL, ''because I tire easily.'' When I was fourteen, I climbed a small mountain with some of my friends. I had to stop for a rest several times on the way, and by the time I reached the top (and the others looked like they had been on nothing more than a leisurely stroll around the block), I was ready for a stretcher. My IC was working at full force. I never again attempted to climb.

Not long ago, in a large informal group I was conducting, the subject of physical limitations came up. Talk centered on the questions, ''Don't we have to face our limitations and learn to live with them?'' A physician in the group brought the discussion to an end by asking, ''Since none of us here was born without arms or deaf and blind, why are we discussing whether or not we would be 'limited' if we had been?''

Fortunately, most of us are not so seriously ''impaired,'' and I have met more than a few individuals who were born with such obvious ''limitations'' who lived in no way a limited life. What about all the lesser IL physical limitations? Who would tell you you were physically limited in what you could do, and why? The ''who,'' of course, might have been anyone—parents, teachers, friends, or the family doctor. And the ''why'' is usually because they believed it and felt it was to your benefit that you also accept the ''realities'' of life.

Dorothy, a woman in her twenties, married with two children, told me she had difficulty keeping up her housework and caring for her babies. ''I have a weak back. I can't lift things, or bend a lot, or by the end of the day I'll feel miserable. Weak backs run in my family. My mother had the same trouble.'' I asked her if doctors had been able to diagnose the problem. ''No,'' she said, ''but that doesn't mean a thing. They weren't able to with my mother, either.'' There is a good probability her IL, ''I have a weak back'' was given her by her mother who in turn may have gotten it from her mother. Or she may at one time have suffered a back strain or some other mild injury which left her sensitive to any exertion which could ''aggravate'' the pre-existing ''condition.''

Family history of a particular illness is often enough to set up an IL for that illness. I heard of a man who had suffered in childhood from migraine headaches "inherited" from his father. At nineteen, he discovered, by accident, the man he knew as his father was not, in fact, his natural parent. The man had married his mother while she was pregnant by another man. The migraine headaches vanished.

Statements such as "I tire easily," "I catch cold every winter," "I'm prone to stomach upsets," are IL's. As such, they are self-fulfilling prophesies. Some years ago, while on vacation in Mexico, I met a neurosurgeon from New York. During his stay, he told me he did not intend to venture from his luxury hotel. He drank only bottled water (even using it to brush his teeth), made sure to peel any fruit he ate, and in every respect practiced scrupulous hygiene. "I don't want to take a chance on picking up a bug," he told me. "I have a sensitive digestive system." That was an IL which locked him in a hotel jail. The day we were leaving, his wife came to say goodbye to us. "My husband asked me to give you his best," she said. "He can't leave the room; he has a terrible bout of Montezuma's Revenge."

The power of these physical IL's is impressive. I frequently wonder how many illnesses are generated by publication in the mass media of findings "proving" the danger of disease from ingestion of pink lemonade or the application of suntan lotion.

IC's associated with physical limitations or chronic "conditions" can be attacked by specific second images and by a maintenance image of robust health. Following is the second image of a housewife in her early thirties, the mother of three small children. She had suffered from frequent minor illnesses and exhaustion.

> "I am now dressing for dinner and an evening out with Jim. I look at myself carefully as I put on my makeup. I look great! My eyes are clear. They actually sparkle. My energy is incredible. To bed late again last

night, and up early this morning, but I feel like a million. I'm able to work and party all day and half the night without tiring. My body is in perfect balance. Strong. I feel the strength through every muscle. And I am in control, total control of my body and my life. All the old tiredness is gone. I am vital and alive and young. Sickness can't touch me. I can keep it at a distance, and I do. God! I feel powerful! And beautiful! And in love! And I can fly through life. Nothing can slow me down. Nothing!"

When you are omnipotent you can move mountains—physically, emotionally, intellectually. You genuinely like yourself, and you do things to your body which feel good. Not unpleasant things the jailers have told you are inevitable or good for you.

People die—physically, emotionally, intellectually—by stages. I was once staff psychologist on a geriatric ward of a mental hospital. We had patients in their late fifties and early sixties who had regressed to infantile behavior. Others had seemingly lost all contact with the world around them. In all areas which are important, they had ceased living. I talked with many relatives of these patients, and I was struck by the similarities in the life histories of these patients. Typically, they had led conventional, routine lives. They were conformists who had fallen into a changeless pattern of existence as early as thirty years of age. Many had taken pride in the changelessness, telling others how many years they had taken their annual vacation at the same place, how many years they had voted the same party ticket, attended the same church, driven the same make of automobile, and had "always said . . ." By thirty-five, they were well on their way toward senile "death." Life was, for them, something which happens *to one*. And they let it happen—until it killed them. Without hope, without the excitement of expecting the surprise of a brand-new day tomorrow and the day after tomorrow, the IL's of society can provide only the security of a grave.

The V.I.F. generates the power which is virtually synonymous with living and well-being. If I am sick or "just naturally weak," I am impotent (perhaps not sexually, although sexual impotence or lowered sexual drive is commonly a symptom of such IL's of inadequacy and vulnerability). I have lost control of my life and the ability to attain what I desire. Inevitably, then, I will experience still more lowering of self-esteem. I will like myself even less. Disliking myself, even if unconsciously, I will punish myself physically as well as emotionally. I will be mean to me.

I know a woman who dislikes her feet. Although she has very normal and attractive feet, she was given an IL by her mother to the effect that "ladies" have feet the size of eight-year-old girls. When her feet grew to normal, not large, proportions, she no longer met mother's definition of "ladylike" feet. She has since developed a pattern of periodically punishing her feet: a badly stubbed toe, a twisted ankle, a heel blister. She has done a number of very mean things to the feet she doesn't like.

These "accidents" are not *conscious* reactions. The victim did not intentionally seek them. Self-destructive IL's, however, can, as most physicians have observed, trigger self-destructive physical reactions.* I am sure her feet are grateful that she is now using the V.I.F. and has stopped acting mean to them.

We are probably all aware of the correlation between physical well-being and self-esteem. We might easily conclude one cannot be present without the other. For this reason, it is important to include a description of a positive physical state in most second images, even if nothing more than, "I am feeling absolutely fantastic." To "see" oneself physically as the picture of health, free of all disease and physical limitations, is essential to feelings of power. A physical description, therefore, can—and should—be a part of every second image, even if it is incorporated only in passing.

* For an interesting expansion on this "psychosomatic" relationship, I recommend *The Mind/Body Effect,* Herbert Benson, M.D., 1979, Simon and Schuster, New York.

10 V.I.F. and Play

I own a very rigid dictionary. Its editors don't believe life should be free or fun. Under synonyms for the word "play," they have the words "diversion," "pastime." And, "Play is the general word for any such form of activity, often undirected, spontaneous, or random." They follow with this italicized sentence: "*Childhood is a time for play.*"

What a sad world they must inhabit. They hold an IC which says, "I can't run out to play," an IM which says, "I have to pursue only serious activities," and an IL which says, "Childhood is a time for play and alas, I am an adult." I don't want to live in that jail, and I doubt that you do. But there are a lot of inmates.

Chances are you and I were raised to believe that jail cell was meant for us. The "play is reserved for children" jail was accepted as the inevitable residence of those who survived their teens. In fact, the IL was handed to us long before that. In childhood, play was accepted and even encouraged. Well, maybe not totally. It never seemed to me I got enough time for play. But at least play was tolerated to an extent. Parents and teachers, however, apparently preparing us for our fate, frequently dropped in cautions such as, "You can't play all the time; there's more to life than play."

From early childhood on, it was all downhill. The number and frequency of play activities seemed to decline as a function of age, approaching zero in adulthood. In those teenage years, the pressure to give up play got really heavy. If you were a girl, it took the form of, "Act like a young lady; you are no longer a little girl." If you were a boy, "Start acting like a man; only babies and sissies play those sorts of games." So a thirteen-year-old girl tries to be a blasé twenty-two-year-old and a thirteen-year-old boy tries to be super-cool. If you have children who have gone through that age you know what I mean. If you have good recall, you know it from experience. A boy who a year before had a wonderful time on the merry-go-round and dressing up for trick or treat, now cannot be bludgeoned into such "little kid" activities.

When I was that age, I was repeatedly hit with the question, "When are you going to start growing up?" Translated, the question was, "When are you going to stop playing and start behaving as a joyless adult?" Had I known then what it took me a long time to learn, I might have answered, "I've decided not to. Being a grown-up looks like a drag." But I didn't. I went along with the "wisdom" of my elders and gave up a lot of activities which were then, and still are, fun. I did, that is, until I got out of that jail and discovered *fun* all over again.

Someone once described a puritan as a person who lives in fear that somewhere out there someone is having fun. You and I are surrounded by a lot of puritans. We grew up in a puritan environment. Puritans are anti-pleasure, not just for themselves, but for everyone. Pleasure, to them, is a creation of the devil. "Hedonism" is what they call it. Play, to their joyless mentalities, is anything short of pain and drudgery. I doubt that any one of us escaped a heavy dose of this puritan philosophy. And the IL's which the Puritans gave us may have resulted in IC's and IM's which keep us from playing. If they don't keep us from playing, they at least extract a price in guilt if we do play.

The whole puritan ethic is, of course, built on guilt. Without strong guilt feelings, no one would ever accept such a put-down, negative, joyless philosophy. When I was a kid, I was told the story of Adam and his problems in the Garden of Eden. Adam and Eve chose to eat what they wanted to and they were punished for it. They were thrown out of

Paradise and from then on got little fun out of life. The quote they read to me was addressed to Adam: "Cursed be the ground because of you; in toil shall you eat of all the days of your life; thorns and thistles shall it bring forth to you, and you shall eat the plants of the field. In the sweat of your brow you shall eat bread 'til you return to the ground, since out of it you were taken; for dust you are and unto dust you shall return."

Now, of course, I'm not Adam, but his guilt was laid on me. Whatever Adam got, they said, I would get, including all that "sweat of your brow" responsibility. The joyless moralists who laid original sin on me as a guilt-trip succeeded for a number of years. Whenever I managed to break loose and have fun, I felt uneasy. Now, fortunately, I can say, "I am sorry, Adam, for the years you spent with those thorns and thistles, but I don't choose to join you."

One sunny day last summer I got a telephone call from a business associate. "I hope I didn't interrupt anything," he said. "Were you tied up?" "Not really," I answered, "I was dropping water balloons from my second story onto my patio." Silence. Then: "Seriously, are you busy doing something?" To this day I'm not sure he believes I was dropping water balloons from the window. But why not? Toy balloons cost very little. Water-filled balloons don't destroy anything, they don't harm anyone, and they are fun. If he doesn't have fun, he has my sympathy. He may believe he deserves the punishment of Adam. I don't. Fun, as I define it, is an activity which makes me feel like laughing, like running and jumping, like shouting with pure glee. My balloon water-bomb play might be acceptable to other adults had I been doing it with my children. Good and noble fathers can sneak in a bit of play now and then so long as their children are involved. Children become one of the few acceptable excuses for adults to play. I have long suspected it is one of the reasons grown-ups involve themselves in Scouting, Little League coaching, and those other activities of "concerned" parents. Does it make any sense, however, that I should need children as an excuse for an activity which I enjoy?

It is sad that even with their children involved, many adults have strong IC's where play is concerned. You can see their IC's in operation if you go to a carnival or zoo. Parents stand around patiently watching the kids enjoy the animals or the amusement rides. But daddies and mommies seldom go on the ferris wheels or through the house of horrors unless they feel obliged to accompany their children. I loved the ferris wheel when I was ten years old. I still love the ferris wheel. Someone said that the difference between children's toys and adult toys is that the latter are more expensive. To which I would add, they are also seldom as much fun. Adults, when and if they do play, approach "play" as a serious—often competitive—endeavor.

If you have no children, or if they are not available to give you an excuse to play, you may find exercise an acceptable rationale for play activities. Every afternoon, thousands of businessmen jump around handball courts "working out." Their wives reserve tennis courts long in advance in order to keep a "trim figure." In the morning, red-faced men in gray sweat suits huff and puff through my suburb. Worried about coronaries, high blood pressure, and waistline, they impose an exercise IM on themselves. But whatever it is they have, an expanded waistline, a coronary, or just a nagging wife, they certainly don't seem to have much fun. We have turned into a nation of adult "exercisers," but not adult players.

No matter what Adam did, he couldn't have fun. He had to serve his sentence of sweat and toil. You may feel you have broken out of the jail cell which confined Adam, and that you do, at least on occasion, play. But do you feel comfortable playing only after you have first earned the "right" to do so through hard work? If so, you have a lot of company. That puritan ethic said "You must feel guilty playing if you have not paid the high price of work for any fun in life." Often the price paid in terms of work is far greater than the pleasure found in the fun activity. If you subtract eight hours a day for work and another eight hours for sleep, you are still left with fifty-six hours each week.

What percentage of that fifty-six hours do you spend in play? Most men and women average less than 10 percent playtime. Suppose we include television watching in our definition of "play." Then it might come to more than 10 percent. But how often does a television program leave you with a feeling of exuberance and laughter? Television is often little more than a distraction, a boring "escape" from the tedium of life. The IM "I have to earn the right to play" is just another way of saying, "I am really worthless." I ask these puritans: Why am I obligated to work for this "reward?" Am I working for you? For the guy down the block? For my family? For what you call the "common good?" Their answers always come down to one thing: a belief in man's inherent worthlessness and guilt. If I were to accept their gloomy views, I would have no reason for not jumping from the top of a ten-story building other than an IM: "I must stay alive to work, sweat, and toil." To hell with that IM. I don't have to "tote that barge; lift that bail" to earn a 10 percent reward in play. I am not worthless. Neither are you. Let the puritans live in their "vale of tears." You and I can go climb trees and build sand castles on the beach.

I took an informal survey of men and women who admitted playing very little. I asked them their reasons. They gave the following:

"*I don't have time to play.*" ("I have too many responsibilities.")
"*I have small children.*" ("My job demands a lot of me.")

These are statements of relative values (work is more important than play) or confessions of ineptitude. If I feel my job demands so much involvement no time is left to play, I must be working solely to benefit someone else. This can be a reflection only of my lack of self-esteem. One man in the group said, "The only free time I have is on weekends, and on weekends I always have chores to do." "What chores," I asked him, "are more important than play? You and I only have so many hours, days, and years to walk around this planet of ours. An hour spent doing a chore [often to please someone else] is an hour which is lost to pleasure. If you had but one week to live, is that how you would spend even a portion of that week? And how do you know that you have even that long a time?" To *play* is to have a sense of one's mortality.

"*I don't have much money.*" ("Entertainment these days costs too much. I'll start having fun when I'm rich.")

First of all, if you want more money, you can always get it. But who says play has to cost money? I have asked scores of couples how often they go out on dates. Over and over again I have heard lack of money offered as the excuse for their IC, "We can't go out for an evening." One more jail! Children can go to a park and play for hours without a cent in their pockets. Why can't their parents? (Incidentally, there is one thing I have found about public parks: there are no children there at night. There is one near where I live. We ride our bicycles to it in the moonlight, take along a bottle of wine, and have a gloriously fun time on the slide and swings.)

"*I would feel foolish playing.*" ("Play seems too childish." "I'd look silly." "I do play sometimes but only at masquerade parties or New Year's Eve celebrations.")

This one is built on the teaching that play is for children. But think about it for a minute. Does it make any sense? Of course not. If you feel foolish enjoying play, you are overly concerned with the opinions of others ("they will laugh at me"). How sad that adults need excuses such as masquerade parties and funny-hats-and-toy-horns New Year's Eve celebrations to let go and play. As you may recall, I said one of the immediate results of the V.I.F. was humor:

everything suddenly seems very funny; all those things you were so concerned about (and this includes the opinions of others) now seem hilarious. People who have employed the V.I.F. never feel foolish playing. They enjoy play, and they recognize the wisdom of playing.

"*I can't play because my husband/wife doesn't want to.*" ("I have nobody to play with." "I'm married to a non-player." "My wife always tells me to cool it.")

This is an expression of a dependency, and like all dependencies, it is a jail. It's saying, "I must rely on someone else for my pleasure." This is never true if you are free and autonomous. Perhaps you like walking in the rain. Does your wife have to get wet joining you when she would rather stay by the fire? Or do you have to stay inside if she doesn't want to go out? If so, you are jailers to each other. There are many play activities you can enjoy fully by yourself. Have you ever watched a two- or three-year-old playing alone? (See the chapter on freedom in marriage.)

"*I'm just not a fun person.*" ("I don't think I know how to play." "I've never played.")

This is one of those IL's which asserts that people are of different types (perhaps from birth). I don't accept the assertion. It is nothing but an IL. You may never have played, although I feel it is probable you played at least in childhood, but that does not mean you cannot play once you break out of the IL-IC-IM jail which says you are not the playing "type." Beneath this IL, I am sure, is a series of IL's which say very negative things about you.

"*I'm too old for that sort of thing.*" ("I tire easily." "I'd probably get sick." "I'm always afraid I'll get hurt." "I have arthritis.")

These are IL's which form the base of a physical jail. I frequently talk to people in their thirties and even in their twenties who leave me feeling I hope I never get *that* old.

Chronologically, I may be old enough to be their parent, but they are often thirty years of age, and one year from eighty-five. I know seventy-five-year-olds who are younger. Age, as well as physical well-being, may be more related to play than to proper nutrition or exercise. It is an important element in "thinking young." We are what we think.

> "*I don't know any place to play.*" ("All places to play are for kids." "If I played, I'd want privacy.")

This one seems to be another way of saying, "Play is for children." Children do not seem to need a specific place to play. They can play anywhere and at any time—unless adults stop them. Play is seldom a matter of "proper" time and place. It's a matter of motivation and the self-esteem essential to being good to yourself—regardless of others.

> "*But I do play bridge.*" (There are some types of play which are acceptable and some which are not.)

It's funny, isn't it, how the "acceptable" forms of adult "play" follow fads? In my area, among the middle and upper-middle class, tennis and skiing are the current "in" things. Bike riding had a certain popularity two or three years ago, and like skiing and tennis it could employ the rationale of "good exercise." The IL, "the opinion of others is all important," is as pervasive in the area of adult play as it is in most other activities. One of the great benefits found in the V.I.F. is loss of these "social acceptance" IL's.

> "*I do have a hobby.*"

A hobby may be play or it may not. It depends upon the approach. For some people a hobby is more like an assigned task. They approach it with grim determination. Perhaps they cannot feel comfortable unless they turn their hobby into work. They may also feel that having invested money in the hobby they have to pursue it. The hobby then becomes an IM. Of course, there are those who feel that only by taking an activity which was initially play and making it extremely complex and challenging, can they justify it as an "adult" activity. I have a friend who owned an electric train. It wasn't a model train and it didn't run on a model railroad. It was just a toy electric train. He ran the track from one room to the next throughout his house. Most of his friends figured he was a harmless nut who had never grown up. He could have joined a model railroad club, spent ten times the money and hundreds of hours in construction of an HO gauge "pike" and have been completely respectable in the adult community. But he didn't. He just played. Perhaps many model railroad builders also have fun, but I *know* he does.

"People who play are unstable and irresponsible."

One woman told me she didn't feel such people were "safe." What she meant, she explained, was that she did not believe playing people could be counted on; they are just not predictable. I tend to believe she's right. *Free* individuals are not the most predictable. Since being free means to have many options, a free person may at any given time exercise one of a number of options. Does this mean, however, the free, playing person is irresponsible? That has not been my observation. I don't "play" by driving down the highway at 90 miles an hour. If I want the sensation of speed in play, I can ride the roller coaster. I can be very responsible yet still enjoy a lot of play. But I probably will never fit into the little boxes other people would like to put me in for their own security.

If the joy of play were the only benefit in discovering freedom, I think it would be worth developing and using the V.I.F. Play, whether in skinny-dipping, skate-boarding or kite-flying, is one of the basic ingredients in living. When you stop playing, you start dying. Others will, you can be sure, try their darndest to keep you from playing. They are not merely trying to keep you in prison, they are trying to kill you off! How many businessmen might be saved from early coronaries if they would only spend time in play. For non-players, retirement is little more than a short period of time, marked off by monthly pension checks, in which to prepare for a funeral.

Play is one of the few activities which, by its very nature, is free of all IC's and IM's. Even when the play is competitive, winning and losing is irrelevant. Play is always for the sake of playing, nothing more. Play is also solitary. You may choose to play "with" someone, but their presence is not essential to your enjoyment. My friend and I may build a sand castle on the beach, but I can build one by myself as well. I am not dependent on a playmate. And my joy in play is mine; it is not something bestowed upon me by another.

There is a high correlation between freedom to play and freedom in all other areas of life. Of the many men and women I have seen in psychotherapy, I cannot recall a single one who spent even a fraction of his time in play activity at the time he sought help—regardless of what the present problem may have been. Ability to play is one of the best indicators of emotional as well as physical health. We have found play as a second image often an excellent first tape. It has the effect of freeing many people to make tapes related to other IC's and IM's. It is for this reason we strongly urge participants in our seminars to make their play tape almost as soon as they learn the V.I.F. Many, however, do not find this easy, conditioned as we all have been to viewing play as silly and childish. The rewards, nevertheless, make the effort more than worthwhile.

Play, entailing as it so often does, imagination, tends to lead to right-hemisphere dominance during the play period. One might say play helps to unlock the creative part of the mind. It is a form of daydream acted out. Remember as a child when you played pirate, policeman, cowboy, doctor, or ballerina? Neurologically speaking, you were in a "different space" while doing so. You created a "new reality" in which anything was possible. Essentially, this is what we do with the V.I.F. Play reinforces the V.I.F. and the V.I.F. increases our freedom to play. Both break us out of our "rational" and "socially proper" jail cells.

Those who have spent time (as staff, patient, or visitor) in a mental hospital are familiar with the lack of play and humor in such institutions. Except for some occasional black humor among the staff, there is seldom laughter. And believe me, there is much to laugh about. Many of the rules and procedures are hilarious. Psychiatric interviews are often the stuff of which situation comedies are made. Psychological evaluations based upon the drawing of a house, tree, and person, and interpretations of the "patient's" associations to a set of ink blots should elicit at least an occasional laugh. But with professionals who take themselves and what they do so very, very, seriously, how can the "patients" laugh? I am convinced their lack of laughter has a lot to do with why so many "patients" (and more than a few psychiatrists and psychologists) have a difficult time "recovering."

Here are two second images of play. The first is by a forty-one-year-old dentist, married, father of three:

> "I am now walking up to the top of the knoll in the park near my office. It is a beautiful, sunny day with just a few clouds and just about the bluest sky I have ever seen. I've taken a two-hour lunch and I have a sack lunch with fried chicken from the Colonel's and a bottle of Chablis. But before lunch, I'm going to fly my kite. I'm excited, really excited. My little box kite is a thing of beauty. I've built it myself and I love it. It's orange and green, and it's small. It will look tiny when the wind carries it up. I put down my lunch and my bottle of cold wine, and I place my kite on the very top of the knoll. I wet my finger and test the wind. It's blowing from the south, not too strong, just perfect kite weather. I let out several yards of string. I'm ready. Here goes! I am running down the hill, looking backwards. There she goes. My little kite is off the ground. It is rising rapidly, up, up, above the trees, up against the sky. Go, little kite! Wow! Look at it go! There has never been a kite that has gone up so fast. Higher!

Higher! Higher! Look, everybody! There it is, my little orange and green kite. I pull the string and I move it to the right and left. My little kite dances. It spins, showing its green and orange. I kick off my shoes and feel the short, cool grass under my feet, and I dance along with my kite. I'm soaring too, right up there with my little kite. Go, little kite, go!"

This one is by a thirty-four-year-old bank auditor, married, mother of two:

"I am now walking out into my backyard. Jim and the kids have gone to a matinee movie. It's a hot day and my clothes are sticking to me. I'm by myself, free to do what I choose. I look out at the lawn. It is green and inviting. I turn on the hose with the sprinkler attachment. The water shoots up in the air. It looks cool and it sparkles in the sun. I unzip my dress, slip it down and fold it over the back of the patio chair. I unhook my bra and slip the straps off my shoulders. The sun is warm on my skin. I know the neighbors can't see me unless they climb up on the fence or peek through the cracks and if they want to go to all that trouble, well, I couldn't care less. I pull down my bikini panties, let them fall around my ankles, and step out of them. I'm naked, with nothing touching my skin except sun and air. It feels great! I run out on the lawn into the water of the sprinkler. I catch my breath when the first drop hits my skin. It's cool, but it feels good. I feel the sticky heat leaving my body. I tingle all over. I jump back and forth over the sprinkler, feeling the water spraying up over my body. I feel like a ballerina, a gymnast. The feeling of freedom is fantastic. I'm doing cartwheels through the spray. And I'm singing, singing out loud. I'm a wood nymph. A sprite. A child of nature. I'm free, and I'm going to play in my magic waters all afternoon!"

11 V.I.F. and Sex

For something which should be fun, sex can create a lot of misery. And almost all of the unhappiness and frustration is due to IL-IC-IM jails. Freud attributed almost all of our hang-ups to sex attitudes, although in some cases he had to stretch his notions a bit far to do so. He may have come close to being right.

When I was doing my internship, one of my supervising psychotherapists said, "In doing psychotherapy, you will become terribly bored listening to patients talk about sex." At the time, I attributed his statement to age and a low sex drive. I was sure I would never tire of talking about such a fun activity. But he knew what he was talking about. Even sex, when discussed hour upon endless hour, can become boring.

If repetition alone can result in boredom, discussion of sex will inevitably bore any of us. No area of human existence is more talked about, more written about, and more worried about. For an "unmentionable" topic, it is almost talked to death. Yet I can predict with certainty this year will see published at least one non-fiction best seller dealing with sex, and several best-selling sex novels. There will be "how-to" books, works devoted to overcoming sex problems, sexual fantasy self-help books, and instructional works to help the reader enhance his or her sexual encounters and/or increase the partner's pleasure. There may be a comparable number of books on food, nutrition, diet, and cooking published each year, and this would be understandable. Hunger and sex are both powerful physical drives. But there is a difference. Tragically, sex can form the walls of the most painful of all prisons. The psychotherapist sees more anxiety, frustration, pain, and depression associated with sex than with any other area of human existence. It is, on the other hand, one of the most rewarding experiences in the life of a therapist to see a patient break out of these painful jails. True sexual freedom can be the most exhilarating of all freedoms.

You and I come into the world as sexual beings. The drive is there, ready to motivate you toward intensely pleasurable behavior. If you are normal, you were born with a nervous system, glands, and sexual organs capable of functioning in a way which can provide many of the greatest satisfactions in life. But then, shortly after birth, your jailers pounce on you. They teach you what is proper and improper, acceptable and unacceptable, "normal" and "abnormal," and "moral" and "immoral" in sex. If their teaching is effective, and it usually is, you learn to limit sexual desire and expression to no more than two percent of the available options.

I don't have too many memories of the first five years of my life, but one that stands out involves me and the little boy who lived next door. We went into the garage one day and decided to show one another our penises. We stood face-to-face and took out our respective organs. I don't remember what his looked like, but I do remember the roof fell in when we were caught by his mother. We had committed a sin falling somewhere between an axe murder and arson of a nursery school. (I was apparently a slow learner because not long afterward I got caught by my mother while engaged in similar activity with a little girl.)

As children, we were taught *everything* and *anything* even remotely associated with sex and genitals (our own as well as those of others) was a no-no. I discovered my genitals were capable of giving me very good feelings. But then I was told touching myself there ("playing," is what they called it) was something I must never, never do. For most of us, that lesson was the first in teaching us there are certain parts of our anatomy which are dirty, ugly, nasty, and, just generally, something to be ashamed of.

From there, it was all downhill. I was taught (as you probably were) to show interest in members of my own sex up to my teen years; after that, I was to pursue the other sex. But not *all* members. I learned limits on age, cultural background, color, marital status, education, nationality, height, weight, and the size and shape of various parts of their anatomy. These limits were rigidly enforced. So rigidly enforced, actually, that I never thought of violating them until I started getting rid of the IC's and IM's. Only then could I recognize how utterly stupid many of these limitations really are.

The IC's and IM's can usually be reduced to a "description" of a person with whom I might permissibly engage in sexual activity, and what I might permissibly do with such a person. Sex was to be limited to those of the other sex who were members of my ethnic group, close to my age, with certain physical and mental qualifications—*within the bonds of matrimony*. What I might licitly do with such a person was limited to a very few actions, all at a proper time and place.

I was given IL's about differences between the sexes and IC's and IM's to accompany them ("I can never expect to understand women," "I have to give the woman an orgasm," "Men are more interested in sex than women are"). These IL's formed all my early dating behavior. "Making out" with a girl became not only an IM ("A girl, after all, expects you to make a pass; if you don't, she may wonder if you are 'gay' "). Her responses to my attempts to "make out" or "score" reflected her IC's and IM's.

Did any of these IC's and IM's make any sense? Probably not, but then almost nothing I was taught about sex made much sense. In sex education class, they taught us how the reproductive systems work. (Remember those films of little ping-pong balls going up and down tubes?)

And they taught us all the dreadful things that can happen if we have fun with sex. Thinking back on it, it strikes me as somewhat like teaching a class in baseball covering only information on what injuries you can suffer sliding into third base, and what permanent effects you may incur if hit in the head by a pitched ball.

Free or not (and I certainly wasn't), I did manage to do some things (all forbidden) with members of the other sex. But I felt guilty about doing them. When I was seventeen, I felt more than the usual amount of guilt because a woman I had sex with was in her thirties. If she had been my age, I might have (undoubtedly would have) felt guilty, but not *as* guilty. Sex with older women (so said my IL) was depraved. Older men having sex with older women was even more depraved. In any case, sex between the unmarried was sinful. So was masturbation. In fact, masturbation was not only sinful; it was sick. It was called the "sin of self-abuse." Others said it was neurotic, and it caused you to withdraw into a world of your own (whatever that meant) and become totally selfish. So if I didn't want to be neurotic or selfish, I would find a girl—but then the moralistic jailers told me I would be "taking advantage" of her. I was lucky, I guess. I was never told it would grow hair on the palms of my hands or make me go blind. I went right ahead and masturbated, and quite frequently. But it took me a long time to enjoy it without subsequent guilt feelings.

A decade or more ago, I saw many people of both sexes, but especially women, who worried about masturbation—whether it was normal, whether it was moral, whether it would have dire results. Today, we hear these concerns expressed less frequently. Psychiatrists and psychologists have been unanimous in assuring the public of the "normality" of masturbation. The majority of therapists have recommended it to women patients as an effective means of discovering and enhancing their sexual response. I still hear parents, however, express distress when they discover their innocent little son or daughter engaged in such activity. And husbands or wives may get upset when they find their partner masturbates. Then the old questions are raised: Is this or that normal? Do others do things like that? If he masturbates, does it mean he is no longer attracted to me? If she is sexually satisfied, what reason would she have for doing that? And the ultimate question: What about *me?*

Have you ever had feelings that you had desires absolutely no one else anywhere at any time ever had? Desires which were so awful, so perverted, you would be locked up if anyone ever knew of them? Psychotherapists, family doctors, and clergy are frequently asked, "Can you tell me if this desire I have is perverted?" Almost always, the question is born in a lot of pain and sweaty palms. I think it is sad anyone ever feels the need to ask such a question. What answer can any "authority" give? Often the answer which is given is nothing but a statement of the "authority's" own freedom or lack thereof.

Some years ago, I counseled a woman who was suffering from depression following her divorce. She loved her husband, she said, but she had divorced him even though he had pleaded with her not to. After two or three years of marriage, she explained, her husband had approached her with the desire for oral sex. "The idea of taking his penis in my mouth didn't turn me off," she said. "I even found thinking about it arousing, but I did have doubts about whether or not it was all right. You see, I have pretty strong religious beliefs. My husband used to call me a fanatic. Maybe I am, but that's the way I was raised. I talked to my pastor, and told him what my husband wanted. He told me he was shocked, that that sort of thing is perverted, and that it proved my husband was a homosexual. He said the sooner I got a divorce, the better. I had a hard time believing it, but then I told myself my pastor knows more about these things than I do, so I moved out that very day, even before my husband came home from work."

Her pastor had succeeded in recruiting another inmate for the jail he himself lived in. Did it answer the question of what is "perverted?" Of course not, and it never will. Because what is "perverted" to me may not be to you, and vice versa.

Penthouse magazine and its spin-off publication, *Forum,*

run a lot of letters from readers who apparently feel a need to express their particular sexual preferences. They publish letters from readers who are turned-on by amputees, or by very fat ladies, or men with numerous tatoos, or by spankings, or enemas. Which ideas are *kinky?* Every idea which doesn't arouse me? Then what if nothing arouses me? What if my sexual drive is so low that nothing—animal, vegetable, or mineral—can get me horny? Wouldn't everything and anything sexual be, for me, a perversion? Maybe that's the explanation for the moralists. They may have no sex drive at all, so of course they see anything you and I do with our genitals as kinky and sinful.

Sexologist and psychotherapist Albert Ellis has said a sexual act becomes perverted when, because of one's hang-ups, it becomes the only sexual expression available. It is not a bad definition. If I feel I am free to have sex only with my wife, at night, in our bedroom, with the lights out and the covers over us, and only in the missionary position, then I am living in a sexual jail. What could be more a perversion of my sexual nature? If she feels the same, we're cellmates. Or co-perverts.

Not long ago, a married woman in her thirties told me she felt sure she had no sexual IC's. I suspected she had not taken a long look at the question. "Then you feel you could enjoy sex with another woman without any problems?" I asked. "Now just a minute," she answered with force, "I'm talking about sex with a man." "All right," I said, "what about sex with a man of a different race?" "I'm not sure I could go that far," she replied. "What about sex with a stranger you had just met?" "No," she said, "I think it would have to be a more meaningful relationship." The conversation never got around to what she felt free to do with those males she felt free to have sex with, but I feel sure it would have turned up even more IC's.

I did a short stint as an intern in the psychiatric facility of a military prison. The officer in charge of prison security, the man responsible for seeing that no prisoner escaped, decided that all convicted homosexuals were to serve their sentence in solitary confinement. His only reason was an IL: "Homosexuals are dangerous." (He couldn't say in what way. Apparently they were dangerous only to his ideas of how the sexual drive should be expressed.) One day they brought in two recently convicted prisoners. One had been apprehended while engaged in a sexual act with another man. Both were adults, and it was a mutually consented act. The other had been convicted of molesting a five-year-old girl. The admitted homosexual had been sentenced to serve the longer sentence. And he was to serve it in solitary. I questioned the reasoning. The security officer said, "Well at least the child molester picked a girl to do it with."

Consider the "logic" behind some of the following:

- A girl has sex with one man other than her future husband before she marries. Thus she has had sex with two men. Nothing "perverted" about that, you say? What if she had sex with the two men in turn the same evening, with both men present at all times?
- A male college student has a picture of a nude "pinup" on the wall of his dorm room? Kinky? What if the model is his sister?
- The leading candidate for President of the United States admits he has "lusted in his heart" after women other than his wife. The statement is "shocking" to some Fundamentalist ministers.
- The publisher of a magazine which features photographs of nude women is sentenced to jail for obscenity. Published photographs of murder victims are seldom "obscene" in the view of the jurists.
- A woman who would think nothing of sunbathing in her yard in a bikini would never dream of answering the doorbell in her slip.
- If I am not sexually turned-on by women, why would I marry one? If my wife is not sexually turned-on by men, what healthy, free reason would she have for

> marrying me? But once we each said, "I do," we were to lose all desires for anyone else? By what magical IL is that supposed to occur?

What would it mean to be free of the sexual jail cells? The answer, when you give it some serious thought, is both simple and mind-blowing. If you were sexually free, you would be able to enjoy sex in all expressions which you *might* find attractive. This could never, of course, include acts which might violate the rights of others since, as I said previously, we are never *free* to violate the rights of others (including any exploitation of another, even if "legitimized" through marriage). Throughout history, sex has been the subject of totally irrational and tyrannical laws which have been enforced with unspeakable cruelty. Many are still codified. Sexuality is an area of your life which you must, therefore, approach with recognition of these legal prohibitions and the voice of your conscience.

Myra, an attractive, cultured woman in her thirties, told me this story:

"I could never have imagined the number of IC's I had where sex was concerned until I started using the V.I.F. Now I know why I was never before able to enjoy sex. I very seldom experienced orgasm. There were all those IL-IC-IM's in my head, and even when I wasn't aware of them, they still held me back. Now, they all seem so incredibly stupid I'd like to lead a campaign to liberate all the women in the world. Do you know that before I used the V.I.F. I never could have gone to a porno movie? I couldn't even have read a book like *Fear of Flying*. Then when I decided to try the V.I.F., I wondered if I would turn into some sort of sexual compulsive if it worked, if maybe I would run around doing everything and anything and then living to regret it.

"You had said getting free to do something you thought you couldn't do didn't mean you were then going to have to do it, but I guess I didn't believe it. Freedom *is* just freedom, isn't it? I've done some things, and there are a lot of things I haven't done. But now I feel free to do them *if* I choose to. And *when* I choose to. And with *whom* I choose. I could enjoy so little of my body before. Now I can enjoy all of it. I never realized how many spots on my body were erogenous, and how many sexual things I can do with them —or enjoy having others do to them. And people! Everything I had been taught about sex tied it to a relationship with special meanings and obligations. And it was all so dumb.

"You know, I once met a man on an airplane. We talked continuously for two hours, and I loved every minute of it. He was interesting, with exciting ideas. I thoroughly enjoyed him. But it never occurred to me then that I could enjoy sex with him. We didn't have a *special* relationship. And my IL said that was essential. Crazy, huh? I used to enjoy looking at the girls in *Playboy,* and some of them were a turn-on, but I never admitted it to myself, and I never would have considered the possibility that I could enjoy sex with another woman. It's all so silly now that I think about it. After all, I enjoyed being cuddled by my mother, and when I hadn't seen a girlfriend for a long time we would hug and kiss, and I knew that felt nice. Let's face it! Bodies feel nice, and what feels nice to my body is sensual, so isn't all sensuality in some way sexual? I like fondling my own breasts. Why shouldn't I enjoy fondling another woman's breasts? Is there anything I wouldn't now do in sex? Yes and no. There are some things which right now—this very moment—don't turn me on. But I might feel different tomorrow—or even by this evening. I'm free to choose what appeals to me at the time. Some possibilities in sex don't sound appealing to me, but I don't feel I have any IC's which prevent me from trying them, and who knows, I might be pleasantly surprised."

The IC's are almost endless. They start even before you *do* anything. You were told you were not even to *think* certain things. Jimmy Carter confessed to lusting after women other than his wife as if it were a crime. Obviously he has an IL which says, "The desire for sex with a woman other than your wife is a sin,'' since he said he knew God had forgiven him for his ''lusting.'' But if you are free of that jail, of course you have desires for sex with persons who turn you on.

I have lived with the same woman for twenty-six years. During those twenty-six years, I think I have come to know her tastes and preferences rather well, just as she has come to know mine. If she fantasizes sex with someone else, does that mean she has rejected me? Not unless she has other reasons for rejecting me (and if she does reject me, isn't that simply an expression of her freedom?). Her fantasy may represent a recollection or the excitement and curiosity of the unknown, but should it matter? If she is free, she not only *can* have sexual fantasies, she will. So will I. We will most probably share our sexual fantasies and desires with one another, just as we do with our other daydreams and wishes.

Daydreaming is a right-hemisphere activity. In no area of human activity is it more essential to satisfaction than in sex. In sex, what one cannot fantasize, one cannot enjoy —or find arousing. Most of us were taught to view sexual (''impure'') thoughts as wrong. But if the thoughts are wrong, then sex is wrong since without the thoughts (*i.e.*, fantasies) any sexual response will be initiated by nothing more than a hormonal ''buildup,'' with no mental functioning involved.

It has been said that the brain is the primary sex organ. I am sure the reader will find this an obvious point. But the puritans would have us turn off our brains (or at least the right hemispheres of our brains which open our personal worlds to fantasies and desires). They would have us believe the thought is always father to the deed, that if I ''fall in love'' with an expensive Italian sports car, I will acquire one even if I have to steal it. Or in other words, that I have no conscious choices; I will always act out my fantasies. What absolute and utter nonsense. Some fantasies may stay fantasies out of choice. I might, for example, enjoy the fantasy of having sex on the beach of a South Pacific atoll, but remembering the sharp coral on such beaches I may choose not to act it out. If I am free, however, the choice will be mine. It will not be dictated by IL-IC-IM's given me by others.

No one owns your body or your genitals, and you don't own anyone else's. Your body is yours to do with as you choose, so long as you do not violate the rights of others. Can you give another person the "right" to exclusive use of your genitals? Sure, but only if you make them your jailer. Our sexual mores are almost all directed toward imprisonment. Monogamy is a prime example. More marriages may be destroyed by the prison of monogamy than by any other single thing. The society you and I were raised in has IC's and IM's which say, "You are not to do anything sexually with anyone until you marry, and from that day on you are permitted to engage in sex [within certain limits] only with your spouse, the one who has exclusive claim on your genitals." And what reasoning is there to support this? Some have argued that sexual exclusivity is "natural," and by implication that desires for sexual enjoyment with any persons other than one's mate for life is somehow "unnatural." In arguing this view once, a college professor cited several species of animals which mate for life. "This is also the nature of man," he said. I mentioned several species which do not mate for life, and that their number is greater than those who practice exclusivity. "But you can't compare man's nature with that of the lower animals," was his reply.

Others argue that since the family is the basic unit of society, monogamy is essential. The argument confuses monogamy and marriage. It makes them synonymous, and they are not. Marriage is a social contract, and as such has nothing to do with sexual desires. There is nothing in the social contract of marriage which demands that it be monogamous, and in other cultures it has not been. But the IL which ties marriage and monogamy together is so well taught, most men and women seem certain marriage could not possibly continue unless monogamous. This view, is, of course, supported by law in many jurisdictions. Until recently, adultery was the only acceptable grounds in a divorce action in New York.

What would happen if marriages were not tied to monogamy? That would depend entirely on whether men and women were free of the IL which presently supports the monogamy clause in the contract. If I view marriage as a contract of mutual ownership, then my spouse is my property. Her body belongs to me, and she is to use it only as I see fit. But to openly proclaim my rights of "ownership" of her might be waving a red flag. She might even tell me to go to hell and walk out. My liberal friends would be outraged by my antediluvian attitudes. So instead, I may choose to join those who demand compliance to the contractual obligation of monogamy by making sex a proof of loving: "You promised to love me, and you say you do. You desire sex only with the one you love, and you can love only one person at a time. Therefore, if you desire sex with someone else, you no longer love me, and you have broken your pledge." By turning sexual relations into "lovemaking" and making proof of love sexual exclusivity (perhaps based on the myth that for every boy there is but one girl), husbands and wives can imprison one another.

The obligation of sexual exclusivity is strongly supported by religious laws and traditions. Religion has, of course, provided a rationale (divine commands) for the mores (practical in continuing the political establishment) of the society. Marriage (and sexual exclusivity, which was a part of the institution) was a socially practical contract. It insured rights of inheritance and legitimacy. In a day in which women were almost universally dependent upon men for support and protection, marriage was the only security for a woman. For a man, it was an assurance of sexual union with a woman for breeding who would bear him children (who were, in an agrarian society, a financial asset). In making marriage a sacrament—holy, blessed by God, and binding until death—the church "raised" marriage above the strictly human, self-interest level. The laity, convinced as they were that the clergy spoke for the deity, had yet another set of IC's and IM's to follow.

But assume for a moment you are married to someone who is sexually "faithful" to you not out of choice, but out of religious command. What does that do to your self-esteem? If the woman to whom I am married engages in sex with me, eats dinner with me, vacations with me, or even shares a glass of wine with me out of obligation rather than choice, my self-esteem will be lowered. And so will hers.

I hope you understand I am not arguing for sleeping around, having affairs, "swinging," or whatever you wish to call it. I am not suggesting anyone *should* do anything. I am not saying you should have sex with anyone or with no one. I am trying only to persuade you to choose freedom. To escape the IC, "I can't have sex with anyone other than my spouse," only to acquire the IM, "I have to go out and have sex with others," lands you right back in jail.

Once you have used the V.I.F. to challenge your sexual IC's you discover two outcomes: First, many additional sexual IC's drop like leaves along with the one you are challenging. And second, you realize how utterly irrational they were. I recently had a woman tell me she didn't feel she was sexually inhibited and she enjoyed sex but she could never bring herself to talk about it with anyone. I asked her if she felt free to talk with a friend about a play she might have recently enjoyed. "Sure," she said, "as a matter of fact, my husband and I just last night were telling these friends of ours how much we enjoyed a movie we saw last weekend." "Why did you tell them about it?" I asked. "We wanted to share it with them. I just knew they would love the movie too," was her answer. "Then if you experienced something new and delightful in sex, why wouldn't you be just as eager to share that?" She paused for what seemed two or three minutes before answering: "It's just not the same."

It isn't the same—but only because of the IL, "Sex is never discussed." The "Sex is a private affair" jail makes no more sense than any other jail. If you find sex thoroughly enjoyable, and you are free, why wouldn't you talk about it? For that matter, if your friends are also free, would any of you be reluctant to enjoy sex in one another's presence? The answer is obvious, isn't it? The IM, "I must have sex only with this one person out of the sight of all others," is another illogical jail cell. Again, that doesn't mean you *have* to do it. It means you should be able to if you want to.

I have dropped this rhetorical question into lectures and the reaction is always the same: shock, revulsion, outrage. To most people, the mental image of sex in the presence of others is "unthinkable." And this is why I raise the question. To challenge my audience to think. Especially to think the "unthinkable." Sex as a social activity can neither be supported nor condemned by rational argument. It strikes me as a bit like eating iguana. The iguana, a large, dragon-like lizard common to Central America, is a delicacy to the natives. It tastes a little like chicken. Few tourists from Omaha, however, could be persuaded to sample it. The very thought of biting into a leg of roast lizard would be enough to upset most Anglo appetites. Yet there is no *logical* reason. *Permitting oneself to think the "unthinkable" in all areas is essential to freedom.* Once free, we can then make our choices on the basis of "I wants." Nothing more.

SEXUAL TAPES

Although in most areas in which the V.I.F. may be used, it is not essential that the first and second images be tied together, it is important in any tapes made to gain freedom in sex that the first image as well as the second narrate sexual achievement. Fortunately, since we have all had some positive sexual experiences, finding a workable first image is seldom hard. Like all first images, it must, of course, include the elements of control of your own life choices and power.

What is meant by achievement and power in a sexual

first or second image is usually somewhat different from what the words mean when used in other areas. As with the second image on any physical tape, the achievement is one of control of one's psychophysical responses. It is never an achievement over someone else. The "achievement" of a sexual "conquest" is not, in other words, what I am talking about.

When I have told seminar participants we have all had some positive sexual experiences, I have occasionally been challenged by a group member who denies ever having experienced anything positive in sex. Generally, this is a problem of definitions: What do we mean by a "positive sexual experience?" It is any sexual experience which resulted in good physical feelings. I could be alone or with someone else, orgasmic or non-orgasmic, resulting from spontaneous or induced arousal. The point is that sometime in the life of each of us, even the most sexually troubled and inhibited, we have experienced good feelings of sexual arousal and/or satisfaction. That can be sufficient for a workable first image. Of course, the more arousing and satisfying the experience, the better. A woman in her mid-thirties, married fourteen years, who had experienced difficulty in sexual arousal with her husband, and even greater difficulty reaching orgasm when they had sex, drew upon a high school experience for the following:

> "I am now parked in Donald's car out on the point near the lake. It's a beautiful night, warm but not too warm. Tonight was so much fun. We danced to Les Brown's band, and Don was so wonderful. He listened to me all evening. Even when his friends showed up he didn't want to join them; he wanted to be just with me. He has fallen in love with me. I don't know exactly what I feel toward him, but I love the feeling of being loved by him. It makes me feel warm all through. And it makes me feel like a woman. Now Don has his arms around me and is kissing me. He runs the tip of his tongue around my lips, slowly, and for a long time. I

want to say, "Damn you! You're playing games with me. You know what I want." But I don't say anything. He slips his tongue into my mouth. The sensations are fantastic. I feel shivers all through me. It feels warm and full between my legs. He is pushing his tongue in and out. My breathing and my heart are both going faster and faster. The feelings are scary but good. Don is rubbing his hand over the outside of my blouse, stroking my breast. I want to say, "Please! Do it to the other one too." But I don't. He is slipping his hand inside my blouse. He may pull the button off, but I don't care. There, he has unbuttoned it, just the one button. He is moving his hand down inside my bra. Damn! It's tight, and he's taking so long. I want his fingers on my nipple. Now he's touching it, moving his fingers over it. God! it feels so good. I'm breathing fast, and I can feel the blood pulsing in my neck. It's so warm. I wish I had all my clothes off, and I want Don to touch me all over. But I don't say anything, of course. I am leaning my head back against the seat, with my eyes shut, enjoying the feelings he is giving me. I know my panties must be soaking wet. Is he going to try to put his hand there? I don't want him to stop. If he stops, I'll die—or scream—or something. I want to go all the way, but I don't want to, I don't want the feelings to stop. Don has unbuttoned my blouse the rest of the way down. He is trying to unsnap my bra but it hooks in back and he can't get it. I don't feel comfortable helping him. Maybe if I lean out, he can get it. There it is. He has it unsnapped. He pushes up the cup on my right breast and runs his hand over my breast. It feels so good, so very, very, good. Now! He's going to! He's going to! He is putting his face down to it, taking my nipple in his mouth. He is moving his tongue back and forth, faster and faster. Now in little circles. I hear a moaning sound, and it takes me a few seconds to realize it is me. I wonder if you can faint from this kind of pleasure. Don is pressing against me. I can feel his hardness against my leg. He is moving his other hand up under my skirt. I put my hand on his to stop him, but I don't. He rubs me through my panties. I hope he isn't turned off by my wetness. God! It feels so good. My legs are shaking. Don is still sucking on my breast. He tries to pull my panties aside but they are too tight, and I don't know if I want his finger inside me. I do, but I don't. It feels so full down there. I feel like I'm shaking all over. It's happening! I can't stop it. My eyes are shut tight. I don't want to scream. It's happening! There it is! That's it! Oh God! Don't stop now, Don, don't stop. Oh! It's going on. And on! And on! Does Don know? Can he tell? It actually happened. I place my hand over his. I want him to stop now. I can't take any more. It happened! It really did! And it was good. It was wonderful.

My first climax with a man. My whole body feels marvelous. I can feel my skin glow all over. My first climax with a man. It happened! I did it! I have a feeling of complete power! I let go! I felt confident. I wanted it to happen, and it did. I can do anything—absolutely anything!"

This first image meets the important essentials of power and responsibility for one's own response. Her orgasm, she recognizes, is not something he *gives* her or "makes her experience." It is something totally within her control, whether the response is triggered during masturbation or a sexual encounter with another. Such *self*-reliance underlies every effective sexual description you create. Any feelings of dependence exacerbate any and all sexual problems. The major sexual problems are, in fact, a direct result of such feelings. This is one reason why the V.I.F., designed as it is to overcome any inadequacy feelings, is so effective in overcoming such problems. The other reason is that sexual problems are "thinking" problems. As a number of sexologists have said, "The most important sexual organ is the brain."

THE SEX DRIVE

Anyone who has ever enjoyed a sexual experience would like to repeat it—frequently. Those who say, "Sex isn't all that important; I can take it or leave it," have never enjoyed a fulfilling sexual experience, and I would challenge them to try to convince me otherwise. Sexually fulfilling experiences begin with sexual arousal and the day-to-day level of the individual's sex drive. The ability to be highly and frequently aroused is desired by all of us, but most of us have a collection of IC's generated by an equal number of IL's which reduce both desire and performance. Following are the most widely held:

- Women have a lower sex drive, and are slower to respond, than men.
- Sexual performance ability reaches its peak in early adulthood and gradually declines thereafter.
- Sexual arousal, being a response to a person and environment, is dependent upon that person(s) and the "right" environment.
- Sexual arousal in women is dependent upon an emotional involvement with the man.
- Sexual arousal and performance cannot be "turned on" or "turned off" at will.

Men and women are equally susceptible to these IL's. Most men over the age of thirty (!), married over a year, have fallen into a sexual performance schedule. It may be daily, three times a week, or twice a month. Sex authorities reassure us we are all within "the normal range," and that we don't have any cause for concern that we may not be up to par—"people just differ, that's all." But what if you would like to be turned on more frequently? Is there any truth in the notion that John Doe is just naturally a once-a-week man while Richard Roe is a once-a-day man? Experience with the V.I.F. says no. A man with the IL, "I desire sex only twice a week," can do a second image of desiring sex and performing satisfactorily once a day—or even more often. Here is the successful second image of a thirty-eight-year-old man who increased his sexual performance from less than twice a week to once a day:

> "I am now standing in the shower letting the warm water pepper my skin. Sandy is waiting for me, lying on the bed, probably on her tummy. Sex was fantastic this morning. I woke up horny as hell, not just an erection that's lost when you go the bathroom, but a desire that ran all the way through me. I wanted to touch Sandy, to pleasure her, to make it, to ball like we haven't been together for a month. She felt so damn good; her skin, her lips, her breasts with her nipples sticking straight out. I moved over beside her and pressed my body against hers. She was so warm and soft. And I started pleasuring her. I played with her breasts, and I kissed her a long time. I was hard right from the start, really hard. It couldn't have been more than seven or eight hours since we had done it, but there I was, ready again. And Sandy loved it. She always loves it when I'm hard and ready, and lately it seems like that's most of the time. I've become a sexual superman, and Sandy is crazy about it. The water on my body and my thoughts of Sandy in there waiting for me are turning me on. I'm ready for another great session."

Frequency is, of course, only one measure of sex drive—and probably the least important. Qualitative measures (if any existed) would be more indicative of where the individual stood in terms of sexual interest than any count of frequency. As we all know, the individual may have sex—even very frequently—for reasons other than satisfaction of sex drive (*e.g.*, ego needs, desire to prove "manliness," desire to please a partner). One may, however, have a desire to increase sexual performance purely and simply because the sex act (or acts) is very pleasurable. And for this, a second image similar to the above can be highly effective.

THE FEMALE RESPONSE

I feel the first point I should emphasize is that the female sexual response and the male sexual response differ more as a result of IL's than anything in the physical makeup of the sexes. So in employing a second image to overcome a lack of response (either in arousal or in attaining orgasm) or in enhancing her response, a woman should keep constantly in mind the inherent "naturalness" of her sexuality. No woman is born non-orgasmic. Nor is she made that way by any emotional "trauma" or by a callous or insensitive lover. She is unresponsive because she lives in an IL-IC-IM jail of her own. With the help of her tapes, she can get out of it.

The key to sexual response in a woman (and in a man also, for that matter) is a total absence of reliance upon another. The sexually turned-on woman is her own woman. She doesn't need a man or woman or parent or anyone to do or say anything in order for her to enjoy arousal and/or orgasm. She is the original "I'll do my own thing" woman. The second image of a woman seeking to increase her response will, therefore, always have a strong element of this independence and "arrogance." She takes total responsibility for her life—not just in sex; in all areas of her existence. She knows (perhaps first in a second image, then later through experience) she can become aroused when and how she chooses, and that her orgasm is hers, it is not something she has (or fakes) to please her lover. Following is the second image of a woman who, prior to using the V.I.F., was rarely orgasmic in sexual intercourse:

> "And I am now rubbing my body with lotion, caring for my skin, making it feel smooth and alive. I like my body. I like touching it, looking at it in the mirror, feeling the air on it. It is sexual skin, the skin of a real

woman. My whole body has become one great big erogenous zone. Every pore of my skin is sexual. It glows with sex. It radiates sex. As I massage my breasts and tummy with lotion, I feel myself turning on. It is getting warm between my thighs, filling with beautiful, erotic, powerful, responses. It spreads. My whole body is becoming one gigantic, erotic organism. I am more than sexual; I *am* sex! And the power is terrific! I don't need anyone to do anything *to* me or *for* me in order to turn on. I can sit in a restaurant, or lie in bed watching television, or spread lotion on myself as I am now, and become intensely aroused. From there, it is just a short step to orgasm—a very short step. And the control is all mine. If I want it, I can have it. When I am in bed with Phil, I don't have to concern myself with what he does for me. What the hell! If he doesn't do something —or anything!—which turns me on, so what? I can do it all myself! And I don't have to lie in bed worrying about whether I am pleasuring him, or whether I have to convince him he is pleasuring me. I can shut my eyes and be anywhere, doing anything, with anyone. It is strictly my body—and I love it. I have the power to make it respond the way I want it to. And I enjoy knowing it is a thoroughly sexual body. I am rubbing the lotion into my breasts with one hand. With the other, I am moving my fingers between my thighs. I feel a feeling of power as I squeeze my thighs together around my fingers. Maybe I'll masturbate. Maybe I won't. The choice is all mine. And I can enjoy the feelings as much and as long and as frequently as I want to."

This second image illustrates an important fact of human sexuality: sexual response, in either sex, is one of the more *self*-centered behavioral responses. It is a *psycho*-physiological response. In eliciting the response, we draw upon our personal fantasies, associations, and learned desires. No matter what a partner may do to us or for us in sex, unless his actions are compatible with the desires we bring to the encounter, we will not sexually respond. Eliminate this essential *self*-interest, approach sex as a self-sacrificing act motivated solely by obligation or the desire to please one's partner, and satisfaction will be lost. Most of us enjoy sexually pleasuring our partner, but we do not diminish our own sexual pleasure in doing so: we increase it. And we do not, hopefully, make of sex anything but an encounter freely entered into by both equal partners, each making individual choices.

There is a further important point to keep in mind in any sexual written description or tape: Sexual responsiveness is dependent upon the goal which is sought. It must be sexual satisfaction for the sake of sexual satisfaction. This might, at first, seem obvious, but most of us have been taught to approach sex for reasons having nothing to do with the physical—sexual—satisfaction of the acts. It may be the desire to be loved, to be made to feel secure, to feel desired, to reduce emotional distance, to "prove" one's masculinity or femininity, to manipulate, or even to fulfill an obligation. Any one of these motivations creates a set of IL-IC-IM's which destroys the ability to fully respond and enjoy. In this respect, it is similar to the motivations one might on occasion have for eating a meal. If I sit down to a dinner not because I am hungry but because I don't want to disappoint my hostess or because my doctor has ordered it or simply because I have an IM, "You have to eat," chances are I will find little satisfaction in the meal. To seek sex with another person out of feelings of obligation or one's ego needs is destructive not only of sexual satisfaction, but also of self-esteem. It is one of the most damaging self put-downs.

THE MALE RESPONSE

Men have a hard time keeping ego and sex in proper perspective. We have all been given a lot of IL's which make sexual performance a proof of manhood (perhaps the most important proof), and "manhood" the sole measure of self-worth. It is enough to create severe anxiety in the adolescent, and depression in the middle-aged male. Men worry about their ability to get an erection, keep an erection, delay ejaculation, and satisfy a woman, to a point where sex becomes a fearful challenge rather than a fun-filled activity.

The majority of men hold an IL, "An erection is something over which I have little control—it just happens" (or fails to happen). The word "impotent," of course, means "powerless," so when we speak of a man being sexually impotent, we are implying that he is powerless to achieve and maintain an erection. Fortunately, this IL, like all IL's, is a myth. In no area of human existence can we find a clearer example of the power of our belief systems: "*If you believe you can, you can; if you believe you can't, you can't.*" Many sexologists and "marriage and family counselors" have added their weight to this IL with such statements as, "An occasional failure [to maintain erection] happens to every man." The statement, first of all, is untrue. Not every man has encountered difficulty maintaining an erection. But even if the statement is true of 99.99 percent of the adult male population, does that establish its "normality" or "inevitability"? Penile erection is triggered through the autonomic nervous system—that same system involved in our "emotional" responses. Therefore, when a man is confronted with something or someone sexually stimulating, the self-sentences pop into consciousness and the mechanism starts to work. If he has negative self-sentences which give rise to fear or anger, they may "short-circuit" arousal and prevent erection (or cause it to be lost). Fortunately, no problem is better suited to the employment of the V.I.F. Of the various "therapies" currently employed in treating problems of sexual potency, I believe none is superior in effectiveness to the V.I.F.

Many men, while not troubled by what could be clinically described as impotence, take a longer time and lengthier stimulation to attain a firm erection than they or their partners might wish. Many find they partially lose the erection during a long session of sex activity. The man who composed the following second image had frequently found himself in this frustrating situation. He said, "The tape worked like some sort of magic, in just one day. Now I play it every day, especially when the occasion calls for it."

> "I am now unbuttoning my shirt. I pull it out of my waist and I unhook my belt. When I unzip my trousers, my erection virtually leaps out. I am hard as an iron bar. It sticks straight up. Firm. Proud. Almost defiantly arrogant. Clair won't have to stroke it or suck on it for a long time to get it up. I get erect as soon as I start thinking sexy thoughts. And I can do long, slow, turn-on things to Clair without it ever going the least bit soft. All the time I am holding her, caressing her, kissing her, going down on her, I stay totally firm and erect. And when I put it in, I can go on as long as both of us want to without the firmness going down at all. I also have incredible staying power. Whatever the position, I have complete and total control of my climax. It never happens unexpectedly or when we are not both ready. I control my penis every bit as much as I control my arm. And I can feel a surge of power go all through my body."

You will note he included control of ejaculation in his second image. So-called "premature ejaculation" is the other most common male problem. Actually, what consitutes "premature" is not easy to say, as Dr. William Masters has pointed out. If it means ejaculation prior to the time the woman is ready for orgasm, then what if she rarely or never climaxes? Practically speaking, however, many men, because of anxiety triggered by negative IL-IC-IM's, "come" much sooner than they would like to—and, of course, sooner than their partner might like. The psychological factors are usually identical with those operating in impotence reactions, so the tapes work just as effectively —which, in these cases, is often like "some sort of magic."

Sally and Matt had been married six years when they told us their story at one of our seminars. Sally was the first to speak.

"I think Matt and I came from the worst possible backgrounds when it comes to sex," she said. "I was raised by parents who were right out of the nineteenth century. I grew up on a farm in southern Illinois, the youngest of five kids. I was the only girl. My mother was the traditional farm wife—with a capital 'T.' She cooked, she sewed, she went to church, and that was it. I guess she loved my father in her own way, and in his, but I don't remember ever seeing any affection between them. And certainly no passion. They sent me to a Catholic school for twelve years. It was co-ed, but that didn't make any difference. I only went out with one boy all through high school. That was to my prom. We double-dated with these other two kids in the class which, come to think of it, was all right with me. He was a short, fat kid who lived on a farm about a mile away from ours. He used to sweat a lot. Anyway, I went to a Catholic girls' college for two years before I met Matt. He was a senior at Notre Dame at the time, and his sister roomed next door to me. Would you believe that when I met Matt I had only kissed one boy in my life! I won't say I knew nothing about sex at that time. I had read enough to know the 'facts of life.' But I didn't give sex much thought. It was just something that went along with marriage. I don't remember ever masturbating, and I'm sure if I ever had I would have remembered it: I would have died with guilt feelings. So you can guess what happened on our honeymoon. It was a big nothing for both of us. Matt was no more experienced than I was."

Matt interrupted. "I was a virgin when we married. Up until a few months ago I would have said it was because I believed sex before marriage was a sin, but I now believe the real reason was that girls intimidated me. I'd listen to the guys talk about making out with girls, but I didn't know how to even start, so I never tried. I guess I felt safe with Sally. But then on our honeymoon, I found out just how much I didn't know. Our wedding night I got over-anxious and came before I ever entered Sally. And then the next night, Sally said it hurt when I tried. She cried, and I guess I wasn't very understanding and, well, we don't have to go into all the gruesome details. After we had been married about two years Sally told me she had never climaxed. I had never asked her. As a matter of fact, I was so dumb about sex, I had never tried to find out. After she told me, I went through a period of feeling hurt and rejected and angry. Then I got a couple of books—you know the kind—but they didn't seem to help much. I'd suggest we try something from one of the books, and Sally would turn it down. She didn't go in for trying new things too much at that time, and she still wasn't reaching a climax. Before we started using the V.I.F., I was about ready to give up on sex altogether—and I think Sally felt the same way."

"I was really scared," said Sally. "I saw my whole marriage falling apart. A friend told me about the V.I.F. I thought the whole thing was pretty far out. At first, I didn't think of trying it out as far as my sex life was concerned, but then one afternoon, I guess I must have figured anything, no matter how kooky it sounded, was worth a try. That's when I called you. You gave me some ideas on writing a second image, and I tried it that afternoon. I have to admit the first time I listened to a tape of my voice describing that kind of things, and especially describing myself enjoying them, I almost came apart. But I'm proud of myself. I stuck to it. I played my tape, and you wouldn't believe what happened." She paused momentarily. "Of course you know what happened. I'm sure you've heard this story before. Anyway, my tape worked!"

"I knew Sally was using the tapes," said Matt, "but she didn't say anything about them, and I didn't ask, until she started to cry one night after we had sex. I started to apologize and I was feeling guilty until she told me she was crying because she felt so happy. I thought, 'My God, this is a miracle!' Sally then told me about the V.I.F. It's funny, but I didn't think about using the tapes to get rid of my sex hang-ups for another couple of weeks. I guess I probably thought Sally's problems were the cause of my problems; that if she got her head straight, I would have no problems. But of course I was wrong. To make a long story short, I made some tapes of my own, and it has turned my whole life around. I've never been happier. I don't even have any regrets for what we have gone through the last six years. It's too much fun thinking about the years ahead. I even have a tape recorder at work and one in my car. A couple of months ago, we went to Hawaii. It was a solid week of the greatest sex you could ever describe."

Sally interrupted. "It was the honeymoon we never had. But you want to know something funny? Matt had made a tape on getting the money for us to make the trip, and sure enough, he won a regional sales contest: a trip for two to Hawaii!"

12 Marital Manacles

The institution of marriage is society's most acceptable jail. The IL "I am married" (or expressed as a joint IL, "We are married") can, and does, support IC's and IM's which allow virtually no freedom whatsoever. It doesn't have to, of course, but so long as men and women accept what society has told them about marriage, it will.

It is really incredible, when you stop to think of it. Otherwise rational adults enter a relationship expecting to give up all freedom. They know marriage will mean prison long before they decide to take the step. Didn't friends greet the announced marriage with, "So you've finally decided to give up your freedom?"

I have asked a number of men and women to list the freedoms they expected to relinquish when they married. They were prepared to give up most—if not all—of the following freedoms:

Freedom to have friends of the other sex.
Freedom to go where I want.
Freedom to quit my job.
Freedom to take the job I might like.
Freedom to choose my friends.
Freedom to handle my own money.
Freedom to go to bed when I want to.
Freedom to choose my clothes.
Freedom to say what I think.

There were others—many others. A husband told of how he had received a job offer by mail. His wife opened the letter, answered declining the offer, signing his name, before telling him anything about it. "She felt that was as much her right as it was mine," he said. He didn't protest.

Marriage as an institution restricting freedom is so widely accepted, it has become virtually heretical to suggest alternatives. Nena and George O'Neill created a shock wave of indignation with the publication of *Open Marriage* (New York: *M. Evans and Company,* 1972). The O'Neills championed a relationship in which partners exercise free choice. If the wife wants to attend the theater on an evening her husband wants to bowl, neither of them feel they have to alter their plans simply "because husband and wife do everything together." The furor seemed to stem from the outrageous (?) suggestion that husbands and wives can have friends of the other sex apart from their friends "as a couple."

I heard comments about their book long before I had the opportunity to read it. The book was then something of a surprise. I expected to find the authors promoting "swinging" and twice-a-week orgies. They didn't. In fact, they were not promoting anything other than relationships in which freedom is a prime value. They were arguing against marital relationships based upon joint IL-IC-IM's. But the assumption of many men and women seemed to be that free of the contractual obligations of the institution of marriage, husbands and wives would seldom choose to love with, live with, and have fun with their spouse. Yet is that an inevitable consequence of freedom? I think not. Such an assumption would seem similar to assuming that if the Ten Commandments were "repealed" we would all run from our houses to rape, pillage, and murder.

The O'Neills spelled out the conditions of the typical closed marriage contract:

Clause 1: Possession or ownership of the mate. (Both the husband and the wife are in bondage to the other: "You belong to me." Belong *to* someone, please note, is very different from the feeling that you belong *with* someone.)

Clause 2: Denial of self. (One sacrifices one's own self and individual identity to the contract.)

Clause 3: Maintenance of the couple-front. (Like Siamese twins, you must always appear as a couple. The marriage in itself becomes your identity card, as though you wouldn't exist without it.)

Clause 4: Rigid role behavior. (Tasks, behavior and attitudes strictly separated along predetermined lines, according to outdated concepts of "male" and "female.")

Clause 5: Absolute fidelity. (Physically and even psychologically binding, through coercion rather than choice.)

Clause 6: Total exclusivity. (Enforced togetherness will preserve the union.)

I do not believe any man or woman goes into marriage conscious of these conditions (and neither do the O'Neills). People get married for security, sex, social approval, companionship, and love. But the conditions are already there, stored in the unconscious of the two partners. They are taught through the example of their parents and their married friends that marriage is a condition of mutual jailer/inmate, each possessing the other. A "good" marriage, as defined by thc "togetherness" school of matrimony, is one in which all opinions and preferences are stated in the first person plural—"*We* like to go to the opera. *We* don't believe in letting bills go unpaid past the tenth of the month."

A woman in her late thirties told me she could not lose weight. "My husband is overweight too, but every time we go on a diet, he blows it, and then of course I go off the diet when he does." I asked why his choices had to dictate hers. "They don't exactly dictate my choices," she answered, "but aren't a husband and wife supposed to support each other? I can't stay away from food if I'm sitting there watching him stuff himself. Besides, if he goes off the diet and I stick to it, I'll make him feel guilty." In virtually every area of her life, a mutually dependent *we* came through. She said both of them felt "alone" and "distant" when they discovered they differed in tastes and opinions.

One or the other would change opinions in order to maintain "togetherness."

In any personal relationship, the participants each attempt to sell their realities to the other. This is particularly evident in the majority of marriages. The husband says, "This is the way the world is," and he expects (demands) she accept his reality. She attempts to do the same to him. This can be on the most trivial of levels. He may leave a movie theater feeling he has sat through the most poorly produced, poorly acted, miserably directed film he has ever seen. His wife, on the other hand, may have found the movie thoroughly delightful. She will be hurt if he refuses to accept her reality. He may become angry if she does not agree with his perception. Beneath this reaction is the belief, "If you loved [respected, cared for] me, you would accept my reality; if you reject my opinions, you are rejecting me."

The institution of marriage itself can become the identity of each partner. They may retain virtually no identity apart from "We are married," their joint IL. We recently escorted a seminar group to the Hawaiian Islands. Most of the group members were married and were going with their spouses. We suggested they each go as if they were single, making their own individual choices as to how they would like to spend their time and with whom. To say the suggestion was disturbing to some would be a gross understatement. It literally terrified them. "I wouldn't know what to do without my husband," was the reaction of one woman. "But we *are* married," protested another, "and I resent the suggestion that everyone run around loose, as if they have no ties at all." A husband asked if we were serious. We said we were. He then said, "Then what is to prevent them from swapping bed partners?" "Nothing that I know of," I said. "You can be sure we are not going to attempt to interfere in anyone's choice; but tell me, why do you assume this will be the outcome?" He thought for a moment before answering, "I just think if you take the restraints off people, that's the sort of thing they'll do."

Did they? I don't know. Whatever the choices of each of

them, I only hope they were *free choices* rather than IC's and IM's. I am intrigued, however, by his assumption that "given" freedom, husband or wife would not choose to be together. He is further assuming marriage must always be the "closed" marriage described by the O'Neills. And that given half a chance, anyone would escape from the restraints of a "closed" marriage.

The institution of marriage, as I frequently see it acted out, strikes me as a case of an ounce of prevention causing a pound of disease. It seems analogous to saying to a child, "I want you to choose carrots as your favorite food so I forbid you to eat anything else." As a result, the child will probably learn to hate carrots, and plot, at every opportunity, to eat something else. If I also demand the child tell me he "loves" carrots, I can never be sure he does not, in truth, hate the vegetable. We humans have a natural resistance to restraints. When told we must do such-and-such or can't do something or other, we tend to rebel—and to resent the one giving the order.

Resenting the person you are living with because of the IC's and IM's of the institution is, however, neither fair nor sensible. He or she didn't make the rules. But just as the army private hates the restrictions of the army and identifies his lieutenant with the hated military establishment, so the spouse incurs the resentment felt toward the institutional bonds of marriage.

I watched a television melodrama in which a teenage girl admitted she hoped to get pregnant when she had sexual relations with her boyfriend. She succeeded. "I want a baby," she told the social worker. "I want something that will belong to just me alone." The social worker's reply should win a prize for irrational counseling. "That's only natural," she said. Not, I would say, unless a totally egocentric attitude toward others is "natural." Since I do not wish to be anyone's possession, I do not wish to possess anyone. And I cannot have the former without the latter. Clause 1 of the "closed" marriage contract—"You *belong* to me"—defines the relationship in terms of ownership of a human being.

Most of us subscribe to the concept of the individual's "inalienable" rights to freedom. But if marriage means I now have a human being who belongs to me, and to whom I belong, I am championing slavery. The woman I am living with is not *my* woman. She is her own woman. I choose to live with her, and I am happy to say she chooses to live with me. Those choices give us no rights of ownership over each other.

If I do not view my marriage as a contract which gives me the rights of ownership of the woman I love, I recognize her freedom in any and all areas and I give up none of mine. She is free to pursue her own interests and goals. She is free to select her own friends. She is free to express her opinions, and free to disagree with mine. She has a right to time, space, and privacy. She has a right to say "no" to my requests and invitations (and at no time do I, by reason of the "contract," have the right to make any demands upon her other than mutual respect of rights). I have no right to exercise "authority" over her. She is free, as I am, to redefine the relationship at any time in terms of her preferences, and we can each, in turn, accept or reject the other's definition.

Since I do not claim ownership of her, I try not to hand her any set of marital IM's and IC's. If I tell her when she is to make an appointment with her dentist, even if I try to justify it as concern for her, I am attempting to play a parental role. She is an adult. She is capable of making such decisions for herself. Even if I feel she is not acting responsibly in caring for her health, those are still her choices, not mine. I have no right to impose an IM on her nor to control her. I can ask a question to draw her attention to a problem, but I can't dictate the answer. I may smoke too much to please her, but does her role as my wife give her the right to tell me I must quit? I don't think so. If my smoke bothers her, she certainly has the right to suggest we work out compromises as to where and when I smoke, perhaps restricting my smoking to the den. The smoking, in such a case, involves her rights. Marriage, however, gives neither of us the right to set down rules of health for the other. Nor does it give us the right to set the bedtime for the other one, or to nag one's spouse into going to church, reading certain books, taking up a hobby, or enjoying our taste in food.

BUT I NEED YOU

If you don't need anyone (in the literal sense of the word) or fear anyone, they can't put you in a prison. "People who need people" are not "lucky" unless you consider it good fortune to be enslaved. In the world in which we live, however, mutual *need* is considered a perfectly good reason for marriage. Each "need" becomes an IM. Or an IC. Or both.

Barbara and Neil both had promising careers when they married. Neil is creative director of an advertising agency. Barbara is a research biologist. Neil was promoted to his present job the week he married. He had been brought along as a copywriter and then became assistant to a very talented and creative advertising man. When his mentor dropped dead of a coronary during a meeting with a client, Neil got his job. Neil had relied heavily on his former boss for advice and approval. Increasingly, he brought his job home with him, looking to Barbara to give him the support he had gotten from his boss. The fact that Barbara had no experience in advertising did not deter Neil from bringing her every problem and idea he had. After a few months, Barbara had had enough. She told Neil she wanted their respective jobs left at work; she no longer wanted to serve as his consultant. It was a position Neil could not accept. "I just can't understand her. She knows how much I rely on her, and she's supposed to be my wife. How can she let me down like this?"

Neil had his reasons for resenting Barbara—almost inevitable reasons. He had created them. If you are dependent upon someone, no matter who it is, you stand a good chance of resenting them. It occurs with most teenagers. They need their parents, but they want to be independent. So they resent the people who represent their lack of freedom. If you *need* someone, for whatever reasons, you are vulnerable. If they withhold whatever it is you have told yourself you need from them, you are frustrated. But even worse, you cannot escape from them. No matter how many jail cells they put you in, you have to stay with them because of your "need."

In the most mutually rewarding marriages, neither husband nor wife needs the other one. He doesn't need her to prop him up, give him encouragement, take care of him, or cook his breakfast. She doesn't need him to protect her, tell her how desirable she is, fight her battles for her, or balance her checkbook. The one need they do not have which surprises their friends to the point of utter disbelief is they do not have a *need* to be loved.

This lack of need is really what autonomy is all about. If you don't have any of those "I shoulds," "I have tos," and I can'ts," you are free. But you can be free only if you do not need others. This usually takes a lot of positive messages to the unconscious, however, since we get so many messages saying "you can't survive without others to take care of you." The messages first came from our parents, and that was understandable, but later we heard the same messages from those who wanted us to be dependent on them, and those who wanted to be dependent on us. Romantic fiction and love songs are loaded with the dependency message. They portray men and women in love as two drowning victims who are hanging onto one another as they go down for the last time.

SEX ROLE HANDCUFFS

Often these created "needs" in marriage are related to sex-role stereotypes. When I was a kid, a very nice man lived in my neighborhood. He and his wife had one child, a grown son. Every day he would walk by my house on his way to the public library. That impressed me. I couldn't figure what people would do in a library every day if they didn't have a teacher who made them write book reports. This man, I learned, was the scandal of the neighborhood. He didn't earn a living. His wife had a job as office manager of some company and he did the housework and prepared the meals. When I got to know him, I found he was an excellent cook, and he and his wife were as happy a couple as you might ever meet. But he created a scandal because he stayed at home and let his wife go out to earn the living. The ladies of the neighborhood lynched him with gossip. His wife was given their pity (mixed with disdain). For many years they were the only couple I knew who dared to violate the role stereotype IL-IC-IM's of husband and wife.

Today, their choices would not be as unusual, but I think they would still get a heavy dose of disapproval. The role of the wife and the duties of a husband were outlined for Adam and Eve when they were evicted from the Garden. Ever since then the roles have been extended and elaborated upon. At least two-thirds of the activities in the home, work and recreation alike, are at least informally assigned as his or hers. IL's all of them.

A Miami housewife, Marabel Morgan, has achieved best-selling author status and has earned over a million dollars with two books (*Total Woman,* Revell, 1973, and *Total Joy,* Revell, 1976) and a "franchised" course for wives. She has even appeared on the cover of *Time*. Ms. Morgan and Helen Andelin (through the latter's course, Fascinating Womanhood) teach their followers a natural inequality of the sexes (women are the weaker sex; men are their protectors; God ordained women to be submissive to their husbands). Starting with scriptural quotations ("Wives be subject to your husbands, as to the Lord," St. Paul, *Ephesians* 6:21), they manage to turn marriage into a multi-celled prison of IL-IC-IM's. They turn the roles of husband and wife into grotesque caricatures of human beings.

But before we write off Ms. Morgan, Ms. Andelin, and their followers for their nineteenth-century views of men and women, you and I might examine the roles acted out in our own marriages. Try answering the following in terms of whether you see the roles as belonging to the husband or the wife.

- Who pays the monthly bills?
- Who sees to the maintenance of the car?

- Who vacuums the carpeting?
- Who makes the beds?
- Who decides on investments?
- Who disciplines the children?
- Who cooks the meals?
- Who mixes the drinks?
- Who mows the lawn?
- Who repairs a leaky faucet?

I'm sure you get the idea. Most of us were raised to believe there were certain tasks and responsibilities belonging to men and others which were women's. It makes sense, of course, for two people sharing a home to divide the chores and responsibilities. Fair is fair. But dividing chores and responsibilities along male/female lines locks you and your partner into a prison in which the IL is a put-down: *You are inadequate*. It may not be apparent at first glance, but think about it for a minute. If I feel I can't iron a shirt because I am a man, I am vulnerable to the time schedule of a woman. So I must be inadequate. A woman married four years told me of how her anger had increased in almost geometric proportions with each day when her new washing machine had not worked properly. She could have called the service department of the store where she purchased the appliance, but she felt that was her husband's task, and when he didn't get around to it, she was frustrated. I don't need to tell you she had less than the best opinion of herself.

Helen Andelin contends a woman loses her "femininity" if she takes on a man's job. Ms. Andelin, incidentally, defines man's work as almost anything which calls for an ounce of brains or the physical strength of a twelve-year-old (except, of course, housework and motherhood). If she does take on a "man's" job, Ms. Andelin suggests she do the job "as a woman." That is, do the job ineptly. According to Andelin, it will make her man feel superior (*i.e.*, manly). Does that tell you something about *her* husband? If I feel I need to have a woman who acts like a moron in order for me to feel like a man, I'm in trouble. My self-image must be low, low, low. If she plays along with that dumb game, she must be (a) really that incompetent, (b) trying to manipulate me into doing everything for her, or (c) hung-up on an equally low image of herself.

If I open the door for a woman, help her on with her coat, and light her cigarette, those actions are probably just social amenities. If she thinks I am doing them because I believe women can't do such things for themselves, she is slightly crazy. If *she* feels she can't do them for herself, she is even crazier. These social-sexual roles do not imprison either sex—unless they become either IC's or IM's. If she feels she cannot put on her own coat without help (IC) because she is a woman (IL), she is not free. (She may stand there, coat in hand, being frustrated for a long time.) If I feel I have to help her on with her coat (IM) because I am a man (IL), I may find her nothing but an annoyance. The first step, then, is to identify any IC's or IM's in your marriage which are built upon the IL "I am a woman" or the IL "I am a man." Then go through the four steps of the V.I.F. (see pages 60–61). Your unconscious will appreciate it.

IL: IT'S FOR LIFE

Marriage, we are told, is "until death do us part." That's the contract. No matter how you look at it, that contract is a jail.

Suppose I offered to build you the home of your dreams. You could pick the architects of your choice and the location, with cost no object. I agree to have it furnished to your specifications and agree to pay all the taxes, upkeep, and utilities. But with one condition: you have to agree to spend the rest of your life there; you can never live anywhere else. I'm sure you can predict what will happen. No sooner do you move in than you start feeling your mansion is, in fact, a jail. It might be the most comfortable, most lavish jail in the world, but it is, nevertheless, a jail. Regardless of how good your friends and relatives may tell you you have it, you will still experience the frustration of a prisoner.

This is what the "death do us part" commitment is all about. It becomes one great big IC or IM.

I had given a lecture on freedom at a university and was in my hotel room packing to catch a plane when I got a phone call from a man who identified himself as a professor at the university. He told me he had been married twenty-three years. "And for twenty-three years," he said, "I haven't had a single day of real happiness. But I cannot accept your talk about freedom. A commitment is a commitment, and I promised to devote my life to my marriage." I asked him why (which seemed to me a sensible question). "That strikes me as a stupid question," he answered. "Marriage is for life."

That's just what the college professor is doing: serving a life sentence. But why? Because that is what marriage is all about. It is an IL: *Once you marry, you stay married.* I have talked to men and women who have decided to divorce only after years of abuse. Invariably, their friends greeted the news as if it was a tragedy. Divorce, in the logic of the IL, is always a tragedy. A failure.

I recently watched a television talk show interview of a psychotherapist-writer of a best-selling book. I have read the book. He makes a lot of sense. When one of the ladies in the audience asked him if he was married, and if so, had he been married only once, he told her he had been married previously and it had ended in divorce. From that point on, the audience seemed to write off what he had to say. A murmur ran through the studio. "How can he talk about how to have a successful, happy life? He couldn't even make a success of his marriage." If he had told the audience he had just celebrated his fortieth wedding anniversary, he would have been applauded. And for what? Perhaps for being a forty-year masochist.

Marriage can be a step toward growth, but so can divorce. I'm not encouraging casual divorce, but I am urging those who believe divorce is a mortal sin to reconsider. Obviously, in many cases divorce is a far better alternative than staying in a marriage that is not satisfying and in fact may be violently destructive.

There has been a lot written in recent years attempting to answer the question, "Can the institution of marriage survive?" Few of these articles ask what I feel is the more important question: "*Should* it survive?" Should *any* institution which deprives its participants of their freedom be perpetuated? I'll leave those questions to the sociologists and philosophers. (I am leading no campaign to reshape the world.) But if my marriage or yours is to be rewarding, some of the traditional conceptions have to go. This doesn't mean I have to walk out on the woman I'm living with. That would be as much an IM as saying I have to stay with her. It does mean we can each be happy only if we are each free. I don't want to live in a relationship in which love does not exist, and love, being a gift, therefore free, cannot exist under coercion. But what if she doesn't want me to be free, and perhaps does not want freedom for herself? How much do I value freedom—and at what price? As I said earlier, anytime I ask the price, I come up with an answer which will be nothing more than a reflection of my self-image.

Over the years, I have talked with hundreds of husbands and wives imprisoned in frustrating marriages, good human beings who were living their lives in multiple IL-IC-IM's because they were unwilling to pay what they were sure would be the price of escape. The three most commonly perceived "prohibitive" prices are financial burdens, loss of children, and loneliness. Husbands see themselves impoverished by alimony and child support payments; wives see themselves forced to apply for welfare. Fathers, and sometimes mothers, see themselves cut off, for all time, from their children. Both men and women feel sure if they divorce they will be doomed to live out their lives in solitude—no one else will have any interest in them.

The last of these IL's—"No one else will have me"—is a heavy one. It almost always generates the IC's and IM's which make marriage such a miserable trap. If you accept the premise of the IL that no one else would have you, and the further IL "We all need someone," it then follows that you will passively permit your spouse to lead you into a jail cell and throw away the key. You may even have married someone who never turned you on simply because "We all need someone." People with negative self-image IL's live out life jail sentences.

Since we only go through life once, and freedom is the only key to happiness, no price should ever be too high, but since consideration of what we tell ourselves *might* be the price may lead to a reluctance to use the V.I.F., the wisest thing is still to avoid thinking about possible price tags.

Another thing: I have never talked with anyone who found the price tag for freedom was what he or she anticipated. Anne and Jim had been married nine years in a typically "closed" marriage. Anne had worked for only a few months before leaving home to marry and she was sure she could not find a job which would pay enough to support herself if she divorced Jim. Also, they had two children and Anne felt she could not care for the children and hold a job. Although she was attractive, and had a good personality, she saw herself as a divorcée sitting home night after night never with any adult companionship. Anne finally decided, however, to take the plunge toward freedom. It came at a time when she was scheduled to go along with Jim on a business trip to Tokyo. This is how she told it:

"I had been on trips like this with Jim before, and they were always the same. I'd sit in the hotel room waiting for him while he was doing his business, or I would go off on a conducted sightseeing and shopping tour with the other wives. God, it was awful! And during the evenings, I would have to go with Jim to dinners with his business associates and their wives. You should have seen those wives. They were catty and boring. They were just something the men dragged along. And I was no different. But before we left for Japan, I wrote out my images in the V.I.F. and put it on a cassette tape. Jim asked why I was taking the recorder along. I said it might come in handy, and he didn't ask any more about it. I think he always felt the husband should indulge some of the wife's childish whims.

"The evening we arrived, I played the tape while Jim was on the phone. I went into the bathroom to do it. The next morning, Jim went off to a conference. I played my tape twice. Then I decided an earplug extension for the recorder would be handy; I could listen to it without Jim overhearing. And you know what I did? Instead of staying in the hotel like the dependent child-bride, I took a cab to the Ginza and strolled the streets until I found a store that sold tape recorders. Then with a little English, a little Japanese, and a lot of pointing and other sign language, I bought the extension.

"For a moment I thought I should get back to the hotel as quick as I could even though I knew Jim wouldn't be through with his business for at least four hours. Then I figured, "What the hell! I am free, totally free! I don't have to do anything I don't want to do," and I went to a little bar where I had a bottle of Japanese beer and a dish of something—I don't know what it was. A man sitting on the next stool was eating some and it looked good. I then did another thing I had never done before. I talked with a stranger, and in a bar of all places! He was Japanese, of course, and thoroughly charming. He suggested a number of sights I might otherwise have missed.

"I met Jim as I was walking into the hotel lobby. He was just returning from his conference. When I told him where I had been and what I had been doing, he acted like he thought I had gone crazy. Then he told me he didn't want me doing that sort of thing again, that I didn't know what kind of men I might run into, that I could get lost, and so on, and so on. I didn't say anything right then. For a little while I felt like a naughty child. But when we got to the room, I went into the bathroom with my tape recorder and my earplug and I played my tape. When I came out, I told Jim I was going sight-seeing the next day—alone. He got really upset, more than at any time I can remember. He said I was trying to pick a fight, that I was trying to manipulate him into ignoring his business obligations to take me to these places, and that he forbade me to do any such thing. And you know something? I felt completely calm while he was carrying on. I didn't get angry and he didn't scare me. I told him I was sorry he felt as he did but that I didn't own him! I wanted him to be free; and he did not own me.

"Jim had made reservations for dinner and we were just about ready to go out. He started telling me I had some crazy women's lib notions and he wouldn't stand for it, when I said, 'I would like to go to dinner with you but I don't care to argue this point, so if you don't care to change the subject, I'll make my own arrangements.' I think it was then he began to see I was serious. He didn't bring it up for the rest of the evening.

"For the next couple of days, he didn't say much; I could tell, though, he wasn't happy with me while I went about doing my own thing. But I just kept playing my tape and visited every shrine, temple, and back alley in Tokyo. We would have breakfast together and meet back at the hotel at the end of the day. A couple of days later, Jim asked me if I would like to go with him to a dinner-dance the Japanese company he was negotiating with was putting on. I think it was the first time in the nine years we had been married that he *asked* me if I would like to go with him rather than just taking it for granted I would go wherever he decided we would go. When the conference ended, he asked me if I would like to visit Kyoto for a couple of days. We ended up staying there five days and we were like a couple of young lovers. While we were there, Jim asked me about my 'change.' I told him about the V.I.F., and he told me how many IC's and IM's he had about marriage. Before we left Kyoto, he asked me if he could borrow the tape recorder. He bought a tape and made his own recording. He even played it with the earplug on the plane flying home. And he ordered champagne and we had an absolutely glorious time under the blankets flying across the Pacific. And to think, I had once been so sure he would leave me if I ever did anything he disapproved of."

A LIBERATION CONTRACT

An unconditional relationship is bound to end up exploitive and frustrating, yet most couples enter marriage with no clearly understood conditions. It is as if they both say, "You can demand anything of me, and I can demand anything of you. Also, I will tolerate anything you may or may not do, and you are to be equally tolerant of me." It has something vaguely to do with "for better or worse" and "accepting one's mate as he/she is." This seldom verbalized unconditional contract carries a further understanding that each partner can demand the other spouse accept his or her perception of reality.

Despite what others may say, and the IL's of "we-ness," marriage need not be such an unconditional contract. In increasing numbers, couples are drawing up new contracts designed to insure their mutual independence. To work satisfactorily, these agreements include (a) a mutual understanding that the partners do not and cannot live in the same reality—at least not at all times and in all areas; (b) a recognition of the independence of each, that marriage carries with it no rights of possession or control of the spouse, and (c) that each partner may set conditions under which they will agree to live together, and that it is understood that if the other partner rejects the conditions, the marriage will terminate.

For two people with healthy self-esteem, sitting down and talking out such an understanding is actually not difficult at all. Both are able, almost at once, to see the benefits to be found in such individual freedom—and the benefits in a relationship based on free choices.

The results of such new contracts should not be surprising. Free of the stifling IM's of marriage, they frequently make more choices of being together than they previously made under compulsion. The fear that, as one woman put it, "we will end up going our separate ways," hardly makes sense. If I like myself, I will not continue to live with someone I don't like to be with, and I won't have the dependency needs which might tempt me to. That is where the V.I.F. comes in. It can be very effective in creating a new reality in which one develops the self-confidence to say, "I do not need to lean on him/her or possess him/her." With that self-confidence, the stage is set for working out a contract of marital liberation. Following are two examples of second images that helped accomplish that. The first was written by a twenty-seven-year-old woman, mother of one, employed as a computer programmer, married eight years.

"I am now going to the Chalet restaurant to meet Roger for dinner, and I'm feeling tickled to death. I'm even singing to myself. I've asked Roger to dinner. Not if he would *take me* out to dinner. I'm taking him, and I've picked the place. I'm dressed in my sexiest best, and I look the part of the stunning, self-sufficient woman I am. My notes are in my purse. I'm ready for our meeting. It's fun to think of it as a business meeting. Finally, Roger and I are going to sit down as two mature, totally equal adults and discuss what we each want. Roger doesn't know. This time, for the first time, I didn't go through that silly business of saying 'Roger, there is something I must talk to you about' in the way that always says, 'I'm unhappy and it's all your fault, and you must do something about it.' This time, Roger doesn't *have* to do anything. And I don't have to do anything. I can choose to do what I want to do, and I can actually mean it when I say I want Roger to feel free to do what he wants to do. I have written out exactly what I want in a new relationship with Roger, and I feel completely in control of my world. I love Roger. I know that now. But I could fall in love with him all over again only when I got rid of all those resentments and all those feelings of being manipulated and taken advantage of. I love him, but I no longer need him. I am my own person, in control of my own present and my own future—financially, socially, and emotionally. I know I can do whatever I want, accomplish whatever I set out to—all on my own. I don't know how Roger will react to the new me, the independent, totally *free* me. I know what I have to offer, and it's a lot. Roger, my love, we can have a love affair that's really free, a no-strings-attached love affair, and I believe we can have a lot of fun together. But the choice is yours. And mine. And my choice is to be independent, free, and capable. I can fly, Roger! And here I come!"

This one is by a thirty-two-year-old man. A commercial photographer, he is the father of three.

"I am now walking down the steps of the Los Angeles Coliseum. I have flown here for a game between the 49'ers and the Rams—by myself. I asked Leeta if she would like to go. I knew her answer. O.K., if she doesn't like football, that's her right. But I do, and this is my choice. Now that we have agreed to live as two human beings not handcuffed to each other, I can choose to go to a football game without dragging Leeta to something she doesn't like or staying home in order to please her. The game is almost ready to start. My God! The stands are filled. There's my seat. The 49'ers are running on the field. Go get 'em, Baby! This is fun. The first football game I've been to without feeling guilty in I don't know how long. I'm really free of all those feelings of guilt and obligation. I can enjoy going to a football game or wherever else I might like to go without any gut feelings of rottenness because Leeta isn't here. She is doing her thing, and I like that, too. Tonight, when we come together again, we can share the excitement of the days we spent without laying any trips on each other. And that's great. The referee is flipping the coin. In a few minutes the game will be starting. I don't know what Leeta is doing right now, she is her own person, free to do what she wants to do. And right now, this very minute, I am free to choose to be sitting here in the Coliseum waiting for the kickoff."

The relationship of marriage gives special emphasis to the truth that one cannot write a second image for someone else. Yet this is the most common temptation for those attempting to use the V.I.F. to resolve their marital problems. If, for example, I want to vacation in the upper Amazon, and I feel reasonably sure my wife is less than enthusiastic about jungle travel, it might be tempting to make a tape in which she is joyfully packing for our South American adventure, mosquito netting and all. But that would be attempting to write a second image for her. And it most likely would not work.

I can, on the other hand, write a second image on successfully presenting my "I want's" to her, and in which I come away from our talk happy with the outcome—even if it means leaving without her. This is nothing more than a recognition of the fact that I alone am responsible for my own happiness—and that I do not wish to impose my wants on someone else.

I am aware that what I have said in this chapter may disturb—even inflame—some readers. They may interpret it as an argument for mass divorce, swinging, or wholesale denial of any responsibility between spouses. It is none of these. I have lived with the same woman, Lois, my co-author, for over twenty-six years. They have been twenty-six of the most exciting, fulfilling, years I feel it has been any human being's privilege to experience. For me, it has been a love affair. Since Lois is, sensibly, concerned with self-interest (what she calls "rational hedonism"), I assume she has found it equally rewarding; otherwise, she would no longer be with me. I have no interest in an affair, no interest in "swinging," and no desire to divorce. But then, I do not feel we have ever married, at least not in the accepted meaning of the word. I don't want to own her; she doesn't want to own me. Lois was once asked by a member of one of our groups how she accounted for the great relationship we have experienced. Her answer said it better, I feel, than I ever could have: "We have never become 'husband' and 'wife.' I am Lois; he's Joe. And we have had one another on probation for over twenty years."

13 Speak Up, Shut Up

Among other bits of "wisdom" I learned as a child was the following: If you keep your mouth shut, you'll stay out of trouble. Never having learned to keep my opinions to myself, I can attest to the value of the advice—depending on how you define "trouble."

"Trouble," as defined by my elders, meant having others upset when one said something with which they disagreed—especially in one of those "sensitive" areas. "Never discuss religion or politics" (to which they added sex, money, and other touchy subjects) gave a message to my unconscious, although it never occurred to me at the time. It was: "Your opinions are unacceptable to others; keep them to yourself!" From there, it was only a short step to the self-sentence, "I am unacceptable to others."

Generally, the only thing college students remember of the philosopher René Descartes is that he said, "*Cogito, ergo sum*"—"I think, therefore I am." I choose to paraphrase it: *What I think is what I am.* Other than our obvious, and rather superficial, physical differences, what makes you different from me and all others is your thoughts, opinions, tastes, values, and goals. Plus, of course, the actions they may motivate. Therefore, if you do not feel free to express them, you do not feel free to be *you*.

When I say "I want to know you," I am inviting you to tell me your thoughts and opinions. I am implying they are of value, whether or not I agree with them. But if I then take offense when you express them, condemning you for holding views with which I disagree, I am telling you I find your views and you of no value. If, for example, I ask for your opinions on affirmative-action programs, I may find that you hold views very different from mine. If, then, I answer, "I disagree with you. May I tell you why?" I show a respect for your opinions and you. But if I reply, "Only a stupid jerk would believe that," I am *attacking* your opinions—and you. On the other hand, if you don't express them out of fear of such an attack, perhaps you don't value yourself as much as you might.

In recent years, there has been an increasing interest in assertiveness. Assertiveness training classes have sprung up throughout the country. In these classes, men and women work to develop skills at stating their views with confidence, and in claiming and maintaining their legitimate rights. While much of the emphasis has been on the problems women, raised to be non-assertive, face, there are possibly just as many men who find it hard to speak out. The importance of assertiveness to self-esteem would seem to be so evident no one would dispute it. But there are apparently some who do.

I recently listened to a radio talk show on which the host interviewed the leader of an assertiveness training program. They discussed the aims of the program and the problems faced by those who felt they could not speak out. Then the host opened the phone lines. Surprisingly, most of the callers were critical. "Aren't there enough abrasive females already!" asked a male chauvinist. "I've taught my children it's polite to let others always go first," said a woman caller. And from another woman, "I don't want to offend anyone, and it sounds like that is what you are encouraging people to do." The show guest asked one caller what he usually did when someone pushed in line ahead of him. "Nothing; I don't say anything," replied the caller. "I always figure I'm not in that much of a hurry and maybe the other fellow is." "But your time should be as valuable as his, shouldn't it?" the assertiveness leader asked. "Why don't you simply tell him you were there first?'' The caller responded non-assertively: ''Gee, I don't know. I suppose you're right.''

In my years of counseling, I have seen many men and women consistently accept punishment rather than stand up on their hind legs. Louise, an attractive woman in her late twenties, told me she dreaded going out in company with her husband. ''He likes to make jokes about my small bust.'' I asked her if she ever objected to his remarks. ''No,'' she said, ''I know he's only kidding. He doesn't intend to hurt me, and maybe it's just that I'm too sensitive.'' I asked her how she felt her husband might react if she came out and told him she definitely did not appreciate his ''jokes'' about her bust. ''I'm not sure,'' she said. ''He might be hurt, or he might be angry.'' And she might have been right, but she will never know if she does not assert herself. Besides, why is it better for her to be hurt or angry than him?

No argument—there are those who will try to punish you for expressing your opinions, values, and even tastes. The insecure individual may interpret any disagreement as a personal attack, a put-down. A neighbor of mine once told me he was supporting a certain political candidate. I told him I planned to vote for the other guy. ''Then you're saying I'm stupid,'' was his reaction. I failed to convince him I was not passing judgment on his intelligence (I suspected he had a low self-image). He walked away angry. It was his way of punishing me.

These punishments include one or more of the following:

- I won't like you anymore.
- I'll make you feel ashamed/guilty.
- I won't talk to you anymore.
- I won't let you belong to my club.

To what extent any of these ''punishments'' may be effective will depend upon our vulnerability to them. If you feel you must have others like you, you probably will keep your opinions to yourself. A year or two ago I spent an afternoon with a man I had known for fifteen years. I had not seen him for several years. As we talked, I expressed my views on several points. Several times he said, "But that isn't what you used to say." I agreed. I admitted my views have changed (and are still changing) in many areas. If none of my views had altered, I would have been frozen in time. Or dead.

By the time he left my hotel, he was visibly angry. He said, "I'm really sorry to see our friendship end this way, but we no longer see eye-to-eye. It seems to me if you valued our friendship you would at least have kept some opinions to yourself." I tried to understand his reaction. "Why," I asked, "should it be necessary that we agree on everything in order to be friends?" He stared at me for a full fifteen seconds before answering. "Well, you know the old saying, 'He that is not with me is against me.' " I haven't heard from him since.

The fear of anger is a dominant middle-class reaction. In "nice," genteel homes, many parents try to teach children anger is never, never ever to be expressed—in fists, words, or otherwise. Which is a teaching which seldom takes. Children do, of course, express anger, sometimes violently. And parents blow up from time to time. The teaching does, however, create a strong fear of anger. In a family (and neighborhood) in which shouting is a common mode of communication, one in which tempers flare and subside almost hourly, the child may never learn to enjoy his parents' anger, but he will learn to live with it, and it will seldom upset him. The child raised in the "genteel" home, however, may grow up to be terrified by his boss, spouse, or friend. Any expression of their anger can trigger his fear response, so he keeps his mouth shut.

Guilt can be an even more effective punishment. "Aren't you ashamed of yourself?" is an all too common punishment for non-conformity. Most of us were raised with so many guilt feelings, all someone else has to do to bring them to the surface is suggest we *should* feel guilty. A woman recently told me I should feel ashamed of myself because I admitted a liking for calf's liver. She was a vegetarian, which is fine with me; that's her thing. It doesn't happen to be mine. I responded with the answer we have suggested to the members of our groups when faced with such guilt-tripping; it isn't said in hostility, just rational self-interest: "I don't need that."

Since guilt is never rational, if you accept a guilt-trip for expressing an unpopular opinion, you are reacting irrationally. To feel guilty about your thoughts and opinions is to feel guilty because you are you. You may regret actions which violate your personal code of ethics and morality, and even resolve not to repeat the actions. But regret and remorse differ from guilt. Guilt is always irrational since it says, "I am no good, and I just proved it once again by what I did." It is a serious devaluation of yourself. It follows, therefore, that those who consistently try to make you feel guilty or ashamed are your enemies.

The threat of terminating the conversation whenever a disagreement arises is a classic punishment among married couples. Let one of them say, "That isn't the way I see it," and the conversation may terminate with a curt, "I don't wish to discuss it further." Especially if the topic is emotionally loaded. If the dissenting spouse is vulnerable to such turn-off punishment, he or she may think twice before disagreeing in the future.

Cutting off the conversation as punishment for disagreement is seldom attempted unless the one trying the ploy is fairly sure it will be effective. If you have a button to be pressed, you can be sure others will press it. We've all met the fellow at the cocktail party who says, "Please don't talk politics; I just can't take it," and in doing so exposes one of his buttons. Then someone brings up the coming elections, and our friend is off the launching pad. If you have a button labeled "I can't take it if he [she] won't talk to me," it might be smart to ask yourself why. Maybe you have an inordinate need to be liked and accepted. Perhaps you can't take rejection. Whatever the reason, if someone can prevent you from expressing your views by the threat of terminating the conversation, you are going to come out of the encounter with those terrible feelings of impotence.

The threat of exclusion from the club is probably the most powerful in our society. Some years ago, sociologist David Reisman wrote of the power of "other-directedness," the neurotic need for acceptance which prevents so many from developing their own personal values and goals. These individuals, and they make up the majority, are so peer-group-directed they become social chameleons: they take on the opinions, values, and tastes of whatever group they may be with at the moment.

The need to belong is inversely related to self-esteem. Many feel the road to liking oneself is through being liked (read: accepted) by others. We are all aware dissenters are seldom accepted in groups. Think (or at least verbalize) what we think, or we will blackball you is the rule.

I gave a lecture before a large audience in Detroit. The name and purpose of the host organization were not familiar to me when I accepted the booking. A week or two before flying to Detroit, I spoke with the chairperson of the organization. I asked her what subject matter she felt her audience might find most interesting. We discussed several, and agreed on one we felt would be of general interest. Questions from the audience following the lecture ranged far and wide, some totally unrelated to the subject matter of the lecture. There were questions about politics, religion, views on marijuana and topless bars. I didn't cop-out; I answered them candidly.

By the time I left the convention hall, the organizing committee had the smell of a lynch mob. The woman who headed the organization said, "If we had known you were not one of us, we would never have invited you to speak." I told her I had never thought to mention I was not a member of her organization, and she had not asked. "Yes," she answered, "but if we had known you held opinions which were not acceptable to us, we would never have invited you. I don't think any of us were offended by the speech, but we were shocked by some of your religious and political views. I think a paid lecturer has an obligation to support the views of the sponsor."

Obviously, I do not agree. If they do not wish to hear my views, fine. But if I am asked to express those views, the fee of a lecture is not going to keep me from saying what I want to say. It is for this reason, among others, I belong to few groups, formally or informally. Even the neighborhood kaffeeklatsch has its firm set of values and opinions to which one must subscribe or be excluded. (Try telling the girls you spent the weekend at a nude beach, and see how soon you are invited back.)

Social exclusion is not, however, all motivated by an in-group intolerance. We all know individuals who *defensively* hold diverse opinions. They verbalize them like a challenge, throwing them down like a gauntlet: "Here's my opinion; want to make something of it?" This isn't merely assertion in self-interest. It is, at best, defensiveness; at worst, a Nixon-style paranoia. I was at a cocktail party when a fellow guest confronted me. "I'm gay. What do you think of that?" I told him that, to be truthful, I didn't think of it at all, and I asked if he felt there was some reason I should give thought to his sexual preferences.

Perhaps there should be non-assertiveness classes as well as assertiveness classes. Speaking out for the sake of speaking out, with nothing else to be gained, is destructive—to oneself as well as others. The self-confident individual does not feel compelled to push views on others. He or she is content to say, "This is me. These are my opinions. If you don't agree, that's fine. I'd like to hear what you think."

Actually, the V.I.F. can work for either "assertiveness" or "non-assertiveness," depending on one's goals. The goal in a second image is always to achieve what one wants. Or in other words, to be free. The object in such descriptions or tapes, then, is to communicate in such ways that our views can be expressed without alienating others, and in ways that can increase the likelihood of achieving our goals. This may mean a tape on assertiveness, or it may mean one on learning when not to "speak up." Perhaps even both.

Jerry L. had worked hard for fifteen years attempting to build his air-conditioning business. While he had built a stable business, he had not attained the success he hoped for. Furthermore, he felt sure he knew the reason. "I had a way of irritating people, employees and customers alike. Two of my best men quit over something I said, and I lost at least one very big contract because I shot off my mouth to the developer. It was almost never anything that had to do with the job. It could be anything—religion, politics, the way to broil a steak. Take that developer. I told him I thought people who liked country and western music were morons. Well, the guy happened to be a nut for that kind of music. It was as if I had to prove that I was the bigger man by putting down the other guy—even if I lost out in the long run. And the crazy part of it was that I often seemed to know I was putting my foot in it while I was doing it. But there was another part of it. At home, I was a different guy altogether. I couldn't speak up to my wife at all. There were times when I'd clench my teeth so tight my jaws would ache. Frankly, I was scared to disagree with her. I don't know what I was afraid of; I think it was just making her angry at me. I was like two different people, one at work and one at home. But you know something? I now think it all came about from the same thing. I didn't have much self-confidence at all."

I asked him what sort of second images he had used for what seemed to be two very different, and opposite, situations. "I made just a single tape," he said. "I didn't want to have a second image in which I was just asserting myself. In my work, that wouldn't have made much sense. I was already asserting myself into a lot of trouble. On the other hand, I didn't see how I could make a tape on keeping my mouth shut and not expressing my opinions. That was giving me ulcers at home. So I figured out what I thought would cover both situations. You see, I really was leading a schizophrenic life." I asked if he would allow me to listen to his tape. The following is a transcription of his second image. He said, "It turned my life around."

> "I am now taking a swim in my pool. It's late in the evening, and as I turn over on my back, I can see the stars. It's a beautiful night. I feel a strength throughout my body as I move through the water. Today was one great day. I liked myself. I really did. I didn't feel I had to prove how smart I am by beating everyone over the head with my ideas. And Shirley and I were able to talk. I was able to tell her exactly how I feel and what I want. I felt comfortable doing it, as if it was the most natural thing in the world. I listened to her, and I feel she listened to me. It was one adult to another. All day I have felt relaxed and good about myself. I like my thoughts and ideas and beliefs, and that's enough."

I didn't question the role his wife may have played in his reluctance to speak freely with her. Perhaps none. There is one common reason, however, why people resist or reject the person who speaks up. They may interpret your expressions of "I wants" as demands upon them. Many people assume if I say, "I want," it means, "I want this from *you*." This interpretation is, of course, either very egocentric, or it is a realistic response to an actual demand. If, for example, I expect my wife to head for the kitchen every time I mention I am hungry, she has every right to feel pressured. If my autonomy is highly visible, however, she will know it is nothing more than a statement of where I am, not a demand on her.

There are, of course, some things we want from others, and we should feel free to express these desires. If others do not feel free to decline, well, that's their problem. Should there be any limitations on what we ask of others? I see no reason for any other than self-interest: If what I ask is excessive or too frequent, I will find I am often turned down (and people will start to avoid me). I assume others are free to respond to me in ways they feel will meet their needs and desires.

There is a final, and most important, reason for expressing yourself with candor, letting others know who and what you are: What you are is your collective values, what you believe in and stand for. If you do not stand up for them, you lose them. If we lose our values, we lose most of our reasons for living. It has been said if we have nothing we are willing to die for, we have nothing worth living for. Our values are the measure of our self-esteem, of how much we recognize the strength within ourselves. If we do not proclaim them, we must not give them—or ourselves—much worth. Then it is only a short step to discarding them.

There are those who claim they can hold onto their values without expressing them in the face of contrary values, but their actions seldom support this claim. It is not that they are hypocritical. They are simply unaware of the erosion of values which results from "discreet" silence. Politicians are notoriously prone to such value erosion. In seeking election, the politician tempers what he says to his constituency. If he says what he believes—all he believes—he will never win an election. So he keeps his real opinions to himself, convinced that once elected, he will vote his conscience. But by then, he has few convictions left. And we are saddled with still one more morally bankrupt politician.

Most people we have spoken with who have made assertiveness (and non-assertiveness) tapes have used them for specific situations (a meeting with the boss, a talk with a parent, child, or spouse, a confrontation with the automobile dealer who doesn't repair the car under warranty). What they found was a developing openness and self-confidence in all areas of their lives. Furthermore, they found a surprising degree of acceptance—even though at that point they had little need of it.

Appendix A

V.I.F. seminars evolved over a ten-year period. During the first years there was much trial and error. Out of large and small group therapy, marathon therapy, and a wide variety of structured and unstructured interaction groups, the basic concepts—the IL-IC-IM—emerged. Following the lead of others, we experimented with exercises in visual imagery and affirmations, all with some success. The final development, the V.I.F., came shortly after.

Although many of the earlier seminars were of five days' duration, usually combined with a trip to Hawaii or Mexico, most of the current seminars are held in northern California (typically, at Asilomar conference grounds near Carmel). These weekend seminars begin Friday evening with an explanation of the IL-IM-IC prisons which account for our frustrations and unhappiness. We then discuss the principles and techniques of the V.I.F.—how to select a first image, how to evaluate the image, techniques of recording, the affirmation, the second image and its limitations, etc.

Those registering for the seminar are advised to bring a cassette recorder and two or three blank tapes. On Friday evening the participants are given a set of printed second images, four to six in number, with instructions that before retiring for the night they record their own, individual, first image, followed by the affirmation, "I can do anything I want to do—absolutely anything." This is to be followed (on the tape) with the set of second images, interspersing them with "I can do anything, etc."

These second images are written in such a way that they would be "I wants" for all participants—at least hopefully (see Appendix B). It is suggested they play their tape twice before turning in for the night, once or twice before the start of Saturday morning meetings, again during the lunch break—all together, several times during the day.

The Saturday and Sunday meetings (the seminar concludes following lunch Sunday) are devoted to discovering our "I want's," use of the V.I.F. in areas of health, education, marriage, sex, emotions, and financial gain, and the development of a powerful new life-style. These meetings are in no way group therapy, nor are they encounter or sensitivity groups. While ample time is devoted to answering questions, self-exposure is neither encouraged nor felt to be desirable. The seminars are not a place to "let it all hang out." They are designed as a learning environment; not a soul-baring one. What each participant chooses to do with the information is his or her own business, not ours or that of other members of the group.

Virtually all members of these first seminars have kept in contact with us and with one another as the V.I.F. has developed further. Some seminar graduates have been meeting weekly for over a year. But why, one might ask, if the V.I.F. leads to autonomy and freedom from a need to rely upon others, would these people—or anyone for that matter—participate in such a seminar? Why would they continue the relationships afterward? First, the seminar itself: Until now, the theory and method of the V.I.F. have not been available in printed form. We could communicate this information only through lectures or seminars. We found a one- or two-hour lecture to be insufficient to cover the material. The seminars have also provided a testing ground for the V.I.F. Many of the questions which have arisen during the course of these weekends we could not have anticipated. As to the continuing group participation, the reasons are perhaps more serious, and they address themselves to the question of why we have included this information on the V.I.F. seminars.

It is not an exaggeration to say we live in a world of impotent people. One of the first things which strikes those who have participated in a weekend seminar is the negativism of those they immediately encounter in the "outside world." It has something of the flavor of a "culture shock." I recall one time we were driving back up the coast from Asilomar. I stopped to have the tank filled. The young man pumping gas said, "Looks like the weather's going to turn miserable again." I told him I felt it had been a beautiful weekend. "Yeah?" he answered. "Well I expect more rain any time, then watch the pileups you get on Highway 17. You headed up that way?" I told him I was. "All I can say is good luck," he said. "The traffic is going to be hell. Hope you make it." We did. It was a delightful drive. The sun continued to shine, and the traffic was the lightest I can remember on that curving stretch of highway. One thing was sure: I didn't need his "downers."

Going back into that world of negative people, and confronting them several times each day, can put a strain on one's tapes. Sure they will work, but in a negative environment I may have to play my tapes twice as frequently just to keep my head above water. A twenty-minute phone call from a gloomy or critical relative may call for three playings of my favorite tape to bring me back up. On the other hand, living around people who are also using the V.I.F. makes life a fun-filled adventure. Nothing can reinforce one's power and confidence more than the company of other omnipotent people. This is not a "support" system. I feel confident I can, with the help of my tapes, resist the jails others would lock me in. It's just a lot easier if I do not have to expend all that energy in doing so.

This can become crucial when one is "involved" in a close relationship with someone who rejects the V.I.F. This might be parent/child, husband/wife, siblings, business partners, or other "significant" relationships. Lois and I had done a radio talk show on KGO, the American Broadcasting Company-owned station in San Francisco. We were enjoying lunch with Owen Spann, the talk-show host and one of the top-rated communicasters in the country. We had been guests on his show several times in promotion of previous books, and had come to know him rather well. He asked questions about the V.I.F. that would have done credit to the best of investigative reporters. In trying to sum up the effect of the V.I.F. on our relationship, Lois said, "Owen, you've seen the relationship Joe and I have had for all these years. Frankly, I know of no relationship that I could consider better in any way, shape, or form. But the V.I.F. has made such a difference in each of us, that if, for whatever reason, Joe stopped playing his tapes today, I'm not sure I wouldn't leave him."

Then what can one do if you find yourself the only one "on the tapes?" There is probably only one answer: Convert them.

We have had men and women participate in the V.I.F. seminar, then return to their homes in cities and towns in which no one had heard of "this crazy business of tape-recording your own voice." One husband and wife from a small town in Oregon were typical. Within a month, they had introduced the V.I.F. to most of their neighbors, many of the husband's business associates, and even the family doctor (who was amazed at the change for the better the wife had made in her "chronic" illnesses). In effect, they formed their own group.

This becomes especially important within a family. I second the sentiments Lois expressed to Owen Spann. In my feelings, it applies as well to children. With all family members using the V.I.F., the atmosphere within the home can come close to being everything a parent (and child) might dream of.

Our commitments have limited the number and frequency of V.I.F. seminars we have been able to offer, and, although we have expanded the program to include "special" seminars for educators, physicians and dentists, sales forces, and high school students, we fully realize problems of time and distance will limit the number of readers who can participate in a weekend seminar with us. For those who can, we welcome you and hope you contact us. If you feel it would, at least for the present, be out of the question, the material in this book will, hopefully, do the job.

Since we are continuing to collect data on all applications of the V.I.F., we would appreciate hearing from you telling of your experiences conducting your own V.I.F. seminar, individually, with family members, business group, or friends. Write to: Joseph and Lois Bird, V.I.F. Seminars, 5150 Graves Avenue, Suite 8B, San Jose, California 95129.

Appendix B

You have just completed the first step in conducting your own V.I.F. "seminar": you have read this book. The next step is to set aside a couple of days to work with the material. In the program to follow, assume you have decided to begin on a Friday evening as we do at Asilomar. (We feel it is most effective when a couple of nights are included to allow your tapes to work while you are resting, and sufficient rest breaks to permit the material to be digested.)

Friday evening: Review the concepts of personal freedom, its relationship to power and happiness, and the jails of IL-IC-IM.

Next, go through the descriptive adjectives listed on pages 241–242. Check those you feel apply to you. The first list—Positive Adjectives—are those associated with achievement, power, and freedom. For this reason, they are adjectives frequently found in first images. The second list—Negative Adjectives—are those associated with feelings of self-loathing, impotence, and negation.

After you have checked those you feel apply to you on both lists, go back over the lists, checking those you feel you would like to have applied to you. If you have checked the adjectives with utmost honesty, you may find you have checked some "negative" adjectives among those you desire. If so, look them over. You may find adjectives which, although they are "impotent," have been taught to you as desirable. We have found this to be most frequently true among women who have been raised with a strong infusion of traditionally "feminine" values. For example, many women checked the adjectives *dependent, emotional, feminine, submissive, suggestible,* and others because they felt these were the "attributes" a woman should have, yet these are adjectives which, if attributed to a man, these women viewed as undesirable.

These adjectives may provide some leads for your "I wants." Further leads for the development of fruitful tapes may be found in answering the questions which follow. Spend the major part of your Friday evening thoughtfully answering them. Then set your answers aside until completion of your seminar weekend. Do not make second images to deal with those questions until you have completed your seminar.

At the conclusion of your Friday evening, write and record a first image. By now, you will have hopefully recalled several such experiences. Follow this first image, of course, with the affirmation, "I can do anything I want to do—absolutely anything." Then record the second images which follow the questions. Not necessarily all of them. You can select three, four, or six. You will be piggybacking these second images. That is, you will record them, one after another, on the same page and then on the same tape (including the affirmation, "and I can do anything . . . ," between them).

Play your tape five or six times each day during your "seminar" (participants at Asilomar play their tapes before and after breakfast, during the mid-morning break, before and after lunch, before and after dinner, and again before turning in for the night).

Lastly, outline your personal "seminar." In this, you can outline the areas relevant to you which may have been raised through reading of the book, the adjectives you checked, or self-analysis. Present an analysis of the areas, one at a time, as if you were talking to a group of friends troubled by similar problems. It may help to clarify your

IL-IC-IM's if you take notes or outline the problems—and solutions—as they become evident.

At the conclusion of your personal "seminar" you will probably have uncovered several "I wants" to which you can apply the V.I.F. Don't wait. Make your tapes. Play them. They will fail to "work" only if you don't press the "play" button on your cassette recorder.

Positive Adjectives—First Image

Active
Adaptable
Adventurous
Affectionate
Aggressive
Ambitious
Appreciative
Assertive
Attractive
Calm
Capable
Cheerful
Confident
Considerate
Courageous
Daring
Dependable
Determined
Efficient
Enterprising
Enthusiastic
Frank
Friendly
Healthy
Humorous
Imaginative
Independent
Individualistic
Intelligent
Logical
Mature
Natural
Omnipotent
Optimistic
Outgoing
Pleasure-Seeking
Poised
Powerful
Rational
Reasonable
Relaxed
Reliable
Sexual
Shrewd
Spontaneous
Stable
Strong
Thoughtful
Trusting
Understanding
Uninhibited
Warm

Negative Adjectives—Refuted in Image Two

Aloof	Forgetful	Self-denying
Anxious	Fussy	Self-pitying
Apathetic	Greedy	Self-punishing
Argumentative	Hostile	Simple
Awkward	Immature	Spendthrift
Bitter	Impotent	Spineless
Careless	Impulsive	Stubborn
Coarse	Inhibited	Submissive
Cold	Intolerant	Suggestible
Complaining	Irresponsible	Sulky
Confused	Lazy	Superstitious
Cool	Masculine	Suspicious
Cowardly	Meek	Tactless
Cruel	Moody	Tense
Deceitful	Nagging	Timid
Defensive	Nervous	Touchy
Demanding	Prejudiced	Unambitious
Dependent	Preoccupied	Unemotional
Despondent	Prudish	Unfriendly
Disorderly	Quarrelsome	Unintelligent
Dull	Quitting	Unstable
Emotional	Reckless	Vindictive
Fault-finding	Resentful	Weak
Fearful	Rigid	Whiny
Feminine	Rude	Withdrawn
Foolish	Sarcastic	Worrying

"SEMINAR" QUESTIONS

Freedom

- Do you feel there are important people in your life (spouse, parent, friend, child) who will not tolerate your freedom?
- Does the concept of freedom seem somehow immoral or dangerous to you?

- Do you sometimes feel you have no right to expect to be happy all the time?
- Do you recognize a "holding back" in yourself when you think of breaking free and getting everything you want in life?
- Do you tend to think of becoming free of certain problems rather than attaining freedom in a total sense?
- Do you find yourself saying, "I have simple tastes and limited goals. I'm happy with my life the way it is. I don't see any reason for going after more," rather than employing the V.I.F. to break free of any and all limitations?
- Do you generally tend to see your successes as the result of a group or "team" effort rather than yours alone?
- Do you feel you have difficulty being good to yourself?
- Do you find yourself saying, in effect, "I may not be living a free existence, but I'm not sure I want to give up the advantage of my present life"?
- Do you feel your commitments to others prevent you from attaining freedom?
- Do you believe life without sorrow and disappointment is an unrealistic dream?
- Do you feel there are some problems you simply have to learn to live with?
- Do you find yourself reluctant to identify significant people in your life as your "jailers"?
- Do you find yourself creating second images which are partially free and are "limited dreams"?
- Do you feel you cannot strive for freedom if your spouse does not desire the same goal?
- Do you have a second image which is more a daydream of a vacation than one of reward for achievement?
- Do you fear a loss of friends and important relationships would follow freedom?

Emotions

- Do you believe you can't help but react when someone "presses your buttons"?

- Do you feel there are times you can't help blowing up?
- Do you feel you can't help but feel blue at certain times of the month?
- Do you feel you are the "jealous type"?
- Do you feel you must express the emotions you feel?
- Do you believe some people can make you angry, even when it is not what you might want to feel?
- Do you feel there are times when you just can't keep depressing thoughts out of your mind?
- Do you suffer guilt feelings for past "sins"?
- Do you tend to spend time on little worries?
- Do the mistakes or inabilities of others make you impatient?
- Do children frequently "bug" you?
- Do you find it hard to unwind?
- Do you find yourself terribly frustrated when not able to do something?
- Do you ever have disturbing thoughts which persist for days?
- Do you have emotional cycles—up one day; in the doldrums the next?
- Do you feel you are always putting your foot in your mouth?
- Do you fear flying or going on water?
- Do you fear snakes or other animals?
- Do you feel you can enjoy an emotional response to music, a novel, or a movie?
- Do you tend to suspect the actions or words of others?
- Do you feel there are things about yourself to which you are particularly sensitive?
- Do you tend to get upset when working under a deadline?
- Do you get upset at thoughts of death, your own or that of a loved one?
- Do you have strong fears of illness or pain?
- Does the sight of an accident upset you for hours?
- Do you get upset or anxious when meeting strangers?
- Do you fear water?
- Do you fear being embarrassed in public?

- Do you become angry when a member of your family publicly disagrees with your views?
- Do you fear "rejection"?
- Do you often dwell on previous misfortunes?
- Do you feel you get carried away by your emotions?
- Do you fear emotional outbursts by others?
- Do you become upset when attempting to work in an environment of people, noise, and movement?
- Do you fear (or hate) certain "types," *e.g.*, ex-convicts, homosexuals, those of a different ethnic group or socio-economic class?
- Do you become depressed when you do not receive approval?
- Do you become upset in a disordered environment?
- Do you worry about past failures?
- Do you fear others finding out about "the real you"?
- Would you be likely to be upset at the thought of making a complete new start—*e.g.*, moving to a different locale, making new friends, beginning a new career?
- Do you fear speaking before a group of people?

Health & Illness

- Do you feel you are as healthy as you can reasonably expect to be?
- Do you believe some periodic minor illnesses (*e.g.*, colds) must be expected?
- Do you suffer from some chronic illness (*e.g.*, allergy, diabetes) which you feel you "inherited"?
- Do you feel limited in some activities because you are "weak"?
- Do you believe you will become ill or emotionally upset if you go without your regular amount of sleep?
- (For Women) Do you believe discomfort (*e.g.*, cramps) inevitably must accompany menstruation?
- Do you believe you are just naturally underweight or overweight and that this cannot be altered other than by rigid dieting?

- Do you believe you have an easily-upset digestive system and hence must watch what you eat?
- Do you believe certain environmental conditions can bring on illness in those foreign to the environment (*e.g.*, gastrointestinal distress in Americans visiting Mexico)?
- Do you believe noise causes headaches?
- Do you believe morning-after hangover is solely physical and nothing psychological can be done to eliminate or reduce it?
- Do you believe nutrition rather than mental health is the primary essential to sound health?
- Do you feel overwork can result in a run-down condition and greater susceptibility to disease?
- Do you feel powerless to cure yourself when you have contracted an illness?
- Do you feel you have to maintain a balanced diet?
- Do you feel there are activities you might enjoy but which you avoid because you have been told they may be injurious to your health?
- Do you feel limited by your age, that there are some activities you are "just too old to do"?
- Do you feel there is nothing you can do to stop the aging process and the toll it takes on stamina and well-being?
- Do you believe if an illness is "going around" you have an increasing chance of "catching" it?
- (For Women) Do you believe severe pain almost inevitably accompanies the contractions of labor?
- Do you feel powerless to stop the course of a common cold, that you must simply "keep warm, get plenty of rest, drink a lot of fluids"?
- Do you feel you can't choose *not* to become sick?
- Do you presently have any illnesses for which you are taking medication and which you feel powerless to fight off even partly by your own will?

Work and Money

- Do you feel trapped in your present job by what others expect of you?

- (For Women) Do you feel your "place" is in the home?
- Do you feel you are limited in earnings by a lack of education?
- Do you feel you have to stay with your job because you have already "invested" so many years in it?
- Do you feel your sex limits your occupational choices or earnings?
- Do you feel you have to play up to the boss or play office politics in order to get ahead?
- Do you believe you are stymied in fulfilling your dreams by a lack of capital?
- Do you believe you have little chance of getting a good job because you have been out of the job market so long?
- Do you feel trapped in a dead-end job by your age?
- Do you feel you cannot quit your job (or take a job) because of objections which would be raised by spouse or parents?
- Do you believe you are barred from certain occupations by lack of "talent"?
- Do you believe financial success demands hard work?
- Do you believe you are held back by rules of seniority?
- Do you feel your work has no value unless you are being paid for it?
- Do you do housework or household chores out of a sense of obligation?
- Do you feel you have no say about your work hours or conditions?
- Do you feel "a job is a job" and that all jobs are tedious?
- Do you feel if you quit your job you would have difficulty landing another which pays as well?
- Do you feel if you were to change occupations you would be "throwing away your education"?
- Do you feel it would be irresponsible to change jobs simply because you don't like your present one even though it pays well?
- Do you feel you have to dress, voice certain opinions, and maintain prescribed "off-duty" behavior in order to keep your job?

- Do you feel you cannot state your conditions on the job, but must accept the conditions set by the employer?
- Do you feel family pressures or financial conditions keep you from going into business for yourself?
- Do you feel your potential earnings are limited by the average of your occupation, union scale?
- Do you believe you must work forty hours a week to make your present income?
- Do you feel limited by social approval in the types of occupations you might seek?
- Do you feel you can't think of any other job you could do?
- Do you believe you would feel guilty if you were not working?
- Do you feel there are "masculine" and "feminine" occupations?
- (For Men) Do you think you would feel less a man if your wife contributed to the family income?
- Do you feel making a lot of money would demand a high price in terms of time, family neglect, health, pressures, values?
- Do you believe work is work and fun is fun, and the two cannot be mixed?
- Do you feel guilty spending money on yourself?
- Do you feel obligated to spend your money helping others?
- Do you fear financial insecurity?
- Would you feel uncomfortable using money to get the best table in the house?
- Do you believe money is the root of all evil?
- Do you believe you are unlucky when it comes to making money?
- Do you feel a need to prove your success to your parents?
- Do you feel comfortable only when purchasing something "practical" rather than "frivolous"?
- Do you feel you do not deserve "easy" money?
- Would you feel uncomfortable staying in the plushest suite of a luxury hotel?

- Do you feel obligated to give a portion of your money to charity?
- Are you reluctant to let people know how much money you have?
- Would you feel embarrassed talking with an old friend who obviously had not been as successful as you?
- Can you see yourself riding up to a top New York restaurant in a limousine?

Religion, and Belief Systems

- Do you have firm ideas about the nature of man, *e.g.*, essentially good, basically evil, fundamentally selfish?
- Do you have sayings or proverbs which you quote to explain some events and advice to others?
- Do you have beliefs and proverbs which describe the opposite sex ("All women are . . ." ". . . well, you know what men are like")?
- Do you attempt to support your convictions by the authority of others—"They say"?
- Do you tend to accept an observation as valid if it is a quote from the Bible?
- Do you look to church leaders or ministers for leadership in areas of life other than theology?
- Do you accept what your religion has taught you about yourself?
- Do you believe you are a sinner?
- Do you believe pleasure-seeking, hedonism, is morally wrong?
- Do you feel you cannot succeed without the support of others—parents, spouse, friends, church?
- Do you feel it is important to look to the church for moral guidance?
- If you succeed (at whatever it might be), do you feel it is the result of God's help?
- Do you read, and rely upon, the readings of your horoscope?

- Do you feel you cannot question the "teachings" of your guru, pastor, or psychotherapist?
- Do you look upon Dear Abby, Ann Landers, or other advice columnists, whatever their "credentials," as authorities?
- Do you doubt your own experience and opinions if an "authority" states an opinion which disagrees with it?
- Do you feel you must attend church on certain days or keep other church commandments because they are commanded by God (rather than arrived at through your own reasoning)?
- Do you believe certain objects are endowed with powers, *e.g.*, good luck charms, religious medals, four-leaf clovers?
- Do you believe you cannot succeed without luck or the help of God?
- Do you believe there are some "truths" which are generally known and accepted by everyone?
- Do you believe good fortune and bad follow one another in cycles?
- Do you believe a few people are gifted with special powers, *e.g.*, ability to see the future, healing powers?
- Do you feel some things are just destined to be—*i.e.*, Fate?

Sex

- Do you believe men and women differ in sexual responsiveness?
- Does it bother you to use or listen to common sexual words, *e.g.*, fuck, screw, cock, cunt?
- Do you feel you could not socialize with others in the nude, *e.g.*, skinny-dip at a party, go to a nude beach?
- Do you feel guilty when sexually stimulating (masturbating) yourself?
- Do you feel you cannot enjoy or be aroused by sexually explicit films or novels?
- Do you feel you cannot permit your partner to watch you masturbate?

- Do you feel you could not respond sexually if there might be a chance of others watching?
- Do you feel you could enjoy sex with another only if you loved him/her?
- Do you feel sex is wrong if it is not an expression of love?
- Would you feel guilty having sex with someone with whom you do not share a commitment?
- Do you find it difficult to talk about sex with members of your sex, those of the other sex, your partner?
- Do you find sex can seldom be enjoyable unless it is proceeded by displays of affection, caresses, kissing, and other "foreplay"?
- Can you enjoy sexual fantasies, even far-out ones, without guilt?
- Do you believe your spouse has exclusive right to the use of his/her body, that marriage gives you no right of ownership over it?
- Do you feel you cannot become sexually turned on unless everything is going right between you and your partner?
- Do you feel you could not enjoy sex with a casual stranger?
- Do you feel uneasy, fearful, or angry when in the presence of someone you suspect is homosexual?
- Do you feel you could never be sexually pleasured by someone of the same sex?
- Do you feel uncomfortable inviting someone to join you in sex?
- Do you believe sex is a private matter, not to be discussed or done in public?
- Do you have sexual desires you feel you could not express to your partner?
- Do you believe you are incapable of orgasm without lengthy stimulation?
- Do you feel you are sexually frustrated due to your partner's lack of technique or unwillingness to do what will turn you on rather than taking the responsibility for your own pleasure?

- Do you believe you cannot reach more than a single orgasm during sex?
- Do you feel you cannot easily and quickly get and maintain an erection without physical stimulation by yourself or your partner?
- Do you feel uncertain as to whether you can consistently control your ejaculation until both you and your partner are "ready"?
- Do you sometimes feel you cannot ejaculate regardless of how long sex continues?
- Do you feel you cannot be sufficiently aroused unless you and/or your partner say or do the "right" things?
- Would you feel guilty fantasizing sex with someone else while having sex with your partner?
- Do you sometimes feel your sex drive is diminishing with age?
- Do you feel you cannot comfortably discuss sex with your children? Your parents?
- Do you find yourself turned off by some sexual acts because you don't consider them "normal"?
- Do you feel repulsed by contact with either male or female genitals?
- Do you sometimes feel you can't satisfy your partner?
- Do you feel you have to engage in sex even though you might at times prefer not to?

Dependence and Independence

- Do you feel dependent upon your spouse for emotional support?
- Do you feel you might not be able to find another partner if you were to terminate your present marriage?
- Do you believe marriage demands you give up certain freedoms?
- Do you feel you have to give emotional support and encouragement to your spouse?
- Do you feel you can't go out for an evening or away for a weekend without your spouse?

- Do you feel you cannot demand privacy in your marriage?
- Do you feel you have to present a "united front" to the world?
- Do you have dreams or ambitions which you feel you cannot express to your spouse?
- Do you feel you cannot tell your spouse when you want to be alone?
- Do you feel you have to feel loved in order to be happy?
- Do you feel that without certain contractual obligations, your relationship would fall apart?
- Do you feel you must sacrifice your personal wants to the greater good of the marriage?
- Do you believe you are bound to your marriage by a lifetime commitment?
- Do you believe you married when and who you did on the basis of your choice, unaffected by, or even in opposition to, the advice and opinions of others?
- Do you feel you cannot detach yourself from his/her family even if you might like to?
- Do you feel you cannot publicly disagree with your spouse?
- Do you feel that should any disagreements arise the decision should be a compromise rather than each of you doing your own thing?
- Do you feel you need marriage in order to feel secure?
- Do you feel reasonably certain you would stay with your spouse if both of you were financially independent? Would he/she stay with you?
- Do you feel obligated to fulfill certain tasks and play certain roles because you are male/female?
- Do you feel free to express your attraction to a member of the other sex to your spouse?
- (For Women) Do you feel you cannot achieve more than your husband in any particular area out of fear of making him feel he is less a man?
- Do you feel you cannot maintain a close friendship with

a member of the other sex outside of the company of your spouse?

- Do you feel friendships must be with other couples whom you both enjoy?
- (For Men) Do you feel an obligation to "protect" your wife against unpleasant "realities"?
- (For Women) Do you feel obligated to protect your husband's "male ego"?
- Do you feel you could not go through divorce without great pain and a sense of failure?
- Do you feel an obligation to look after your spouse's health, *e.g.*, suggest diet, doctor appointments?
- Do you feel you cannot openly state what you want—sexually, conversationally, recreationally?
- Do you feel you cannot tell your husband/wife the ways in which you would like to be free?
- Do you believe you are presently married for no reason other than the fact that you want to live with him/her, and that it has nothing to do with dependency needs—sexual, social, emotional, moral, or financial?

General

- Do you feel there is no space in your home you can claim for privacy?
- Do you find it difficult to close the door on a salesman or neighbor who wants to take up your time?
- Do you feel you cannot reserve time each day simply for pleasuring yourself doing what you want to do?
- Do you feel you cannot do your own thing when the family is around?
- Do you feel you can claim exclusive use of your own things (pen, tools, typewriter)?
- Do you feel free to go where you want to go even if others don't want to join you or might not approve?
- Do you feel free to decline invitations from friends (*e.g.*, a wedding) without offering an excuse?
- Do you feel free to turn away drop-in guests?

- Do you feel free not to answer a letter?
- Do you feel free to decline a conversation with a family member?
- Do you feel free to let someone know when you are using a space (*e.g.*, "I'd like to be alone in the den for a while")?
- Do you feel free to refuse to lend things which are yours?
- Do you feel free to go out for the evening with no more explanation than, "I'm going out for a while"?
- Do you feel free to go to bed when you want to rather than when your spouse suggests it?
- Do you feel you could receive mail or a telephone call without being questioned about it?
- Do you feel obligated to provide an explanation if, upon arriving home, you are asked, "Where have you been?"
- Do you feel you can demand that your purse or pockets not be invaded without permission?
- Do you feel the choice of how and where you spend a day off, a free weekend, or a vacation is your choice, and your choice alone?

YOUR SEMINAR SECOND IMAGES

The participants in your weekend V.I.F. seminar will, of course, all have their own experiences of achievement which they will compose into first images. All will employ the same second images, "piggy-backed" all on one tape. Following are three second images typical of the type we have distributed to our seminar participants for use throughout the seminar weekend.

SAMPLE IMAGES

"I can do anything I want to do—absolutely anything."

"I am now standing before my mirror. I woke up this morning free of all anxiety, free of all worry, free of all pressures, and free of all guilt. I have shed them, just like dropping a heavy weight from my shoulders. Nothing can bother me. No one can lay a trip on me because it is my world and I refuse to have depressions, fears, and guilt enter it. No one can threaten me because I rule the world, and it's fun to look in the mirror and smile at a totally powerful person."

"*I can do anything I want to do—absolutely anything.*"

"I am stepping from my shower, feeling the tingle and coolness still on my body. I *like* my body. I like what it can do. And I like the control I have over it. Age can't affect it because I'm ageless. I can be as loose and playful as a ten-year-old, or strong and active as a twenty-year-old. My body's immune system is in my control. No injury or disease can penetrate the shield I have erected around it. I drive out illness! I wake up in the morning feeling fantastic, and I go to bed feeling the same. What difference does it make how late it is? I don't tire. My body is mine, and it does what I want."

"*I can do anything I want to do—absolutely anything.*"

"It's Sunday afternoon, a beautiful Sunday afternoon, and the conclusion of the seminar. I'm walking outdoors, breathing in the fresh air deeply. Everything looks somehow new and alive. And I feel alive, more alive than ever before. This weekend has opened a score of doors for me. I am beginning to see where I want to go and where I am going in all areas of my life. It's a feeling of power and control. I like the person I am right now, this very moment, and the person I will be tomorrow and the day after."